Programming in BASIC
for Business

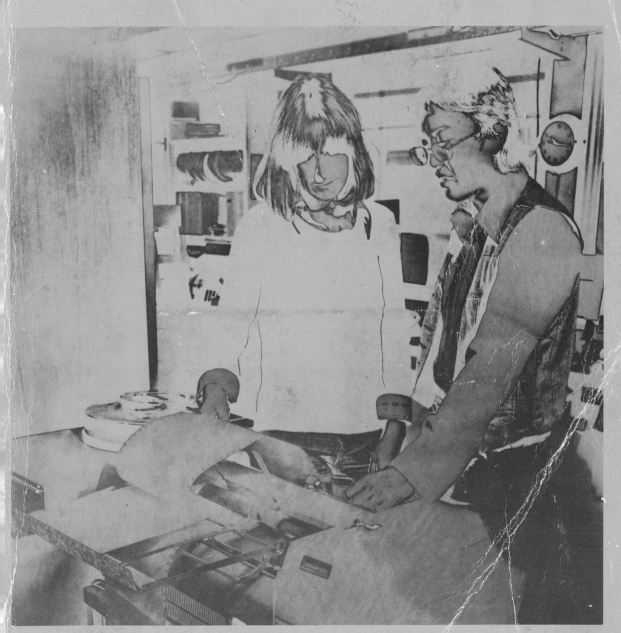

BRUCE BOSWORTH   **HARRY L. NAGEL**

Summary of BASIC Statements

Statement (Chapter)	Purpose	Example
DATA (4)	Supplies data to program Used with READ statement	90 DATA 8, J.DOE
DEF (9)	Defines a function	20 DEF FNA(N)=P*(1 + R)↑N
DIM (8)	Defines maximum size of arrays and matrices	10 DIM X(20), A(4,15)
END (3)	Last statement of program	999 END
FMT (11)	Format used with PRINT USING	50 FMT X = 9,999.99
FOR/NEXT (7)	Controls statements for a loop	30 FOR I=2 TO 30 STEP 3 . . . 80 NEXT I
GO SUB (9)	Branches to a subroutine	75 GOSUB 800
GO TO (6)	Branches unconditionally	45 GO TO 15
IF/THEN (6)	Branches conditionally	30 IF A=B THEN 250
INPUT (4)	Requests data from terminal and assigns to variables	20 INPUT N$,H,R
INPUT:FLNAM: (13)	Assigns data from named file to variables	20 INPUT:PAY:N$,H,R
LET (5)	Assigns values of expressions to variables	10 LET S=0 50 LET N=N+1
MAT (12)	Matrix operations	
INPUT	Fills matrix with data supplied from terminal	10 MAT INPUT A
READ	Fills matrix with data supplied from DATA statement	15 MAT READ B
PRINT	Prints out a matrix	20 MAT PRINT N
=	Equivalence of matrices	30 MAT A = B
+	Addition of matrices	25 MAT A = B + C
−	Subtraction of matrices	25 MAT X = Y − Z
*	Multiplication of matrices	25 MAT C = D*E
( )*	Multiplication by a scalar	40 MAT D = (K)*E
INV	Inverts a matrix	50 MAT B = INV(A)
TRN	Transposes a matrix	50 MAT B = TRN(A)
ZER	Fills matrix with zeros	50 MAT A = ZER
CON	Fills matrix with ones	50 MAT A = CON
IDN	Creates identity matrix	50 MAT A = IDN
ON/GO TO (6)	Branches to one of several lines based on the value of a variable	25 ON X GO TO 30,40,15

BRUCE BOSWORTH
HARRY L. NAGEL
St. John's University, New York

Programming in BASIC for Business

SCIENCE RESEARCH ASSOCIATES, INC.
Chicago, Palo Alto, Toronto
Henley-on-Thames, Sydney, Paris, Stuttgart

A Subsidiary of IBM

Library of Congress Cataloging in Publication Data

Bosworth, Bruce.
   Programming in BASIC for business.

   Includes index.
   1. Basic (Computer program language)   2. Business—
Data processing.   I. Nagel, Harry L., joint author.
II. Title.
HF5548.5.B3B67   001.6′424   76–48291
ISBN 0–574–21090–3

Contents

Preface

This book was written to introduce students to the BASIC programming language. Although there are other texts in BASIC, they are general in their approach and seldom cover business applications. This book fills the need for a comprehensive treatment of the BASIC language with a business orientation.

Each chapter of the book completely explains a few BASIC statements at a time. Each statement is presented in illustrative programs complete with output. Small cases reinforce the meaning of each statement. Students will find numerous programming exercises of varying difficulty at the end of each chapter to test their programming ability. After mastering the first eight chapters, they can try the larger application programs in Chapter 14.

Many aspects of the BASIC language differ from computer system to computer system. This text has indicated many of these differences. The programs in this book were prepared on the RAPIDATA Timesharing System.

This book can be used in a course completely devoted to computer programming. It can also be used as a supplement in a course on data processing. Much of the material in the book has been used in class over a period of several years. All of the programming exercises and the larger case problems in Chapter 14 have been class tested and were well received by students.

Following a brief introduction to programming, flowcharting, and time-sharing in Chapter 1, a complete set of chapters (2 through 9) sufficient for a short course in BASIC is presented. Chapters 10 through 13 provide advanced aspects of BASIC, including string variables, PRINT USING, matrices, and data files. The material in these chapters will differ from system to system. Individual "advanced" chapters may be omitted as the particular situation dictates.

We are indebted to Marilyn Bohl of IBM for her detailed review of the manuscript and the many helpful suggestions she made. Several other persons reviewed the manuscript and also helped improve it by their comments: William Claffey (Cypress College), Robert C. Hopkins (Los Angeles Pierce College), Gordon Howell (Georgia State University), Joan Ramuta (Joliet Junior College), Robert Rademacher (Colorado State University), and Stuart J. Travis (Ferris State College). Special thanks to Anthony Ingrao, our graduate assistant, who prepared and executed numerous BASIC programs for us.

We would like to thank Rosemarie Realmulto, who typed the initial manuscript with zeal and a high degree of accuracy. We are also grateful for the assistance and support given to us by Dr. Joseph Giacalone, Associate Dean of the College of Business Administration, St. John's University.

Introduction to Timesharing and BASIC

Since the early 1950's we have witnessed a rapid increase in the use of computers in our everyday lives. Today, computers are common in government, education, and business. Look at your driver's license or telephone bill. In all probability it was processed by computer. Examples like this are all around us.

To be useful, computers must be told not only what to do but also how to do it. This is the purpose of programming. A *program* is a detailed set of instructions that direct the computer to do its job. A *programmer* is a person who prepares such programs. Programs are typically referred to as *software*. *Hardware* constitutes the physical components of a computer system, i.e., the equipment.

COMPUTER LANGUAGES

There are a number of computer languages in which a programmer can write the detailed instructions needed to get the computer to work. The names of some of these languages are BASIC, FORTRAN, COBOL, Assembler, and PL/I.

Learning how to program a computer is similar to learning a foreign language. In the BASIC language, however, there are 30 verb-words so vocabulary is no problem. Programming is like playing chess. There are only six different kinds of pieces on a chessboard but an infinite number of combinations of moves. Thus, with the verb-words in the BASIC language we can write programs to do such diverse things as:

1. Help a person find a mate.
2. Prepare a payroll for a company including the writing of the checks, determining the appropriate federal, state, and local tax deductions, social security tax, pension deductions, insurance deductions, etc.
3. Process applications for credit cards to determine who is eligible.
4. Maintain a running balance of the inventory of a company with many products.
5. Explore different marketing strategies by creating a hypothetical environment to test them in.

PROGRAMMING WITH DATA CARDS

The most common approach used to enter data and programs into a computer is by means of punched data cards. Processing data and programs punched on cards generally follows this sequence: (1) write your program on special coding paper; (2) submit it to a keypunch operator to have a deck of cards produced; (3) submit the completed deck to the computer

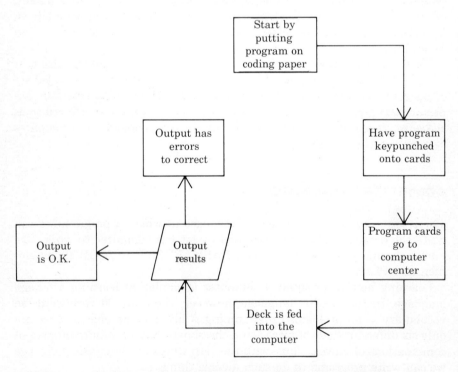

FIGURE 1.1 Sequence for Programming with Punched Cards

center, where it is placed on top of a batch of other decks waiting to be fed into the computer; (4) later in the day, or tomorrow or maybe next week, pick up your results, the *output*.

If you are lucky, the output is okay. If the program had an error in it, you have to correct it and start the sequence over again. Figure 1.1 illustrates the sequence described above.

TIMESHARING

A major problem with the punched card approach is that users do not have ready access to the computer. This means that fast and immediate results cannot be obtained. In the 1960's timesharing systems were developed to overcome the problem of getting access to the computer and obtaining output results. Such systems consist of terminals (which often look like typewriters) connected by telephone lines to computers in other locations. In this manner many people can be connected to one computer. Figure 1.2 shows the general scheme of a timesharing system.

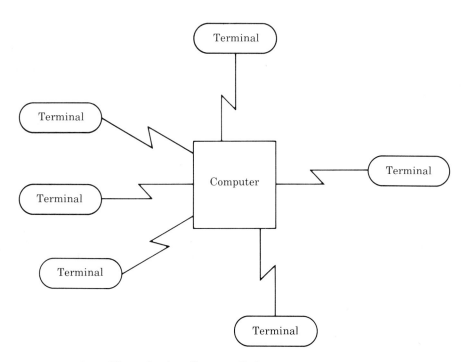

FIGURE 1.2   A Timesharing System Scheme

The computer, which works very quickly, can process many people's instructions in much the same way that a chess master can play "simultaneously" many players. He makes one move against each opponent, and by the time he has moved against all of his opponents, the first player is ready again with his next move.

With timesharing, programs can be processed almost immediately. Obvious errors can be corrected on the spot. Output can be obtained in minutes, rather than hours or days.

Because timesharing is a convenient and easy method of interacting with a computer, the use of such systems is on the rise. Typical timesharing users are in banking, health and medical care, airline, hotel, and car rental reservations, and other areas where a speedy response is required.

PURPOSE AND PLAN

The most widely used terminal-oriented programming language is BASIC (*B*eginners *A*ll-purpose *S*ymbolic *I*nstruction *C*ode). This book introduces the student to the BASIC language, one step at a time. The early chapters introduce simple programming concepts that, when applied, will build up the student's confidence and his ability to go on. In this way BASIC is easy to learn. If the time is taken to study each chapter and to do the many exercises at the end of each one, the student can easily move forward.

THE SYSTEM USED FOR THIS BOOK

The programs in this text were prepared on a Model 33 ASR data terminal like the one shown in Figure 1.3. Some programs were prepared on a paper tape before being transmitted to the computer over an acoustical coupler that links the terminal to the computer by telephone lines. Appendix A explains how a paper tape can be prepared by those students who will have to work with paper tapes.

The BASIC language discussed in this text is the BASIC found on the RAPIDATA System. Since some aspects of BASIC may differ from system to system, differences are noted throughout the text. Students are advised to refer to the appropriate system manual so that they can understand any differences encountered.

RECENT COMPUTER DEVELOPMENTS

In recent years portable desktop computers that are no bigger than an office typewriter have begun to appear. Many of these small computers feature

FIGURE 1.3   Model 33 ASR Teletype (Courtesy of Teletype Corporation)

the BASIC language for programming to solve problems. Figure 1.4 shows such a desktop computer.

FLOWCHARTING

A useful aid in understanding the logic of a program is a diagram showing the logic, called a program flowchart. For simple programs a flowchart is not necessary since the logic is apparent. The more involved the program, the more necessary the flowchart.

Typically, a programmer will make a rough diagram as a flowchart to help with the writing of the program. Ultimately, a final flowchart will be developed showing the logic of the final program. This final flowchart serves

FIGURE 1.4   IBM 5100 Portable Computer (Courtesy of IBM Corporation)

as documentation so that at some later date you, or other programmers, can understand the program it represents.

The standard flowcharting symbols used in this book are defined in Figure 1.5.

QUESTIONS

1. What are some applications of computers that you are aware of?
2. Discuss the advantages and disadvantages of timesharing.
3. What is meant by the term *computer program?*
4. What is meant by the terms *hardware* and *software?*
5. What is the purpose of program flowcharting?

Symbol	Meaning
Terminal	Stop, start, or end the program
Process	Calculations, assignments, or other operations
Input/Output	Input/Output: reading or writing
Decision	Compare, test, examine, and decide
Preparation	Initialize, set an index, perform an operation on the program for control
Connector	To go to, or come from, another part of the chart
Flow lines	Direction or flow, or sequence of operations

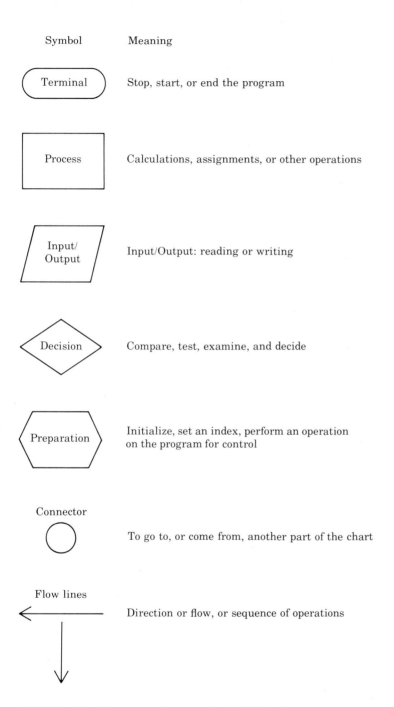

FIGURE 1.5 Flowchart Symbols and Meanings

2

BASIC Program Elements and Structure

STATEMENT NUMBERS

A program in BASIC consists of a series of statements. Each statement is an instruction that stands alone as a single line. Each line in the program starts with a line number. These numbers are necessary to tell the computer the sequence of the program statements. A simple program illustrating some statements in BASIC and the idea of line numbering is shown in Program 2.1.

PROGRAM 2.1 Line Numbering in a BASIC Program

```
10 REM AN ILLUSTRATION OF A BASIC PROGRAM
20 PRINT "BASIC IS NOT A DIFFICULT LANGUAGE TO LEARN"
30 READ A
40 DATA 573.8
50 PRINT A
60 END
```

Notice that every line in Program 2.1 has a different number. The numbers go from low to high. The available range is from 0 to 99999.* Typically,

---

*On some systems this range is smaller; on others it is larger.

spacing is suggested when numbering so that additional programming statements can be inserted if necessary. Line numbering such as

1
2
3
4
5

does not allow changes or additions to the program to be easily made. For example, a line cannot be added between lines 3 and 4. If the line numbering had been:

10
20
30
40
50

then a line could be added between existing lines if desired. For example, a line 25 can be inserted between the above lines 20 and 30. Line numbers are integer values only. Each line number is followed by a BASIC statement as shown in Program 2.1.

CONSTANTS AND VARIABLES

A *constant* is a value that remains fixed. Many computations use formulas that incorporate constant values. For example, compound interest is found using the formula $A = P(1 + r)^n$, where P is the principal or starting amount, r is the interest rate, n is the number of time periods, and A is the final result. The "1" in this formula is a constant. Examples of what constants can look like in BASIC are:

-6.345	.005214	3.1416
105138	2.71828	2

Program 2.2 illustrates the use of the above compound interest formula (with constants in the formula) to determine the total cost of a $3,000 loan, at 9 percent interest, compounded yearly for 6 years.

PROGRAM 2.2   Finding Compound Interest: Constant Values

```
10 LET A = 3000*(1.0 + .09)↑6
20 PRINT A
30 END
```

When processing numerical data in BASIC, leading plus and minus signs and decimal points appropriate to the numbers being used are acceptable. Here are some unacceptable data values:

$100 . . . the dollar sign is not permitted
−58.32.6 . . . two decimal points are not allowed
4,365 . . . a comma between characters is not allowed
228− . . . the minus sign should not be at the end

A *variable* represents a value that is not fixed. In the compound interest formula shown earlier, the components *P, r,* and *n* represent factors that can change and thus are variables. For compound interest we may want to find the value of *A* for numerous sets of variables *P, r,* and *n.* For example,

P	r	n
$1,000	5%	5 years
2,000	6	10
4,000	8	12

In BASIC any single alphabetic letter from *A* to *Z,* or any alphabetic letter followed by a numeric value from 0 (zero) to 9, may be used to specify a variable. This gives a total of 286 possibilities for variable names: 26 single letters, plus 10 times 26 combinations of *A*0 to *A*9, . . . , *Z*0 to *Z*9. Some examples of acceptable variable names are:

A	*B*	*X*	*Z*3	*B*2
*C*9	*F*1	*D*5	*X*7	*M*8

Some unacceptable variable names are:

5*X* . . . alphabetic character must be first
*A*22 . . . only a single numeric is allowed
JOE . . . only a single alphabetic is allowed
B− . . . either a single alphabetic or an
 alphabetic followed by a numeric
 is permitted

Program 2.3 shows how the compound interest for many sets of variables can be found. The above values for *P, r,* and *n* are used.

PROGRAM 2.3 Finding Compound Interest Using Variables

```
10 READ P,R,N
20 DATA 1000,.05,5,2000,.06,10
30 DATA 4000,.08,12
40 LET A = P*(1.0 + R)↑N
50 PRINT A
60 GO TO 10
70 END
```

Note that the variables in BASIC as well as the words in each line of Program 2.3 are capitalized. This is because most computer systems will only print with uppercase letters. Therefore, throughout this book all BASIC programs and examples will be in uppercase letters. When you write a BASIC program, all lowercase letters should be capitalized.

COMPUTATIONAL OPERATIONS

To direct the computer to perform a computation, the symbols for such computation must be used. These symbols in BASIC are as follows:

Operation	BASIC Symbol	Arithmetic Examples	BASIC
Exponentiation	↑	$X^2, 17^{1/2}$	X↑2,17↑.5
Multiplication	*	$A \times B, 2.14 \times D$	A*B, 2.14*D
Division	/	$\dfrac{50}{Z}, L \div M$	50/Z, L/M
Addition	+	$A + B + C, 15 + X$	A+B+C, 15+X
Subtraction	−	$X - Y, B - 1.5$	X−Y, B−1.5

Besides knowing the symbols for computations, the programmer must know how expressions are evaluated by the computer. The order of priority is to do first any exponentiations; second any multiplications or divisions; and third any additions or subtractions. An expression is evaluated from left to right, following the order just described. Some examples are:

Expression	BASIC	Sequence of Operation
1. $A^2 - B + 4$	A↑2−B+4	$\overset{\boxed{1}}{A}\overset{\boxed{2}}{↑2}−\overset{\boxed{3}}{B+4}$
2. $X + Y^2/Z^3$	X+Y↑2/Z↑3	$X+\overset{\boxed{4}}{Y}\overset{\boxed{1}}{↑2}/\overset{\boxed{3}}{Z}\overset{\boxed{2}}{↑3}$
3. $3/P - A \times C$	3/P − A*C	$\overset{\boxed{1}}{3/P} −\overset{\boxed{3}}{A}\overset{\boxed{2}}{*C}$

Notice in example 1 that subtraction is done before the addition. This sequence is because they are on the same level and, going from left to right, whichever comes first is done first.

In example 2, going from left to right and by order of priority, the exponentiation operations are carried out first and second, the division third, and the addition last. In example 3, going from left to right, the division is done first, the multiplication next, and the subtraction last.

Another concept that needs to be understood is the use of parentheses, or brackets, in an expression. Operations that are placed within parentheses will be performed before those that are not in parentheses. The sequencing described above will still apply to items in the parentheses. Below are several examples:

Expression	BASIC	Sequence
1. $a^2 + \dfrac{b}{2a}$	A↑2+B/(2*A)	$\boxed{2}\ \boxed{4}\ \boxed{3}\ \boxed{1}$ A↑2+B/(2*A)
2. $P \times (1 + r)^n$	P*(1+R)↑N	$\boxed{3}\ \boxed{1}\ \boxed{2}$ P*(1+R)↑N
3. $(2 + X) \times (Y - 4)$	(2+X)*(Y−4)	$\boxed{1}\ \boxed{3}\ \boxed{2}$ (2+X)*(Y−4)
4. $K \times \dfrac{(L + M)^2}{4}$	K*((L+M)↑2/4)	$\boxed{4}\ \boxed{1}\ \boxed{2}\boxed{3}$ K*((L+M)↑2/4)

Notice in each example that if the parentheses were not present the sequence of evaluation would change. Here is what the interpretation by the computer would be:

1. $a^2 + \dfrac{b}{2} \times a$

2. $P \times 1 + r^n$

3. $2 + X \times Y - 4$

4. $K \times L + \dfrac{M^2}{4}$

Each expression is now something very different from the original form.

Note that in the earlier BASIC example 4, K*((L+M)↑2/4), the items L+M that are contained within parentheses are themselves within parentheses. This inner expression L+M is evaluated first, followed by the remaining items within the outer parentheses.

SUMMARY

A program in BASIC consists of statements each starting with a line number. Programs can contain both constants and variables.

Possible variable names are the 26 letters of the alphabet, and each letter followed by a single numeric, zero to nine—for a total of 286 variable names.

When directing the computer to perform computations the following rules should be understood:

1. Higher order operations are done before lower order ones, the order of priority being (1) exponentiation, (2) multiplication and division, (3) addition and subtraction.

2. Expressions are evaluated from left to right.

3. Operations within parentheses are performed before those outside parentheses according to order priority in rule 1.

4. With multiple parentheses the order of evaluation starts with the innermost parentheses and proceeds outward.

EXERCISES

2.1 Which of the following constants are acceptable in BASIC?
   a. $-.00567$ c. 1,281.3   e. 161.00   g. $\$+28.56$
   b. $+8.1302$ d. $2.61-E3$ f. $+\$28.56$ h. -459176

2.2 Which of the following are unacceptable BASIC variables and why?
   a. $X11$ c. $-M5$ e. PI g. $K9$
   b. $I3$ d. $C.2$ f. N h. $D+8$

2.3 Write the following expressions using BASIC notations:
   a. $\frac{1}{2}bh$ e. $6XY$ i. $-0.2X^3 + 10X$

   b. $b^2 - 4ac$ f. $X^2 + 2XY + Y^2$ j. $.35X \div 200$
   c. $P(r + 1)^n$ g. $g - n + K$
   d. t^{2n+2} h. $.80^5$

2.4 Rewrite each of the following expressions in BASIC symbols and notation, and solve using the values $a = 5$, $b = 3$, $c = 4$, $d = 2$:

   a. $\frac{b - 2}{d + a}$ d. $a(b + 1)^d$ g. $-abc^d$

   b. $c^2 - \frac{b}{2 + a}$ e. $\frac{2a}{b + d} - \frac{a - b}{d^2}$ h. $\frac{(-abc)^d}{5d}$

   c. $\frac{b}{3} - ac$ f. $5^d - \frac{a}{-b+c}$

2.5 Use appropriate variables and notation to write a BASIC expression that will give you net pay, which is gross pay less a deduction equal to 22 percent of gross pay.

2.6 In inventory analysis we attempt to find what is called the *economic order quantity*. This quantity can be calculated using the following formula:

$$\sqrt{\frac{2 \times \text{annual required units} \times \text{cost per order}}{\text{Cost per unit of item} \times \text{percent carrying cost}}}$$

Rewrite this expression with symbols and notation acceptable to BASIC. It is helpful to note that the square root of a number is equal to that number raised to the one-half power.

2.7 The Cobb-Douglas production function often encountered in macro-economics has the form:

$$\text{Output} = A \times L^{\alpha} \times K^{1-\alpha}$$

where A is technical progress, L is the employed labor force, K is the stock of capital for production, α (alpha) is the fraction of total output earned by labor, and $1 - \alpha$ is the fraction of total output earned by capital. Write the function as an expression in BASIC. Remember that α is not an acceptable BASIC symbol.

3

END, PRINT, and REM

You can begin writing programs in the BASIC language almost immediately. Only two statements are required to generate output. This chapter shows how it is possible, with the use of the PRINT and END statements, to start programming. The third statement described in this chapter (REM) does not generate output.

THE END STATEMENT

Every program written in BASIC must conclude with a statement indicating termination. The END statement does this. It is assigned the highest line number in the program.

The general form of this statement is

line # END

For example, 999 END is a complete END statement.

THE PRINT STATEMENT

The PRINT statement produces printed output. In general this statement can be used within a program in three different ways: (1) labeling and providing headings, (2) carrying out computations where it is not necessary to store and identify the computation, and (3) showing the end result of the computation carried out as a separate operation using a LET statement.*
In this chapter, only items (1) and (2) will be covered.

—————
*See Chapter 5.

The PRINT statement has the general form

$$\text{line \# PRINT} \begin{Bmatrix} \text{labels or headings} \\ \text{computations} \\ \text{values or numbers} \end{Bmatrix}$$

Printing Literals

A literal is an expression, label, heading, or term made up of alphabetic or numeric characters or a combination of both. For example, a description of a part and the number of units in stock could be made up by alphabetic and numeric characters as illustrated by the following:

Alphabetic	Numeric	Combination
Red Pins: Stock	1,458	Red Pins: Stock 1,458

Both alphabetic and numeric literals can be printed by placing the items to be printed in quotes. For example,

5 PRINT "RED PINS:STOCK 1,458"

A numeric can also be printed without being placed in quotes as long as it does not include any special characters such as commas. For example,

5 PRINT 1458

Programs 3.1 through 3.3 illustrate literal printing.

The output for each program is found after the word RUN. This word is a system command that is typed on the computer terminal and causes the program to be executed, that is, to have the program processed by the computer.*

PROGRAM 3.1 Printing Alphabetic Literals

```
5 PRINT "RED PINS:STOCK"
9 END


RUN
RED PINS:STOCK
```

---

*Appendix B describes some of the system commands that appear in this text. These commands are generally similar to those in most other systems. It is always a good idea to read the appropriate system manual so that you understand all system commands.

PROGRAM 3.2   Printing Alphabetic and Numeric Literals

```
5 PRINT "RED PINS:STOCK 1,458"
9 END


RUN
RED PINS:STOCK 1,458
```

PROGRAM 3.3   Printing a Numeric Literal without Quotes

```
5 PRINT "RED PINS:STOCK"
7 PRINT 1458
9 END


RUN
RED PINS:STOCK
 1458
```

Program 3.1 shows the alphabetic literal. Program 3.2 presents the combined alphabetic and numeric literal. Program 3.3 illustrates how a numeric does not have to be quoted to be printed.

It is a common error to forget the closing quotes when using the PRINT statement. An error message, such as "ILLEGAL EXPRESSION," may indicate that this has occurred.* Check all PRINT statements if such a message appears.

Blank spaces can improve the appearance of a BASIC program. Since blanks outside of the quotes are ignored by the computer, it would be better from a reading standpoint to have

5 PRINT "XYZ COMPANY FINANCIAL STATEMENT"

rather than

5PRINT"XYZ COMPANY FINANCIAL STATEMENT"

even though both statements are the same to the computer.

Those blanks that are included in the quotes are *not* ignored; they result in a space for each blank as part of the output. To see this effect, refer back to Programs 3.1 and 3.2 and the resulting output.

---

*After running a program you may find that the output contains a message indicating that something is wrong with your program. Such error messages direct you to correct whatever is wrong. Since messages differ from system to system, the system manual should be studied for the appropriate error messages and their meaning.

E Format

When values are printed out, they are generally limited to six character spaces, plus a decimal point if required.* For numbers that exceed these space limits, the *E format* may result. This scientific format indicates that the number to the left of the *E* should be multiplied by 10 raised to the power of the number after the *E*. For example, the value 2,000,000 in *E* format is 2.0*E*6. The interpretation, 2×10^6, tells us to multiply the 2 times 10 raised to the 6th power, which is the same as adding six zeros after the 2 to give 2,000,000.

If the *E* format is positive, to return to the full value equivalent move the decimal point to the right the number of places shown after the *E*. So for 2.0*E*6 we have

$$2.000000.$$

in which the decimal point is moved to the right six places. A value such as .00000456 in *E* format would be expressed as 4.56*E*−6. The *E* followed by a minus sign means that the value on the left is divided by 10 raised to the power to the right of the minus sign. In this example we have

$$\frac{4.56}{10^6} \quad \text{or} \quad \frac{4.56}{10000000}$$

To return from an *E* minus format to the full decimal equivalent, move the decimal point to the left the number of places indicated by the number after the *E* minus. So for 4.56*E*−6 we have

$$.000004.56$$

where the decimal point is moved to the left six places.

Numerical data in *E* form can be included in a PRINT statement. Program 3.4 shows data in line 5 that is in *E* form; lines 10 and 20 show data that are very large and very small in value. The output illustrates what happens when these types of data are printed.

PROGRAM 3.4   Printing with E Format

```
5 PRINT 5.5E4,.283E-2
10 PRINT 1000000,2500000
20 PRINT .0000456,.052146721
99 END


RUN
  55000          .00283
  1E 6           2.5E 6
  4.56E-5        5.21467E-2
```

*Space limits differ from system to system.

Computational Printing

The PRINT statement can be used to direct the computer to perform computations. All of the symbols and operations described in Chapter 2 can be incorporated in a PRINT statement. Programs 3.5–3.7 demonstrate computational printing using the information from Case 3.1.

CASE 3.1 The tax on sales in a certain state is 5 percent of the total value of the items purchased. Suppose two items were purchased for $5 and $10, respectively.

PROGRAM 3.5 Case 3.1, A Single Computational PRINT Statement

```
2 PRINT (5+10)*.05
10 END


RUN
.75
```

The output of Program 3.5 is a result of the computation performed based on line 2 of the program. Only the tax on the total is printed out. Note the use of parentheses to ensure the addition is carried out first, then followed by the multiplication.

Typically, the output desired has headings or labels. Programs 3.6 and 3.7 show how headings and labels can be added. Observe that both programs show that more than one computation is possible in the PRINT statement (line 40).

PROGRAM 3.6 Printing Headings, Multiple PRINT Computations

```
10 PRINT "TOTAL","TAX"
20 PRINT "SALES","TOTAL"
40 PRINT (5+10),(5+10)*.05
50 END


RUN
TOTAL        TAX
SALES        TOTAL
 15           .75
```

PROGRAM 3.7 Underlining Headings, Multiple PRINT Computations

```
10 PRINT "TOTAL","TAX"
20 PRINT "SALES","TOTAL","GRAND TOTAL"
30 PRINT "-----------------------------------------------"
40 PRINT (5+10),(5+10)*.05,(5+10)+(5+10)*.05
50 END


RUN
TOTAL        TAX
SALES        TOTAL        GRAND TOTAL
---------------------------------------------
 15           .75          15.75
```

Observe that none of the computations carried out with the PRINT statements in Programs 3.6 and 3.7 have quotes around them. A computation placed in quotes would result in the quoted expression being treated as a literal, not a computation.

Many times a computer output should have blank lines to improve the appearance of the output. Such a blank line can be obtained by inserting a PRINT statement as shown in Program 3.8, line 60.

PROGRAM 3.8 Skipping Lines Using the PRINT Statement

```
20 PRINT "TOTAL SALES"
40 PRINT "------------"
60 PRINT
80 PRINT "    $";(5+10+20)
90 END


RUN
TOTAL SALES
------------

   $ 35
```

For every blank PRINT in a program, a line is skipped. By properly inserting these PRINT statements, as many lines as desired can be skipped.

OUTPUT SPACING

The timesharing terminal output page commonly has a capacity of 75 character spaces from the left to the right margin. When a PRINT statement indicates that more than one item will be printed on a line, the spacing is regulated by the computer. Two punctuation marks can be used with the PRINT statement to control how the output is spaced. These punctuation marks are the comma and the semicolon.

The Comma

In a PRINT statement the comma sets the spacing at a field width of 15 spaces.* If you look back at the output of Programs 3.6 and 3.7, you will see spacing based on the commas in lines 10, 20, and 40 of both programs. In each program the literal headings and computational prints have been separated by commas.

---

*Some systems may set spacing in a slightly smaller or slightly larger field width.

　　With 75 character spaces to a line, the use of the comma permits up to five fields of 15 spaces for output. Program 3.9 has generated output that shows all five print fields being used.

PROGRAM 3.9　Print Field Positions Using Commas

```
5 PRINT "PRINT POSITION SHOWN BY NUMBERS BELOW"
10 PRINT
20 PRINT"12345678901234567890123456789012345678901234567890123456789012345678901"
30 PRINT"FIELD 1","FIELD 2","FIELD 3","FIELD 4","FIELD 5"
40 END

RUN
PRINT POSITION SHOWN BY NUMBERS BELOW

12345678901234567890123456789012345678901234567890123456789012345678901
FIELD 1         FIELD 2         FIELD 3         FIELD 4         FIELD 5
```

　　The output from Program 3.9 shows the location of each of the five print fields. This can be summarized as follows:

Print Field	From Left Margin Starting Position
1	1
2	16
3	31
4	46
5	61

Literals and negative values will be printed starting in these positions. Positive values are printed one space farther to the right to allow for the fact that a + sign was not printed (but can be assumed). The output of Program 3.7 illustrates where literals and numerics have their starting positions.

　　It may be desired to skip a field so as to have output spaced across the entire page. Such field skipping can be accomplished by using a blank quote as shown in line 5 of Program 3.10.*

PROGRAM 3.10　Skipping Fields

```
5 PRINT "FIELD 1"," ","FIELD 3"," ","FIELD 5"
10 END

RUN
FIELD 1                         FIELD 3                         FIELD 5
```

---

*On some systems, quotes are not needed; only an extra comma is required.

An additional feature of the comma is its use as a means of continuing output printing on one line even though two or more PRINT statements are used in a program. If a PRINT statement ends with a "dangling comma," the output paper will not advance to the next line. Instead, the output of the next PRINT statement will follow on the same line as the preceding output. This continuation is shown in Program 3.11.

PROGRAM 3.11   Commas at the End of a PRINT Statement

```
 5 PRINT "GROSS WAGE",
10 PRINT "+ OVERTIME",
15 PRINT "= TOTAL WAGE",
20 PRINT "- TAXES",
25 PRINT "= NET WAGE"
99 END


RUN
GROSS WAGE      + OVERTIME      = TOTAL WAGE    - TAXES         = NET WAGE
```

Observe that the output from Program 3.11 is spaced in conformance with the five print field positions described earlier.

The Semicolon

The semicolon, when used in a PRINT statement between positive numerical data, will result in two blank spaces being placed between the printed output.* One blank is from the semicolon, the other represents the positive sign. If a semicolon is followed by a negative numeric, only one blank space will result. Using the semicolon instead of the comma enables output to be "packed" on a line. This packing can be seen in the output of Program 3.12. Line 25 of the program shows various numerical values separated by semicolons.

PROGRAM 3.12   Printing Packed Output Using the Semicolon

```
25 PRINT 1;2;3;4;5;6;7;8;9;10;100;2000;-888;12.6+83
99 END


RUN
 1  2  3  4  5  6  7  8  9  10  100  2000  -888  95.6
```

Program 3.13 shows a mixture of commas and semicolons in PRINT statements.

---

*Not all systems follow these spacing patterns.

PROGRAM 3.13   Mixing Commas and Semicolons

```
5 PRINT 100/2;100/3,100/4;100/5
10 PRINT 100/2,100/3;100/4;100/5
99 END

RUN
 50    33.3333    25   20
 50               33.3333   25   20
```

When used with literals the semicolon does *not* provide extra spacing. The effect of a semicolon between literals is the same as using a hyphen in a word break at the end of a line. If the semicolon is at the end of a PRINT statement, the output paper will not advance. Program 3.14 shows the "dangling semicolon" at the end of line 10 with the resulting output. Program 3.15 shows what can happen to the output when the dangling semicolon is used between literals. Extra spacing is needed to make the output correct. Such spacing is supplied by using blanks within the quotes as shown in lines 20 and 30 of Program 3.16.

PROGRAM 3.14   Semicolon at the End of a PRINT Statement

```
10 PRINT "                        UNITED STATES OF A";
20 PRINT "MERICA"
99 END

RUN
                        UNITED STATES OF AMERICA
```

PROGRAM 3.15   The Semicolon between Literals

```
10 PRINT "THE SEMICOLON DOES NOT";
20 PRINT "PROVIDE SPACING"
99 END

RUN
THE SEMICOLON DOES NOTPROVIDE SPACING
```

PROGRAM 3.16   The Semicolon between Literals with Spacing

```
10 PRINT "TO USE THE ; WITH LITERALS";
20 PRINT " YOU CAN PROVIDE";
30 PRINT " THE EXTRA SPACES NEEDED."
99 END

RUN
TO USE THE ; WITH LITERALS YOU CAN PROVIDE THE EXTRA SPACES NEEDED.
```

To understand the spacing that results when literals and numerics are separated by semicolons, study Program 3.17. A literal followed by either numerics or a computation, and separated by a semicolon, will be printed out with a single space after the literal if the numeric/computation is positive, and no space if negative. A numeric/computation before a literal, separated by a semicolon, will provide a single space between the printed output.

PROGRAM 3.17   The Semicolon between Literals and Numerics

```
10 PRINT "ENDING INVENTORY";200-15;"UNITS"
99 END


RUN
ENDING INVENTORY 185 UNITS
```

THE REM STATEMENT

Very often it is desirable to provide statements within the written program that spell out in some detail the purpose of the program as well as describe what various sections are supposed to do. These remark, or REM, statements are part of program documentation. This kind of documentation is useful to the programmer and to others who want to review and better understand the program.

Lines 5 and 10 in Program 3.18 illustrate how comments are put into a program by using REM statements. The output is not affected by these statements because they are ignored by the computer.

PROGRAM 3.18   REM Statements in a Program

```
5 REM THIS PROGRAM WAS WRITTEN BY B. BOSWORTH IN BASIC
10 REM IT ILLUSTRATES SOME ASPECTS OF PRINTING.
20 PRINT "SALES TAX IS";5;"% OF TOTAL"
30 REM COMPUTATIONAL PRINT IN LINE 40.
40 PRINT "TOTAL $";25+30+5.15
99 END


RUN
SALES TAX IS 5 % OF TOTAL
TOTAL $ 60.15
```

Program 3.19, using the information in Case 3.2, illustrates the many things that the PRINT statement can do by itself.

CASE 3.2 The annual interest on corporate bonds is found as follows:

$$\text{Annual interest} = \text{par value} \times \text{annual interest rate}$$

An investor having the following bonds would use such a formula to compute the interest on each bond.

Total Par Value	Interest Rate
$4000	$6\frac{1}{4}\%$
7000	$7\frac{5}{8}$
3000	$6\frac{1}{2}$
8000	$8\frac{1}{8}$

Program 3.19 calculates the interest for each bond in Case 3.2. Later on we will see that it is possible to solve problems like the above with less involved PRINT statements.

PROGRAM 3.19 Case 3.2, Computing Bond Interest with PRINT

```
5 REM PROGRAM TO COMPUTE BOND INTEREST
10 PRINT "    TOTAL","INTEREST"," ANNUAL"
15 PRINT "PAR VALUE"," RATE","INTEREST"
20 PRINT "------------------------------------"
30 PRINT "$4000","6 1/4%","$";4000*.0625
40 PRINT "$7000","7 5/8%","$";7000*.07625
50 PRINT "$3000","6 1/2%","$";3000*.065
60 PRINT "$8000","8 1/8%","$";8000*.08125
90 END
```

```
RUN
    TOTAL        INTEREST        ANNUAL
 PAR VALUE         RATE         INTEREST
------------------------------------------
 $4000          6 1/4%          $ 250
 $7000          7 5/8%          $ 533.75
 $3000          6 1/2%          $ 195.
 $8000          8 1/8%          $ 650
```

SUMMARY

Every BASIC program must have an END statement which has the highest line number in the program.

PRINT statements can generate alphabetic, numeric, and alphanumeric output. They can also perform computations. Output is printed from the left margin.

Commas in a PRINT statement will typically generate output spacing in five fields of 15 character spaces each. A comma at the end of a PRINT statement will not let the paper advance to the next line if space is available. The next PRINT statement will use any available space and then continue to a new line if it is needed.

Semicolons in a PRINT statement leave:

1. One blank space if placed after a numeric and before a numeric or a quoted item.

2. No blank spaces if placed after a quoted item and before another quoted item or a numeric.

Remarks in the form of REM statements provide comments and descriptions (documentation) about a program. They can be placed anywhere in the program. They do not generate output.

EXERCISES

3.1 For the information listed, write a PRINT statement in BASIC that generates one line of output.
   a. Earnings for 3rd Quarter.
   b. In field two, Division; in field four, Sales.
   c. A heading with each item in a separate field; name, social security number, date of birth, number of dependents.

3.2 The following PRINT statements contain errors; correct them.
   a. 10 PRINT "FINANCIAL REPORT   e. PRINT "HELP"
   b. 20 "PRINT INVENTORY LEVEL"   f. PRINT 279, UNITS
   c. 30 "JANUARY"   g. 50 PRINT 10 + 62.5 =
   d. "40 PRINT CURRENT ASSETS"   h. 60 PRINT 20(485,000)

3.3 Convert these values from E format:
   a. .528 $E-5$ d. $3.41791E-02$
   b. $.0153E-5$ e. $7531E7$
   c. 4.68 $E6$ f. $-1.23658E-02$

3.4 Write and run a program that will show your name, address, and course number.

3.5 Using the digits in your social security number, write and run a program that will:
   a. print out the number
   b. sum up the digits of the number
   c. calculate the average digit
   d. show the sum of the digits squared

3.6 Sales are $5, $10, and $15. The tax rate is 5 percent. Write a program using the PRINT statement that when it runs has the output under the following heading:

Sales	Tax	Total

3.7 Redo exercise 3.6 with "$" signs in the output.

3.8 Redo exercise 3.7 with the output in the following format:

Sales	$	$	$
Tax			
Total	$	$	$

3.9 The area of a triangle is found by using the expression $\frac{1}{2}\,bh$, where b is the base dimension and h is the height of the triangle. Write a program to find the area for each of the following triangles:

Base	Height
5	7
10.5	6.2
100	78

Your output should have labels for all the variables and the areas found.

3.10 To find the roots of an equation, $a + bX + cX^2$, the quadratic formula can be used. That is,

$$X = \frac{-b \pm (b^2 - 4ac)^{1/2}}{2a}$$

Suppose $a = 5$, $b = 2$, and $c = 3$; write a program that uses this formula to get the roots of the equation with these values.

3.11 Redo exercise 3.10 so that the output shows all values a, b, c, and X with labels.

3.12 Write a program using the computational PRINT to evaluate each of the following expressions, given that $a = 3$, $b = 6$, and $c = 3$:

a. $a + \dfrac{b}{c}$

c. $\dfrac{(a + b)^2}{c}$

b. $\dfrac{a + b}{c}$

d. $a^2 + \dfrac{b}{c}$

3.13 Redo exercise 3.12 such that the output shows each of the expressions that were evaluated, the values used, and the final answer.

3.14 Many marketing promotions consist of computerized letters sent through the mail. Write a program that generates the following letter:

Dear Student: Today's Date
 Stop by the computer lab for a demonstration of the timesharing equipment being used. Before coming, please read the chapters in the text that I have assigned. Looking forward to seeing
you in the lab.

                                     _____
                                     Your Instructor

3.15 Revise exercise 3.9 to include REM statements describing the program.

3.16 In accounting, one measure of a company's financial condition is the current ratio. This ratio is computed as current assets divided by current liabilities. Below are several years of data for the GIGO Computer Company, Inc.:

	1970	1971	1972
Current assets	$370,000	$400,000	$450,000
Current liabilities	160,000	100,000	150,000

Write a program that will output this data as well as the current ratio for each year. Have the current ratio appear on a line below the current liabilities for each of the years shown.

3.17 Redo exercise 3.16 so that output follows this format:

Year	Assets	Current Liabilities	Ratio
1970			
1971			
1972			

3.18 A firm estimates that 5 years from now it will need $2 million to purchase some new equipment. To accumulate this sum, it is decided to set aside an amount each year. The firm can earn 9 percent compounded annually on their cash. To find the amount that must be deposited at the end of each of the 5 years to accumulate the $2 million the following formula is used:

$$A = F\left[\frac{r}{(1 + r)^n - 1}\right]$$

where A is the amount to be deposited at the end of n years, with the annual interest rate of r, and F is the future sum needed. Write a program that will find A. Include REM statements in your program. In addition to A, have the output show F, r, and n.

READ/DATA, RESTORE, and INPUT

Chapter 3 showed how the PRINT statement could be used to generate specific output based on numeric data that is placed in PRINT statements. Only limited amounts of data can be placed into a program using the PRINT statement. To enter larger amounts of data into a program the READ/DATA statements can be used. In this chapter, we will see how numerical data can be entered into a BASIC program and assigned to variables by means of the READ/DATA and INPUT statements.

THE READ AND DATA STATEMENTS

The general forms for the READ and DATA statements follow:

line # READ variable name list
line # DATA data list

Each variable name except the last one in the READ statement is followed by a comma. No punctuation is required at the end of the READ statement. The DATA statement has items separated by commas and, like the READ statement, requires no ending punctuation.

Program 4.1 illustrates the READ/DATA statements. The READ A, B in line 10 will have the values in line 15 assigned to the variables *A* and *B*, respectively. Variable *A* will take on the value 5, and variable *B* will take on the value 10.

PROGRAM 4.1   READ/DATA Statements

```
5 REM THIS PROGRAM ADDS TWO NUMBERS
10 READ A,B
15 DATA 5,10
40 PRINT "A=";A;"B=";B,"SUM=";A+B
99 END


RUN
A= 5 B= 10      SUM= 15
```

The variable names and items in READ/DATA statements have to be matched on a sequential one-for-one basis. Thus, if we have three values, we could write three variable names:

$$10 \text{ READ } X, Y, Z$$
$$20 \text{ DATA } 10, -6, 5.2$$

X is set equal to 10, Y is set equal to -6, and Z is set equal to 5.2. If there were additional data in line 20, say

$$20 \text{ DATA } 10, -6, 5.2, 16, 38$$

the values 16 and 38 would not be read since only three variables are specified in line 10. If the data was

$$20 \text{ DATA } 10, -6$$

the program execution would terminate since the data set has only two items while the READ requests values for three variables. An "OUT OF DATA LINE 10" message would appear as output.* Program 4.2 illustrates what happens when the program has excess data or insufficient data.

PROGRAM 4.2   Excess Data and Insufficient Data

Excess Data	Insufficient Data

```5 PRINT "X","Y","Z"```
```10 READ X,Y,Z```
```15 DATA 10,-6,5.2,16,38```
```20 PRINT X,Y,Z```
```99 END```
	```5 PRINT "X","Y","Z"```
	```10 READ X,Y,Z```
	```15 DATA 10,-6```
	```20 PRINT X,Y,Z```
	```99 END```

```
RUN                                 RUN
X            Y           Z          X              Y              Z
  10          -6          5.2

                                    OUT OF DATA- LN #   10
```

Program 4.3 shows various READ/DATA statement arrangements. Since the computer matches variables and data on a sequential one-for-one basis,

---

*This output is not true of all systems. Check your system manual to see what the output will be.

breaking up the READ and DATA statements as shown in Program 4.3b
and 4.3c does not change the output.

PROGRAM 4.3   READ/DATA Statement Arrangements

(a)
```
10 READ A,B,C
15 DATA 5, -7, 9
20 PRINT A,B,C
40 END


RUN
   5                  -7                 9
```

(b)
```
5 READ A
10 READ B
20 READ C
30 DATA 5, -7, 9
35 PRINT A,B,C
40 END

RUN
   5                    -7                    9
```

(c)
```
10 READ A,B
15 DATA 5, -7
20 READ C
25 DATA 9
30 PRINT A,B,C
40 END


RUN
   5                  -7                 9
```

As seen in Program 4.3, the DATA statement can be placed either before
or after the READ statement, as long as it is before the END statement.
This point is made in Program 4.4. The output for Program 4.4a–c is the
same regardless of where the DATA statement is located. If the data list
is to be changed, it is easier to have the data in statements just before the
END statement (Program 4.4c).

PROGRAM 4.4   Positions of the DATA Statement

(a)
```
5 REM DATA BEFORE READ
10 DATA 15,6,7
20 READ A,A1,A2
30 PRINT A,A1,A2
40 END


RUN
  15                 6                 7
```

(b)
```
5 REM DATA IMMEDIATELY AFTER READ
20 READ A,A1,A2
25 DATA 15,6,7
30 PRINT A,A1,A2
40 END


RUN
  15                 6                 7
```

(c)
```
5 REM DATA JUST BEFORE THE END
20 READ A,A1,A2
30 PRINT A,A1,A2
35 DATA 15,6,7
40 END


RUN
  15                 6                 7
```

Printing a variable before a value has been assigned to it can, on some systems, result in an error message such as, "UNDEFINED VARIABLE IN LINE #." On the RAPIDATA System all undefined variables are assigned a value of zero. Program 4.5 illustrates the printing of an undefined variable, A, in line 10.

PROGRAM 4.5   Printing an Undefined Variable

```
10 PRINT A
20 READ A
30 DATA 38 1
40 END


RUN
 0
```

Since the computer retains only the current value of a variable, a PRINT statement with a variable in it will result in output for the current value of the variable. Program 4.6 illustrates this point. Line 10 of the program reads variable A twice, first assigning $A = 7$, and then $A = 3$. When line 20 (the PRINT statement) is executed, the value for A that is printed out is 3, as shown by the output.

PROGRAM 4.6   Printing the Current Value

```
10 READ A, B, C, A
20 PRINT A, B, C
30 DATA 7, 9, 6, 3
40 END


RUN
 3               9               6
```

The use of the READ/DATA statements in a programming application is shown in Program 4.7. This program is based on Case 4.1.

CASE 4.1   Total profit is found by subtracting total cost from total revenue. Total revenue is found by multiplying revenue per unit (price) times the number of units sold; and total cost is obtained by multiplying the cost of each unit sold times the number of units sold. Symbolically, we can write $T = P \times U - C \times U$.

Program 4.7 obtains the total revenue, total cost, and total profit if the selling price per unit is $10, cost per unit is $6.50, and 225 units are sold.

PROGRAM 4.7   Case 4.1, Finding Total Profit, READ/DATA Statements

```
5 REM PROGRAM TO FIND TOTAL PROFITS.   TOTAL PROFITS = TOTAL REVENUE -
10 REM TOTAL COST.   WHERE P=PRICE PER UNIT, C=COST PER UNIT,
15 REM AND U=# UNITS SOLD AND BOUGHT
30 READ P,C,U
40 DATA 10,6.50,225
65 PRINT
68 PRINT
70 PRINT "TOTAL PROFIT REPORT"
75 PRINT
80 PRINT "NUMBER OF UNITS SOLD";U
85 PRINT "PRICE PER UNIT";P,"COST PER UNIT";C
90 PRINT "TOTAL REVENUE";P*U
92 PRINT "LESS TOTAL COST";C*U
95 PRINT "---------------------------------"
100 PRINT "TOTAL PROFIT";P*U-C*U
199 END


RUN


TOTAL PROFIT REPORT

NUMBER OF UNITS SOLD 225
PRICE PER UNIT 10               COST PER UNIT 6.5
TOTAL REVENUE 2250
LESS TOTAL COST 1462.5
-----------------------------------
TOTAL PROFIT 787.5
```

Program 4.7 demonstrates one advantage of using READ/DATA statements. Specifically, when the program is generalized so that it can be used over and over again, with different sets of data each time, only the data lines have to be changed. If computational PRINT statements were used instead of the READ/DATA statement, such a program would be impractical as well as troublesome to change each time new data had to be used.

THE RESTORE STATEMENT

There are times where it is necessary to reread data previously read in a program. Data once read cannot be read again unless the DATA lines are repeated or a RESTORE statement is used. The RESTORE statement has the form

line # RESTORE

This statement causes the data initially read from storage to be replaced in storage. Program 4.8 shows a simple program using the RESTORE. The data was initially read in and corresponds to the variables A, B, and C. The RESTORE in line 20 restores the data of line 10 for use again. Line 25 causes the data 1, 2, 3 to be assigned to the variables X, Y, and Z, respectively.

PROGRAM 4.8   RESTORE Statement

```
1 PRINT "A","B","C"
5 READ A,B,C
10 DATA 1,2,3
15 PRINT A,B,C
18 PRINT
20 RESTORE
22 PRINT "X","Y","Z"
25 READ X,Y,Z
30 PRINT X,Y,Z
99 END


RUN
A               B               C
 1               2               3

X               Y               Z
 1               2               3
```

If the RESTORE was not inserted at line 20, the READ statement at line 25 could not be executed since no data would be available to read.

THE INPUT STATEMENT

One of the major advantages of using a terminal is the ability to carry out a "conversation" with the computer via the program being run. Such "conversational programming" permits direct and almost immediate response from the computer. Real time systems, such as airlines reservation systems, employ this kind of interactive programming.

To write a program where a dialogue between the terminal user and the computer takes place, the READ/DATA statements are replaced by an INPUT statement. This statement has the form

line # INPUT variable list

A simple program using INPUT is shown in Program 4.9.

PROGRAM 4.9   INPUT Statement

```
10 INPUT A,B
20 PRINT "SUM OF";A;"AND";B;"IS";A+B
99 END


RUN
?5,10
SUM OF 5 AND 10 IS 15
```

When the INPUT statement is executed by the computer, a "?" mark appears as the initial output as shown in Program 4.9. The programmer or program user must then type in the values for A and B. In this case 5 and 10 are typed in, separated by a comma and without any ending punctuation.

```
RUN                                      RUN
?5                                       ?5,10,7

INCORRECT FORMAT - RETYPE--              INCORRECT FORMAT - RETYPE--
?5,10                                    ?5,10
SUM OF 5 AND 10 IS 15                    SUM OF 5 AND 10 IS 15
```

**FIGURE 4.1   Insufficient   FIGURE 4.2   Excess Data
Data Inputted   Inputted to
to Program 4.9   Program 4.9**

Note that inputting of data is similar to the placement of data in a DATA statement.

If the program user fails to type in all of the data as needed to conform to the INPUT statement, an error message will appear indicating more data is needed. This is shown in Figure 4.1. Figure 4.2 shows what happens when too much data is typed. An error message "INCORRECT FORMAT — RETYPE" has occurred because the data input does not conform to the variable list in line 10 of Program 4.9. Once the data is typed in and conforming to the variable list, the execution of the program continues as though no error was made.

Since application programs are often utilized by persons other than the programmers who write them, an INPUT statement in a program should be preceded by some statements that will explain to the user the format of the data to be inputted. Otherwise, the "?" could be meaningless to the program user when it appears. Thus, the programmer should write additional PRINT statements as shown in Program 4.10, which is a conversational version of Program 4.7.

PROGRAM 4.10   Case 4.1, Finding Total Profit, INPUT Statement

```
5 REM PROGRAM TO FIND TOTAL PROFITS.  TOTAL PROFITS = TOTAL REVENUE -
10 REM TOTAL COST.  WHERE P=PRICE PER UNIT, C=COST PER UNIT,
15 REM AND U=# UNITS SOLD AND BOUGHT.
25 PRINT "TO GENERATE OUTPUT FROM THE TOTAL PROFIT PROGRAM"
30 PRINT "WHEN THE ? APPEARS TYPE AFTER IT THE FOLLOWING ITEMS"
35 PRINT "EACH SEPARATED BY A COMMA:  PRICE PER UNIT, COST PER UNIT,"
38 PRINT "NUMBER OF UNITS SOLD."
39 INPUT P,C,U
65 PRINT
68 PRINT
70 PRINT "TOTAL PROFIT REPORT"
75 PRINT
80 PRINT "NUMBER OF UNITS SOLD";U
85 PRINT "PRICE PER UNIT";P,"COST PER UNIT";C
90 PRINT "TOTAL REVENUE";P*U
92 PRINT "LESS TOTAL COST";C*U
95 PRINT "---------------------------------"
100 PRINT "TOTAL PROFIT";P*U-C*U
199 END


RUN
TO GENERATE OUTPUT FROM THE TOTAL PROFIT PROGRAM
WHEN THE ? APPEARS TYPE AFTER IT THE FOLLOWING ITEMS
EACH SEPARATED BY A COMMA:  PRICE PER UNIT, COST PER UNIT,
NUMBER OF UNITS SOLD.
?10,6.50,225
```

Program 4.10 continued

```
TOTAL PROFIT REPORT

NUMBER OF UNITS SOLD 225
PRICE PER UNIT 10                COST PER UNIT 6.5
TOTAL REVENUE 2250
LESS TOTAL COST 1462.5
------------------------------------
TOTAL PROFIT 787.5
```

There are no limits to the number of INPUT statements that can be placed in a program. Multiple INPUTs are possible as illustrated by lines 15 and 25 in Program 4.11, which is based on Case 4.2.

CASE 4.2   As one part of controlling and analyzing its inventory system, the ABC Company has a program that is run each week. This program takes as input data the inventory level at the end of the previous week, as well as the number of units sold each day of the current week. As output the program generates for each day of the week, the beginning inventory, the number of units sold, and the ending inventory; it also shows the total number of units sold during the entire week.

PROGRAM 4.11   Case 4.2, Inventory Analysis, Multiple INPUTs

```
10 PRINT "WHAT IS BEGINNING INVENTORY?"
15 INPUT I
20 PRINT "WHAT WERE SALES FOR EACH DAY OF THE WEEK?"
25 INPUT M,T,W,T1,F
30 PRINT
35 PRINT "BEG. INV.";I;"UNITS"
40 PRINT
45 PRINT "                    DAILY SALES"
50 PRINT "                    ----------- "
55 PRINT "MON.","TUES.","WED.","THUR.","FRI."
60 PRINT M,T,W,T1,F
65 PRINT
70 PRINT "NUMBER OF UNITS SOLD THIS WEEK";M+T+W+T1+F
75 PRINT "ENDING INVENTORY";I-(M+T+W+T1+F)
99 END


RUN
WHAT IS BEGINNING INVENTORY?
?150
WHAT WERE SALES FOR EACH DAY OF THE WEEK?
?20,30,15,25,10

BEG. INV. 150 UNITS

                    DAILY SALES
                    -----------
MON.            TUES.           WED.            THUR.           FRI.
20              30              15              25              10

NUMBER OF UNITS SOLD THIS WEEK 100
ENDING INVENTORY 50
```

A program can have both READ/DATA and INPUT statements in it. The conversational part of the program will be based on the variable list of the INPUT statements. Other data that is required for the program can be entered by the READ/DATA statements.

Program 4.12 shows a program that converts miles to kilometers. The conversion factor is 1.609 kilometers to a mile. This constant is entered into the program by the READ in line 10. The INPUT statement is used to enter the number of miles to be converted to kilometers.

PROGRAM 4.12   A Program with Both READ/DATA and INPUT Statements

```
10 READ K
20 DATA 1.609
30 INPUT M
35 PRINT
40 PRINT M;"MILES IS EQUIVALENT TO";K*M;"KILOMETERS"
50 END


RUN
?2000

 2000 MILES IS EQUIVALENT TO 3218 KILOMETERS
```

Another example of a program containing both READ/DATA and INPUT statements is Program 4.13 based on Case 4.3.

CASE 4.3 An individual retirement account (IRA) permits an annual contribution of up to $1500 a year. The total accumulation for such an account is calculated by the formula

$$F = A\left[\frac{(1 + R)^N - 1}{R}\right]$$

where F is the total, A is the amount paid into the account each year for N years, and R is the rate of interest.

If $1500 a year is put into an IRA at 7.5 percent compounded annually for 10 years, what is the total accumulation?

Treating R as a constant and A, N as variables to be entered by an INPUT statement, Program 4.13 supplies the answer. The flowchart for this program is shown in Figure 4.3.

PROGRAM 4.13   Case 4.3, Finding the Accumulation in an IRA Account with READ/DATA and INPUT Statements

```
10 READ R
20 DATA .075
30 PRINT "AFTER THE QUESTION MARK APPEARS TYPE THE"
40 PRINT "ANNUAL CONTRIBUTION, AND THE NUMBER OF YEARS IT"
50 PRINT "WILL BE PAID INTO THE IRA ACCOUNT."
60 PRINT
70 PRINT "WHAT IS THE ANNUAL CONTRIBUTION, AND HOW MANY YEARS"
80 PRINT "WILL IT BE PAID IN";
90 INPUT A,N
100 PRINT
110 PRINT"A YEARLY CONTRIBUTION OF $";A;"FOR";N;"YEARS"
120 PRINT"COMPOUNDED AT 7.5% EACH YEAR, GENERATES A TOTAL"
130 PRINT"IRA ACCOUNT OF $";A*(((1.0 + R)↑N - 1.0)/R)
140 END


RUN
AFTER THE QUESTION MARK APPEARS TYPE THE
ANNUAL CONTRIBUTION, AND THE NUMBER OF YEARS IT
WILL BE PAID INTO THE IRA ACCOUNT.

WHAT IS THE ANNUAL CONTRIBUTION, AND HOW MANY YEARS
WILL IT BE PAID IN ?1500,10

A YEARLY CONTRIBUTION OF $ 1500 FOR 10 YEARS
COMPOUNDED AT 7.5% EACH YEAR, GENERATES A TOTAL
IRA ACCOUNT OF $ 21220.6




RUN
AFTER THE QUESTION MARK APPEARS TYPE THE
ANNUAL CONTRIBUTION, AND THE NUMBER OF YEARS IT
WILL BE PAID INTO THE IRA ACCOUNT.

WHAT IS THE ANNUAL CONTRIBUTION, AND HOW MANY YEARS
WILL IT BE PAID IN ?1000,15

A YEARLY CONTRIBUTION OF $ 1000 FOR 15 YEARS
COMPOUNDED AT 7.5% EACH YEAR, GENERATES A TOTAL
IRA ACCOUNT OF $ 26118.4
```

Note that the output for Program 4.13 shows two sets of results. The second set was obtained by running the program again with a different set of inputs for A and N. Thus, results for different sets of contributions and years can be calculated by running the program over again.

Also observe the dangling semicolon at the end of line 80. This symbol causes the INPUT question mark to appear on the same line as the output of the PRINT statement.

SUMMARY

Data can be entered into a program by using either the READ statement or the INPUT statement, or both.

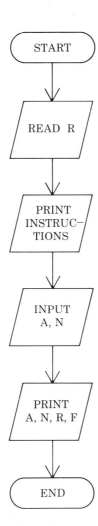

FIGURE 4.3 Flowchart for Case 4.3, IRA Account Program 4.13

When using the READ/DATA statements there must be enough data to agree with the variable list in the READ. Too little data will result in an error message.

A RESTORE statement can be used so that the DATA statements of a program can be reread.

Interactive or conversational programs use the INPUT statement. When data is typed in response to an INPUT statement, it must be typed in exact conformance with the variable format. Too much or too little data will result in an error message.

EXERCISES

4.1 What output will result from the following program:

    10 DATA 60,4,20
    20 READ A, B, C
    30 PRINT A+B+C/B
    40 PRINT (A/B)*C+B
    99 END

4.2 What output will result from each of the following programs:

a. 5 READ A   b. 5 READ A,A
    10 PRINT A;   10 PRINT A,A
    15 DATA −32   20 PRINT A;
    20 READ A   25 PRINT A
    25 PRINT A   30 DATA −32,7
    30 DATA 7   99 END
    99 END

4.3 Write programs using READ/DATA statements for the following Chapter 3 exercises:

a. 3.6   b. 3.9   c. 3.10   d. 3.16

  2.9   2.12   2.13   2.19

4.4 Real estate brokers are often compensated on a straight commission basis. Their total earnings are computed this way:

$$\begin{pmatrix} \text{Value of real estate} \\ \text{property sold} \end{pmatrix} \times \begin{pmatrix} \text{commission} \\ \text{rate \%} \end{pmatrix} = \begin{pmatrix} \text{commission} \\ \text{on sale} \end{pmatrix}$$

If there is a 6 percent commission rate on all property sold less than $100,000, write a program that computes the commissions for the following salespersons on each of the properties they sold:

Person	Value of Property Sold
A. Smith	$40,000
	62,500
	47,500
J. Jenkins	76,250
	49,500
	57,500

4.5 The United Computer Company pays its salespersons a monthly salary of $1000 plus 1½ percent commission for equipment sold during the month. The table below shows the sales figures by person for last month.

Salesperson	Amount Sold
1	$13,500
2	21,000
3	9,600
4	24,400

a. Write a program that will produce a table containing the above information plus an additional column that shows the total salary plus commission on sales. Have the sales, percent, and salary in one DATA line.

b. Why is it practical to have the salary and percent as part of your DATA line instead of using these values in a computational PRINT?

c. When would it be practical to have two DATA lines, one for sales and one for salary and percent?

4.6 The ABC Company has four divisions selling various products. Management wants to know what percent of total sales volume is generated by each division. Below are the gross sales figures for the last year by division.

Division	Sales (million $)
1	2.85
2	7.62
3	3.57
4	2.81

Write a program that reads in the sales data and generates as output a table that (1) shows the above with total sales and with a third column headed "% OF TOTAL", and (2) shows the percent for each division. The last column will sum to 100.0.

4.7 For the program below what will the output look like?

```
10 READ A, B, C
20 DATA 2, 4, 6
30 PRINT (A+B)/C
40 RESTORE
50 READ B, A, C
60 PRINT (A+B)/C
70 RESTORE
80 READ C,A,B
90 PRINT (A+B)/C
100 RESTORE
110 READ C,B,A
120 PRINT (A+B)/C,
130 RESTORE
140 READ A,C,B
150 PRINT (A+B)/C
199 END
```

4.8 Below are a set of investments that are to be increased by the same three interest rates, first by 7 percent, then by $7\frac{1}{2}$ percent, and then by $8\frac{1}{4}$ percent. Write a program that will increase this set of investments by these three rates.

One year investments: $3,000; $10,000; $12,500; $17,000

4.9 Do exercise 4.8 making use of the INPUT statement.

4.10 Do exercise 4.5 making use of an INPUT statement for the sales, the salary, and the commission's percent.

4.11 The ABC Company (see exercise 4.6) anticipates that, for this year and the next 2 years, sales in each division will grow above last year's sales by the following percentage growth rates:

	Last Year-1	This Year-2	Next Year-3	Year After-4
Percent	100.0	108.0	114.2	121.3

Write a program that will generate for each of the divisions the expected sales for the years involved. Your output should have the following headings:

Three Year Sales Forecast–ABC Company

Division	Year 1	Year 2	Year 3	Year 4
1				
2				
3				
4				

Put both the sales and the percents in DATA lines.

4.12 In macroeconomics one often encounters the Cobb-Douglas production function which takes the form:

$$\text{Output} = AL^{\alpha} K^{1-\alpha}$$

where A is technical progress, L is the employed labor, K is the stock of capital for production, α is the fraction of total output earned by labor, and $1 - \alpha$ is the fraction of total output earned by capital.

If A is 15, L is 500, K is 250, and α is .5, write a program that reads in this data and computes output. The program should also print out all of the components that went into the function.

4.13 A balance sheet in accounting is divided into two parts. On the left are the "assets" and on the right are the "liabilities and capital." Assets consist of current plus fixed assets. Suppose the XYZ Company has current assets of $45,000, fixed assets of $78,000, current liabilities of $32,000, and capital of $91,000; write a program that reads in this data and prepares a balance sheet with a heading and labels for all the items mentioned including totals for both parts.

4.14 There is a mathematic property that states: for a set of data the sum of the deviations about its mean is equal to zero; or $\Sigma (X_i - U) = 0$, where Σ is the sum of, X_i is each data value, and U is the average or mean of all the X_i. For the following data, write a program that illustrates this property. (*Hint:* First compute the mean, then INPUT the mean.)

$$5, -3, 7, 8, -2$$

4.15 In statistics there is a measure of variation called the *standard deviation* which has the formula:

$$\sigma = \sqrt{\frac{\Sigma (X_i - U)^2}{N}}$$

where N is number of data values. Write a program to find the standard deviation for the data in exercise 4.14. *Note:* $\sqrt{X} = X^{1/2}$. See hint in exercise 4.14.

4.16 Suppose in Program 4.11 the PRINT statements in lines 10 and 20 ended with semicolons after the quotes. How would that affect the program? If you are not sure, first try this program:

10 PRINT "TYPE A AND B VALUES AFTER THE ? MARK";
20 INPUT A, B
30 PRINT "A + B = "; A + B
99 END

4.17 Revise Program 4.10 treating price (P) and cost (C) as constants entered by READ/DATA statements.

5

LET

THE LET STATEMENT

In the previous chapter, we studied how to assign values to variables with the READ/DATA and INPUT statements. Another way in which we can assign values to variables is with the LET statement. The LET statement is also used to evaluate expressions. The form of the LET statement is

$$\text{line \# LET \{variable\}} = \begin{Bmatrix} \text{constant} \\ \text{variable} \\ \text{expression} \end{Bmatrix}$$

The LET statement evaluates the expression on the right side of the equal sign and assigns that value to the variable on the left side of the equal sign. An expression here means any variable or constant or a valid combination of variables, constants, and operators ($+$, $-$, $*$, $/$, and $\uparrow$).

Some examples of the LET statement are given below:

1. 100 LET N = 5
2. 100 LET Y = A*X↑2 + B*X + C
3. 100 LET A = B
4. 100 LET J = J + 1

Example 1 assigns the value of 5 to variable N, even if N had some other value prior to the execution of line 100.

Example 2 evaluates the expression $A*X\uparrow2 + B*X + C$ and assigns the value of that expression to the variable Y. The variables $A, B, C,$ and X must have been assigned values prior to the execution of line 100. Again the previous value of variable *Y,* if any, would be replaced by the value of the expression.

In example 3 the value of variable *B* is assigned to variable *A*. That is, if variable *A* had the value 2 and variable *B* had the value 3, after line 100 is executed both variables have the value of 3.

Example 4 requires that variable *J* have been defined previously. It takes the old value of variable *J,* adds 1 to that value, and assigns that increased value to the variable *J.* Thus, if prior to line 100 variable *J* had the value 10, then after line 100 is executed variable *J* has the value of 11.

Note that the symbol "=" in the BASIC language does not mean equal. Example 4 clearly demonstrates this, since *J* is never equal to *J* + 1. It means, rather, assign the value on the right to the variable on the left.

Below are some examples of invalid LET statements.

1. LET 5 = N
2. LET A*X↑2 + B*X + C = Y
3. LET J + 1 = J

These examples are all invalid since the left side of the "=" can only contain a single variable.

Thus, while $A = B + C$ is the same as $B + C = A$ in mathematics, in the BASIC language

$$\text{LET } A = B + C$$

is a valid statement, but

$$\text{LET } B + C = A$$

is invalid. Program 5.1 illustrates the LET statement.

PROGRAM 5.1 The LET Statement

```
10 READ A,B,C
15 LET X=A+B+C
20 PRINT X,X↑2,X↑3
25 DATA 1,2,3
30 END


RUN
 6               36              216
```

Note that in Program 5.1 it would have been possible to omit line 15 and replace line 20 with Figure 5.1.

$$20 \text{ PRINT } A + B + C, (A+B+C)↑2, (A+B+C)↑3$$

FIGURE 5.1   PRINT without Using LET in Program 5.1

One advantage of Program 5.1 is that it avoids the lengthy statement in Figure 5.1. Another advantage is that the statement in Figure 5.1 requires the computer to add $A+B+C$ three times. The computer does not remember the sum of A, B, and C unless it is assigned to a variable. Thus, Program 5.1 requires less computations than a program having the statement in Figure 5.1.

Another application of the LET statement arises when lengthy computations are required. Suppose we wish to compute the value of

$$\frac{A^2 + B^2}{C(B - A)} \div \frac{(D - A)B}{C^2 - D^2}$$

Figure 5.2 shows us how. An easier way is illustrated in Figure 5.3.

10 PRINT ((A ↑ 2 + B ↑ 2)/(C*(B − A)))/(((D − A)*B)/(C ↑ 2 − D ↑ 2))

FIGURE 5.2 Lengthy Computations without Using LET

10 LET X1 = A ↑ 2 + B ↑ 2
15 LET X2 = C*(B−A)
20 LET X3 = (D−A)*B
25 LET X4 = C ↑ 2 − D ↑ 2
30 PRINT (X1/X2)/(X3/X4)

FIGURE 5.3 Lengthy Computations Using LET

Programs with statements like those in Figure 5.3 are much less prone to error than programs with statements like the one in Figure 5.2.

Program 5.2 has no practical application, but it does illustrate some of the ramifications of the LET statement.

PROGRAM 5.2 Several LET Statements

```
10 READ A, B, C, D
20 LET C= A
30 LET A= B+C
40 LET D= A+D
50 LET B= A
60 PRINT A, B, C, D
70 DATA 1, 2, 3, 4
80 END

RUN
  3            3            1            7
```

The variables changed as follows:

Line	A	B	C	D
10	1	2	3	4
20	1	2	1	4
30	3	2	1	4
40	3	2	1	7
50	3	3	1	7

Note that the order in which the statements are executed makes a considerable difference in the final output. Consider Program 5.3; this program consists of the identical statements of Program 5.2 but the output is completely different.

PROGRAM 5.3   The Order of the LET Statements

```
10 READ A, B, C, D
20 LET B=A
30 LET A=A+C
40 LET C=A
50 LET D=A+D
60 PRINT A, B, C, D
70 DATA 1, 2, 3, 4
80 END


RUN
 4              1              4              8
```

If we have the statement

$$10 \text{ LET } X = A + 1$$

and A has not been given a value previously, an error message will be printed such as "UNDEFINED VARIABLE ACCESSED ON LINE 10" referring to variable A. Some systems, though, will automatically assign the value zero to any undefined variable. Applications of LET statements are given in Cases 5.1 and 5.2.

CASE 5.1   One method of measuring inventory management is by finding the merchandise inventory turnover ratio and comparing it to the ratio of prior years or with similar industry measures. This ratio can be computed by taking the cost of goods sold and dividing by the average inventory. First, average inventory must be obtained. It is determined by taking the sum of the beginning and ending inventory and dividing by 2. The ratio can be found this way:

1. Average inventory $= \dfrac{\text{beginning inventory } + \text{ ending inventory}}{2}$

2. Merchandise inventory turnover ratio $= \dfrac{\text{cost of goods sold}}{\text{average inventory}}$

If your business has sold over a period of time $480,000 worth of goods, and beginning period inventory was $40,000 and ending period inventory was $20,000, what is the inventory turnover at cost?

Program 5.4 shows how the merchandise inventory turnover ratio can be obtained using only LET statements. These statements are found in lines 15–50.

Program 5.5 also calculates the merchandise inventory turnover ratio, but this program uses READ/DATA statements to place the data into the program rather than LET statements as in Program 5.4.

**PROGRAM 5.4   Case 5.1, Merchandise Inventory Turnover, Using LET
                Statements**

```
5 REM PROGRAM TO CALCULATE MERCHANDISE
10 REM INVENTORY TURNOVER AT COST
15 LET C=480000
20 LET B=40000
25 LET E=20000
30 LET I=B+E
40 LET A=I/2
50 LET T=C/A
60 PRINT "COST OF GOODS SOLD $";C
70 PRINT "BEG. INVENTORY $";B
80 PRINT "END. INVENTORY $";E
90 PRINT "AVERAGE INVENTORY $";A
100 PRINT
110 PRINT "MERCHANDISE INVENTORY TURNOVER AT COST $";T
199 END


RUN
COST OF GOODS SOLD $ 480000
BEG. INVENTORY $ 40000
END. INVENTORY $ 20000
AVERAGE INVENTORY $ 30000

MERCHANDISE INVENTORY TURNOVER AT COST $ 16
```

PROGRAM 5.5   Case 5.1, Merchandise Inventory Turnover, Using READ/DATA Statements

```
5 REM PROGRAM TO CALCULATE MERCHANDISE
10 REM INVENTORY TURNOVER AT COST
20 READ C,B,E
25 DATA 480000,40000,20000
30 LET I=B+E
40 LET A=I/2
50 LET T=C/A
60 PRINT "COST OF GOODS SOLD $";C
70 PRINT "BEG. INVENTORY $";B
80 PRINT "END. INVENTORY $";E
90 PRINT "AVERAGE INVENTORY $";A
100 PRINT
110 PRINT "MERCHANDISE INVENTORY TURNOVER AT COST $";T
199 END


RUN
COST OF GOODS SOLD $ 480000
BEG. INVENTORY $ 40000
END. INVENTORY $ 20000
AVERAGE INVENTORY $ 30000

MERCHANDISE INVENTORY TURNOVER AT COST $ 16
```

An illustration of both LET and INPUT statements is found in Program 5.6, which is based on Case 5.2.

CASE 5.2   One method of determining the depreciation of an item is by the straight line approach. In this approach, annual depreciation is found by dividing the cost of the item (less any salvage) by the estimated years of life of the item. This can be stated in the following way:

$$\frac{\text{Cost} - \text{salvage value}}{\text{Estimated years of life}} = \text{depreciation per year}$$

Suppose the XYZ Construction Company at the start of the year purchases a piece of equipment that costs $36,000. The useful life of this type of equipment is 3 years. At the end of that time the resale or salvage value is $1,200. It is desired to calculate the annual depreciation for the equipment.

Program 5.6 computes the annual depreciation. This "conversational" program uses an INPUT statement in line 20 to place the required values into the program. Line 25 calculates cost less salvage, and line 30 finds the depreciation. If another depreciation result is needed, we can type RUN and the program will start over again.

The flowchart for Program 5.6 is shown in Figure 5.4. Note the numbers placed in the upper right-hand corner of the flowchart symbols. These numbers correspond to the line numbers of the program and provide a means of cross-reference between flowchart and program.

PROGRAM 5.6 Case 5.2, Depreciation, Using LET and INPUT Statements

```
1 REM CONVERSATIONAL PROGRAM FOR STRAIGHT LINE
5 REM DEPRECIATION DETERMINATION
10 PRINT "****STRAIGHT LINE DEPRECIATION DETERMINATION****"
12 PRINT
15 PRINT "AFTER ONE ? MARK, TYPE IN THE FOLLOWING ITEMS EACH"
16 PRINT "SEPARATED BY A , :  COST, SALVAGE VALUE (TYPE Ø IF"
17 PRINT "NONE),EST. YEARS OF LIFE"
18 PRINT
20 INPUT C,V,L
25 LET T=C-V
30 LET D=T/L
35 PRINT
40 PRINT "WITH A COST OF $";C;", A SALVAGE VALUE OF $";V;
50 PRINT " AND A USEFUL LIFE OF";L;"YEARS"
60 PRINT "THE ANNUAL DEPRECIATION FOR THIS ITEM IS $";D
99 END

RUN
****STRAIGHT LINE DEPRECIATION DETERMINATION****

AFTER ONE ? MARK, TYPE IN THE FOLLOWING ITEMS EACH
SEPARATED BY A , :  COST, SALVAGE VALUE (TYPE Ø IF
NONE),EST. YEARS OF LIFE

 ?36000,1200,3

WITH A COST OF $ 36000 , A SALVAGE VALUE OF $ 1200  AND A USEFUL LIFE OF
 3 YEARS
THE ANNUAL DEPRECIATION FOR THIS ITEM IS $ 11600
```

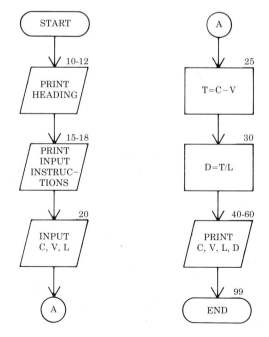

**FIGURE 5.4 Flowchart for Program 5.6,
Case 5.2, Depreciation, Using
LET and INPUT Statements**

SUMMARY

The LET statement, like the READ and INPUT statements, can be used to assign constant values to variables. In addition, the LET statement can be used to evaluate expressions and assign the values of those expressions to variables.

EXERCISES

5.1 Show what the following program will print when it is run:
```
10 READ A,B,C,D
15 DATA 1,2
20 LET X = A + B
25 LET B = X + A
30 LET A = X↑B/C * A − 5
35 DATA 4,5,6
40 PRINT A,B,C,X
45 END
```

5.2 What will the program in exercise 5.1 print if lines 25 and 30 are interchanged?

5.3 Write a program that reads in values for A, B, C, and D and then calculates

$$Y = \frac{(A + B)\uparrow 2}{C\uparrow 2 + D\uparrow 2} \div \frac{1/D + 1/B}{C\uparrow A - B}$$

Use LET statements to evaluate each of the numerators and denominators. The data to be used is 1, 2, 3, 4.

5.4 Rewrite Program 4.7 using LET statements to evaluate total revenue, total cost, and total profit. Assign the variable $T1$ to total revenue, $T2$ to total cost, and T to total profit.

5.5 Rewrite Program 4.11 using LET statements to evaluate the number of units sold this week using variable N, and the ending inventory using variable E.

5.6 Write a program to READ an employee's number, the number of hours that he worked, and his hourly rate, and prepare a table showing his number, his salary (number of hours $\times$ hourly rate), his federal tax (20 percent of his salary), his social security tax (.05478 $\times$ his salary), and his net salary (i.e., gross salary − all deductions). Use the LET statement. Data for the program is: number, 3542; hours worked, 37; and rate, 4.50.

6

GO TO, IF/THEN, Computed GO TO, and STOP

If the only capability of computers were statements like PRINT, READ/DATA, LET, and INPUT, the importance of computers would be similar to the importance of electronic calculators. It is the branching statements that are introduced in this chapter that give computers their immense power.

In all of the programs in the previous chapters, the statements were executed sequentially; that is, the first statement to be executed was the first statement in the program, the second statement executed was the second statement in the program, and so on, until the END statement was encountered. The branching statements of this chapter change this normal sequence of statement execution. There are two types of branching statements. The type discussed first is the unconditional branch—the GO TO statement.

THE GO TO STATEMENT

Consider Program 6.1, which presents an example of how the GO TO statement changes the normal sequence of the execution of the statements.

PROGRAM 6.1 GO TO Statement

```
10 READ X
15 PRINT X,X↑2,X↑3
20 GO TO 10
25 DATA 2, 4, 5, 10, 8, -3
30 END


RUN
 2              4              8
 4             16             64
 5             25            125
10            100           1000
 8             64            512
-3              9            -27

OUT OF DATA- LN #   10
```

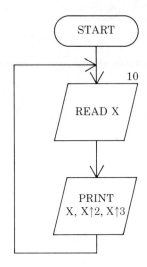

FIGURE 6.1 Flowchart of Program 6.1

In line 10 the READ X assigns the number 2 to the variable X. The PRINT statement on line 15 then prints the numbers 2, 4, and 8. The GO TO 10 on line 20 tells the computer to execute line 10 again. This time, the READ X assigns the number 4 to variable X since the first number in the DATA statement, the number 2, was already read. The program then prints the current values of X, X^2, and X^3, namely, 4, 16, and 64. When the GO TO 10 is encountered a second time, it again sends the computer looping back to line 10 to read another value of X. This procedure continues until there are no more numbers in the DATA statement that can be read. When the computer is told to read a number from the DATA statement and all of the numbers in the DATA statement have already been read, the computer prints "OUT OF DATA" in the line that tries to do the reading. The above program is an example of what is called a *loop*. See the flowchart in Figure 6.1.

Thus, the GO TO statement changes the normal sequence of the execution of the statements. It tells the computer what is the next statement to be executed. Program 6.1 will work for as many numbers as there are in the DATA statement(s). We are beginning to see the power of the computer.

The form of the GO TO statement is

line #1 GO TO line #2

When line 1 is encountered, the next statement to be executed will be line 2. Line 2 may be greater than line 1, in which case we wish to skip some statements; or, as in Program 6.1, line 2 may be less than line 1, in which case we want to repeat a number of statements.

We need never have statements like

$$100 \text{ GO TO } 101$$
$$101$$

Statement 100 accomplishes nothing since the next statement to be executed would be 101 anyway.

Program 6.2 has no practical importance other than illustrating the GO TO statement. The line numbers are executed in the following order: 10, 15, 45, 50, 35, 40, 55, 60, 20, 30, and 99, resulting in the printing of the statement EVERY GOOD PERSON DOES FINE.

PROGRAM 6.2 Several GO TO Statements

```
10 PRINT "EVERY";
15 GO TO 45
20 PRINT " FINE";
30 GO TO 99
35 PRINT " PERSON";
40 GO TO 55
45 PRINT " GOOD";
50 GO TO 35
55 PRINT " DOES";
60 GO TO 20
99 END


RUN
EVERY GOOD PERSON DOES FINE
```

Case 6.1 shows a program that uses a GO TO loop sequence of operation.

CASE 6.1 Because of increased labor and raw materials costs, the Global Manufacturing Company has decided to revise its prices on the items listed below. The price increase for each item is to be 6.6 percent above the current price.

Item Number	Current Price	Item Number	Current Price
218	$ 200	406	$ 179
233	1,456	407	1,000
345	545	557	267
367	248	679	470
401	225	887	359

Program 6.3, using a GO TO loop, generates a revised price list for Case 6.1.

PROGRAM 6.3   Case 6.1, Revising Price List

```
5 REM PROGRAM TO UPDATE PRICE LIST
10 PRINT "ITEM","CURRENT","REVISED"
11 PRINT "NUMBER","PRICE","PRICE"
15 READ I,P
20 LET R=P*1.066
30 PRINT I,"$";P,"$";R
40 GO TO 15
50 DATA 218,200,233,1456,345,545,367,248,401,225,406,179
55 DATA 407,1000,557,267,679,470,887,359
90 END
```

```
RUN
ITEM           CURRENT         REVISED
NUMBER         PRICE           PRICE
 218           $ 200           $ 213.2
 233           $ 1456          $ 1552.1
 345           $ 545           $ 580.97
 367           $ 248           $ 264.368
 401           $ 225           $ 239.85
 406           $ 179           $ 190.814
 407           $ 1000          $ 1066
 557           $ 267           $ 284.622
 679           $ 470           $ 501.02
 887           $ 359           $ 382.694

OUT OF DATA- LN #  15
```

Program 6.4 illustrates how the LET statement can be used as either a counter of items or as an accumulator of values. Variable C in the program, line 18, is being used to count the number of times the program cycles through the GO TO loop. Each time line 18 is executed, a constant value of 1 is added to the prior value of C. Line 5 gives an initial value to variable C of zero. This defining of a variable is often referred to as *initialization*.

PROGRAM 6.4   A Counter and Accumulator

```
5 LET C=0
10 LET S=0
12 PRINT "C","X","S"
15 READ X
18 LET C=C+1
20 LET S=S+X
25 PRINT C,X,S
30 GO TO 15
35 DATA 7,3,5,6
99 END
```

```
RUN
C              X               S
 1             7               7
 2             3               10
 3             5               15
 4             6               21

OUT OF DATA- LN #  15
```

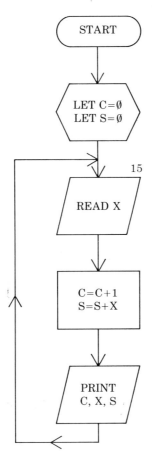

FIGURE 6.2   Program 6.4
Flowchart

Variable S is used in Program 6.4 to accumulate the sum (hence the variable name S) of the values in the DATA statement. The purpose of line 10 is to initialize the variable S to zero so that it can be used to accumulate the values of variable X in line 20 later on. More about initialization will be discussed later in this chapter.

When line 15 is executed the first time, the variable X is assigned the value 7. In line 20, variable S, which was zero because of line 10, becomes 7 since $0 + 7 = 7$. Line 25 prints the values of X and S, which are both 7, along with C, the counter, which is 1.

The GO TO 15 on line 30 causes the next value of X to be changed to 3 from 7, since the second entry in the DATA statement is 3. Line 20 now changes the value of S from 7 to 10 since $7 + 3 = 10$. Note that S did not become zero again since line 10 was only executed the first time. Line 25 then prints the current values of *C, X,* and *S* which are now 2, 3, and 10. This program will continue until all of the numbers in the DATA statement have been read. When GO TO 15 is then encountered, the computer attempts to read another *X* from the DATA statement and, since there is no data, the computer says "OUT OF DATA," as it did in Program 6.1. Figure 6.2 is a flowchart of Program 6.4.

Program 6.5 is another illustration of the GO TO statement.

PROGRAM 6.5   An Infinite Loop

```
10 LET X=1
15 PRINT X,X↑2,X↑3,X↑.5,1/X
20 LET X=X+1
25 GO TO 15
99 END
```

```
RUN
1          1          1          1          1
2          4          8          1.41421    .5
3          9          27         1.73205    .333333
4          16         64         2          .25
5          25         125        2.23607    .2
6
```

The execution of Program 6.5 will not stop unless the "plug is pulled out of the machine" or the computer reaches a number that is too large. Actually, you should never pull the plug. Each system has its own method for branching out of an infinite closed loop, as in Program 6.5. On the RAPIDATA System, you must type the letter *S* followed with a carriage return.

Line 10 initializes, that is, assigns initially to the variable *X* the number 1. Line 15 then prints the value of 1, 1^2, and 1^3, $\sqrt{1}$, and 1/1. In line 20, the variable *X* is increased by 1 so that it now assumes the value 2. Line 25 returns the execution to line 15 where 2, 2^2, 2^3, $\sqrt{2}$, and 1/2 are printed. *X* is then increased by 1 to 3 and the process is repeated. Note that no data is required in this program and hence the program will never run "OUT OF DATA" as Program 6.1 did. Thus, with a program of only five statements, we can get, theoretically, an infinite amount of information, namely, the squares, cubes, square roots, and reciprocals of all of the positive integers. With this program we see the real power of the computer. We can tell the computer to repeat a series of statements an infinite number of times. The computer, unlike people, does not get tired.

Program 6.6, which is based on Case 6.2, provides another illustration of the GO TO statement.

CASE 6.2 To calculate simple interest, the following formula is used:

$$\text{Interest} = \text{Principal} \times \text{Rate} \times \text{Time}$$

where the interest is the amount charged for the loan, the principal is the amount borrowed, the rate is the annual percentage charge, and the time is the fractional part of a year.

Given the following amounts that have been borrowed, the above formula could be used to determine the interest on each loan.

Loan	Principal	Rate	Time
1	$1,200	7%	7 months
2	850	9.5	6
3	11,250	9.25	9
4	8,566.50	11.75	4
5	2,500	10.50	8
6	925.75	8.25	5

Program 6.6 shows how the interest for the above loans can be calculated. A counter is used in this program (line 65) rather than including the loan number with the data. Note that in line 50 the interest rate is converted into decimal form by dividing by 100, and that the time, T, is divided by 12 to obtain the fractional part of the year.

PROGRAM 6.6 Case 6.2, Calculating Interest on Loans

```
5 REM PROGRAM TO FIND INTEREST ON LOANS
10 LET L=1
20 PRINT "LOAN","PRINCIPAL","RATE-%","TIME","INTEREST"
25 PRINT
30 READ P,R,T
50 LET I=P*(R/100)*(T/12)
60 PRINT L,"$";P,R,T;"MOS.","$";I
65 LET L=L+1
70 GO TO 30
90 DATA 1200,7,7,850,9.5,6,11250,9.25,9,8566.50,11.75,4
95 DATA 2500,10.5,8,925.75,8.25,5
99 END
```

```
RUN
LOAN            PRINCIPAL       RATE-%          TIME            INTEREST

1               $ 1200          7               7 MOS.          $ 49.
2               $ 850           9.5             6 MOS.          $ 40.375
3               $ 11250         9.25            9 MOS.          $ 780.469
4               $ 8566.5        11.75           4 MOS.          $ 335.521
5               $ 2500          10.5            8 MOS.          $ 175.
6               $ 925.75        8.25            5 MOS.          $ 31.8227

OUT OF DATA- LN #  30
```

THE IF/THEN STATEMENT

Whereas the GO TO statement branches unconditionally, that is, no matter
what, the IF/THEN statement will branch only if a particular condition
is true. Otherwise, it will not branch but will execute the next statement in
the sequence. That is, it will only branch conditionally.

The form of the IF/THEN statement is

line #1 IF{expression 1}relation{expression 2}THEN line #2

The kinds of relationships available on the computer are

Symbol	Example	Meaning
$<$	$A < B$	A is less than B
$<=$	$X <= 5$	X is less than or equal to 5
$>$	$A + B > C$	$A + B$ is greater than C
$>=$	$Y >= P + 5$	Y is greater than or equal to $P + 5$
$=$	$N = 10$	N is equal to 10
$<>$	$K <> L + M$	K is not equal to $L + M$

An example of an IF/THEN statement is

50 IF N = 10 THEN 80
60

Statement 50 says, test if the variable N is equal to the number 10. If it is,
then execute line 80 next. If the variable N is not equal to the number 10,
then execute the next statement in sequence (the one following this IF),
which is 60 in this example.

PROGRAM 6.7   The IF/THEN Statement

```
10 REM   THIS PROGRAM READS TWO NUMBERS AND PRINTS
15 REM   THE LARGER OF THE TWO
20 READ A, B
25 IF A>B THEN 40
30 PRINT B
35 GO TO 99
40 PRINT A
45 DATA 7, 3
99 END

RUN
7
```

Program 6.7 assigns the number 7 to variable A and the number 3 to variable B in line 20. Then A is compared to B by line 25. Since A is greater than

B, the next statement to be executed is line 40 which prints the value of *A*, which is 7. If the DATA statement in line 45 was 45 DATA 4, 12, variable *A* would have been assigned the value 4, and variable *B* would have been 12. Now when line 25 is encountered, the condition $A > B$ is not true so that line 40 is not executed next but line 30 is executed next instead. In line 30, the value of the variable *B*, which is 12, is printed. The GO TO 99 in line 35 prevents both numbers from being printed when *B* is the larger number.

Program 6.8 is another illustration of the IF/THEN statement.

PROGRAM 6.8 Summing Numbers and Their Squares

```
10 REM THIS PROGRAM READS 5 NUMBERS FROM THE DATA STATEMENT
20 REM AND PRINTS THE NUMBERS, THE SQUARES OF THE NUMBERS,
30 REM AND THE SUMS OF THE NUMBERS AND THEIR SQUARES.
40 LET S=0
45 LET S2=0
50 LET N=1
55 READ X
60 LET S=S+X
65 LET S2=S2+X↑2
70 PRINT X,X↑2
75 IF N=5 THEN 90
80 LET N=N+1
85 GO TO 55
90 PRINT "---","---"
95 PRINT S,S2
100 DATA 7,2,3,4,1
999 END


RUN
 7          49
 2           4
 3           9
 4          16
 1           1
 ---        ---
 17         79
```

Variables *S* and *S2* will accumulate the sum of the numbers and the sum of the squares of the numbers, respectively. These sums are initialized to zero, in lines 40 and 45. Variable *N* is used as a counter to count the number of data values that have been read in. *N* is initialized as 1 before the first number is read in. Lines 60 and 65 accumulate the sum and the sum of the squares of the numbers, and line 70 prints the number and its square. In line 75, we test if $N = 5$. That is, we see if we are finished processing all five numbers. If *N* is not 5, we proceed to line 80 where 1 is added to the variable *N*, and then we go back to line 55 to read the next number from the DATA statement. We repeat this process until all five numbers have been read, at which time *N* is equal to 5 and control is transferred to line 90.

Program 6.8 is a typical illustration of a program designed to do something a fixed number of times. The flowchart of this program appears in Figure 6.3.

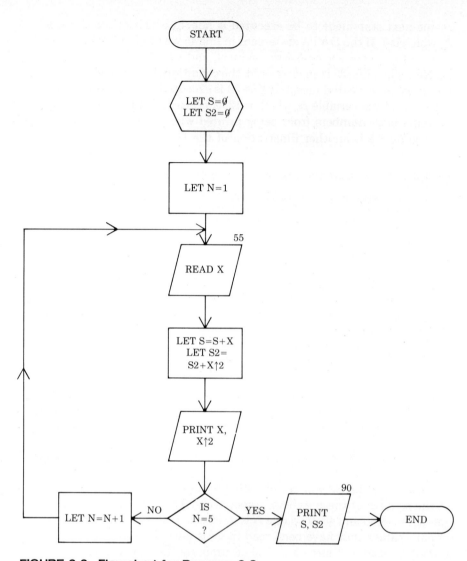

FIGURE 6.3 Flowchart for Program 6.8

Sometimes, we may not know exactly how many times we are to perform an operation but we want to keep performing it until we have used up all of the data. This is illustrated in Program 6.9.

PROGRAM 6.9 Testing DATA to End Program

```
10 REM THIS PROGRAM ACCOMPLISHES THE
15 REM SAME THING AS PROGRAM 6.3 EXCEPT
25 REM THE DECISION TO END IS MADE DIFFERENTLY
40 LET S=0
45 LET S2=0
50 READ X
55 IF X=999 THEN 30
60 LET S=S+X
65 LET S2=S2+X↑2
70 PRINT X,X↑2
75 GO TO 50
30 PRINT "---","---"
35 PRINT S,S2
90 DATA 7,2,3,4,1,999
999 END
```

```
RUN
 7        49
 2         4
 3         9
 4        16
 1         1
---       ---
17        79
```

Note that Program 6.9 has the same output as Program 6.8. Program 6.8 will work for any five numbers in the DATA statement. Program 6.9 will work for all numbers in the DATA statement up to the number 999. Thus, if line 90 were changed to

$$90 \text{ DATA } 7, 2, 3, 999, 4, 1$$

the numbers 4 and 1 will not be read by the program since as soon as the 999 is encountered the totals are printed. Similarly, if there are 50 numbers in the DATA statement followed by a 999, all 50 numbers would be processed.

Any number can be used to signal the end of the DATA. Thus, if line 55 were changed to

$$55 \text{ IF } X = 1000 \text{ THEN } 80$$

and the DATA statement was

$$90 \text{ DATA } 7, 2, 3, 4, 1, 1000$$

the output would also be identical to the output of Programs 6.8 and 6.9.

Case 6.3 shows an application of the IF/THEN and GO TO statements.

CASE 6.3 The ABC Company computes salesperson's monthly earnings on the following basis: monthly earnings are 20 percent of total sales; plus a bonus of $12\frac{1}{2}$ percent of any amount sold in excess of $5000. There are nine salespersons in the company and last month their sales were as follows:

Person	Monthly Sales
1	$4,000
2	6,250
3	4,750
4	4,800
5	7,125
6	6,050
7	8,300
8	3,500
9	9,625

Program 6.10 shows how earnings and bonuses can be found. Note that the program ends when the number -9999 is encountered in the DATA statement. In this case, we could not use the number 999 to signal the end of the DATA as was done in Program 6.9 since it is possible for a salesman to sell exactly $999 worth of merchandise, which would cause the program to end prematurely. A flowchart for Program 6.10 appears in Figure 6.4.

PROGRAM 6.10   Case 6.3, Calculation of Bonuses

```
5 LET P=0
8 READ E
11 IF E=-9999 THEN 99
12 DATA 4000,6250,4750,4300,7125,6050,3300,3500,9625,-9999
13 LET P=P+1
14 REM TEST FOR BONUS
15 IF E>5000 THEN 50
20 LET E1=.20*E
30 PRINT "PERSON";P,"NO BONUS THIS MONTH","EARNINGS $";E1
37 PRINT
40 GO TO 8
45 REM COMPUTATION OF BONUS
50 LET B=.125*(E-5000)
60 LET E1=.20*E+B
70 PRINT "PERSON";P,"BONUS    $";B,"EARNINGS $";E1
72 PRINT
80 GO TO 8
99 END


RUN
PERSON 1       NO BONUS THIS MONTH        EARNINGS $ 800

PERSON 2       BONUS    $ 156.25          EARNINGS $ 1406.25

PERSON 3       NO BONUS THIS MONTH        EARNINGS $ 950

PERSON 4       NO BONUS THIS MONTH        EARNINGS $ 960

PERSON 5       BONUS    $ 265.625         EARNINGS $ 1690.63

PERSON 6       BONUS    $ 131.25          EARNINGS $ 1341.25

PERSON 7       BONUS    $ 412.5           EARNINGS $ 2072.5

PERSON 8       NO BONUS THIS MONTH        EARNINGS $ 700

PERSON 9       BONUS    $ 578.125         EARNINGS $ 2503.13
```

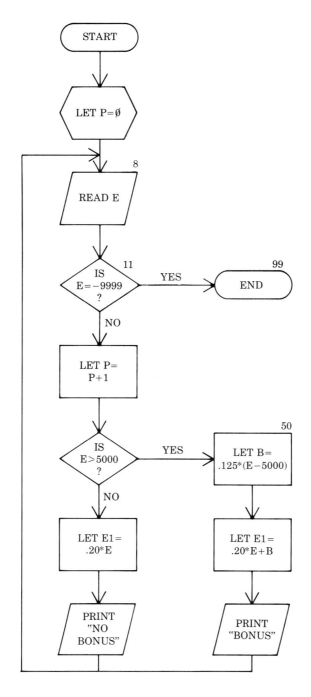

FIGURE 6.4   Flowchart for Case 6.3, Bonus Program 6.10

Case 6.4 shows how several IF/THEN statements can be combined to perform involved decisions.

CASE 6.4 The ACME Company wishes to print a list of the employee numbers of all employees who are eligible for retirement. In order to be eligible for retirement, any one of the following conditions must be satisfied:

1. The employee must be at least 65 years old.
2. The employee must have worked at least 30 years with the company.
3. The employee must be over 60 years old and have worked at least 25 years with the company.
4. The employee must be over 55 years old and have worked at least 20 years and have a salary of at least $30,000 per year (early retirement for executives).

We will now write a program that will read an employee's number, age, years employed with the company, and salary. We will then determine if he or she is eligible for retirement. If so, we will print his or her number. If not, we will go on to the next employee. We will continue until we have processed the data for all of the employees. The DATA for the last employee is followed by zeros to signal the program to end. Note that we also need zeros (or any number) for the variables A, Y, and S since the READ on line 10 reads all four variables.

The variables that we will use in this program will be:

Variable	Explanation
N	Employee number
A	Employee's age
Y	Years employed with the company
S	Employee's salary

Since there are many decisions in this program, we will first draw a flowchart. See Figure 6.5. Once the flowchart is drawn, the writing of the program follows readily, as shown in Program 6.11.

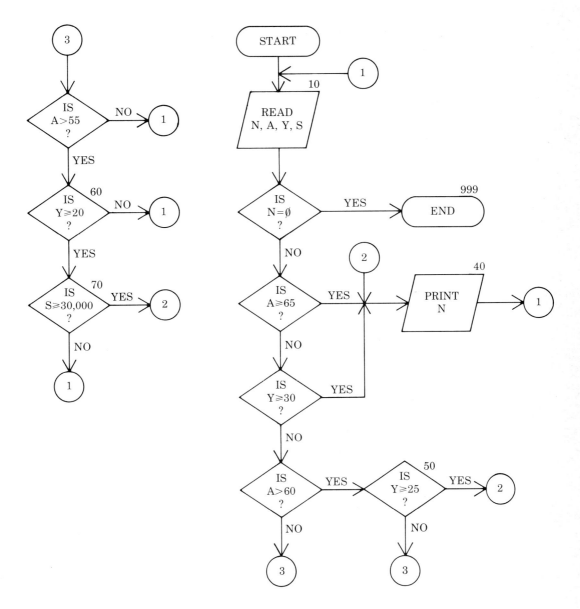

FIGURE 6.5 Flowchart for Program 6.11

PROGRAM 6.11   Case 6.4, Eligibility for Retirement

```
10  READ N,A,Y,S
12  IF N=0 THEN 999
15  IF A>=65 THEN 40
20  IF Y>=30 THEN 40
25  IF A>60 THEN 50
30   IF A>55 THEN 60
35  GO TO 10
40  PRINT N
45  GO TO 10
50  IF Y>=25 THEN 40
55  GO TO 30
60  IF Y>=20 THEN 70
65  GO TO 10
70  IF S>=30000 THEN 40
75  GO TO 10
80  DATA 1234,40,5,12500,1235,61,25,15000
85  DATA 1236,56,21,30000,1237,71,15,18000
90  DATA 1238,62,19,41000,1239,59,30,11000
95  DATA 1240,20,10,10000,1241,56,22,29000
100 DATA 1242,57,18,31000,1243,62,24,35000
101 DATA 0,0,0,0
999 END


RUN
 1235
 1236
 1237
 1239
 1243
```

Note the way the program follows the flowchart. We first read N, A, Y, and S in line 10 (note the 10 outside the upper right-hand corner of the READ N,A,Y,S box), and then we test if $N = 0$, in which case there is a branch to the end. Then we test if $A >= 65$. If this condition is true, we then GO TO 40 which is the PRINT statement. If this condition is false, we then test if $Y >= 30$, and so on. Observe that there are four statements that say GO TO 10, and note also that there are four arrows pointing to a 1 in the circles, which refers to the READ N,A,Y,S corresponding to line 10.

THE COMPUTED GO TO STATEMENT

Whereas the GO TO statement branches unconditionally to the indicated line number, the computed GO TO will branch to any one of several indicated line numbers depending on the value of a particular variable or expression. For example, the statement:

$$100 \text{ ON X GO TO } 50, 200, 75, 30$$

will branch to line 50 if $X = 1$, to line 200 if $X = 2$, to line 75 if $X = 3$, and to line 30 if $X = 4$. If X has any value less than 1, or 5 or more, an error message will be printed. If X has a fractional part, it is truncated. An illustration of the computed GO TO statement appears in Program 6.12. Note that if

$X = 3.6$, the program transfers control to line 50 where "THREE" is printed. It does not round X to the nearest integer. Also note that when $X = 5$, the error message "ON -5 LN # 15" was printed.

PROGRAM 6.12   Computed GO TO Statement

```
10 READ X
15 ON X GO TO 30,20,50,40
20 PRINT X;"TWO"
25 GO TO 10
30 PRINT X;"ONE"
35 GO TO 10
40 PRINT X;"FOUR"
45 GO TO 10
50 PRINT X;"THREE"
55 GO TO 10
60 DATA 1,2,3,4,1.5,4.8,3.6,2.2,5
99 END


RUN
 1 ONE
 2 TWO
 3 THREE
 4 FOUR
 1.5 ONE
 4.8 FOUR
 3.6 THREE
 2.2 TWO

ON- 5 LN #  15
```

THE STOP STATEMENT

The STOP statement does just what its name implies—it stops the program. If the END statement is on line 999, a STOP statement anywhere in the program is the same as a GO TO 999. The STOP statement differs from the END statement in that there can be several STOP statements anywhere in the program but there can be only one END statement and it must be the very last statement in the program. An example of the STOP statement is in line 35 in Program 6.13. Instead of 35 STOP we could have had 35 GO TO 99, which would have done the same thing, and is identical to Program 6.7.

PROGRAM 6.13   The STOP Statement

```
10 REM SAME PROGRAM AS 6.7
15 REM BUT USES THE STOP STATEMENT
20 READ A,B
25 IF A>B THEN 40
30 PRINT B
35 STOP
40 PRINT A
45 DATA 7,3
99 END

RUN
 7
```

SUMMARY

The GO TO and the IF/THEN statements are important statements in the BASIC language. The GO TO statement transfers control unconditionally to the indicated line number, and the IF/THEN statement transfers control to the indicated line number only if a certain condition is true. If the condition is not true, the statement following the IF/THEN statement is executed next. The relations that can be used in expressing conditions that can be tested are >, >=, <, <=, =, and <>.

The computed GO TO statement allows a programmer to transfer control to any one of several different line numbers based on the value of a particular variable. The STOP statement stops the program, just as a GO TO the END statement would.

EXERCISES

6.1 What would Program 6.1 do if line 20 were changed to
   a. 20 GO TO 15
   b. 20 GO TO 30

6.2 What would Program 6.2 do if all of the GO TO statements in lines 15, 30, 40, 50, and 60 were removed?

6.3 What would Program 6.4 do if
   a. line 35 were changed to 35 DATA 1,2,3,4,5,6?
   b. line 30 were changed to 30 GO TO 10?
   c. line 30 were changed to 30 GO TO 20?
   d. line 30 were changed to 30 GO TO 25?
   e. line 30 were changed to 30 GO TO 99?
   f. line 20 were changed to 20 LET X = X + S?
   g. line 20 were changed to 20 LET S = S + X↑2?
   h. a line 40 were added that read 40 DATA −4, −9, −8, −1?
   i. line 30 were eliminated?
   j. line 20 were eliminated?

6.4 What would Program 6.5 do if
   a. line 10 were changed to 10 LET X = 5?
   b. line 20 were changed to 20 LET X = X + 2?
   c. line 25 were changed to 25 GO TO 10?
   d. line 25 were changed to 25 GO TO 20?

What changes are necessary to change Program 6.5 so that the output prints the results for

e. only the even numbers. (*Hint:* Lines 10 and 20 must be changed.)

f. only the odd numbers.

g. the numbers 5, 10, 15, 20, ...

6.5   What is wrong with the statement:

$$50 \text{ IF } A > B \text{ THEN } 50$$

6.6   What would happen to Program 6.7 if

a. line 20 were changed to 20 READ B, A?

b. line 35 were omitted?

6.7   Write a program to print the sum of the odd numbers between 7 and 33.

6.8   Write a program to read three numbers and print the largest of the three.

6.9   Write a program to read three numbers and print the median (e.g., the median of 8, 12, 2 is 8).

6.10 Write a program to read numbers until 999 is encountered. Then have the computer print the average of the numbers.

6.11 Write a program to read 10 numbers that are grades in a programming examination. Have the computer print the average passing grade, the average failing grade, and the class average. Grades of 60 or above are considered passing. The data values to be used are: 60, 59, 40, 88, 98, 75, 90, 72, 82, and 77.

6.12 Rewrite Program 6.11 to test for the following conditions for retirement:

1. Age must be at least 62, or
2. Age must be at least 60 and the years employed must be at least 20, or
3. Years employed must be at least 20, or
4. Age must be at least 58 and years employed must be at least 20 and salary must be at least $25,000.

6.13 Write a program that reads in an employee's number, the number of his or her dependents, the number of hours that he or she worked during the week, the hourly rate that applies, and a code number of 0, 1, or 2 to indicate that the employee carries no insurance, personal insurance only, or family insurance, respectively.

Have the computer calculate the employee's wages. This should be number of hours $\times$ the hourly rate if the number of hours worked is 40 hours or less. If the number of hours worked is greater than 40, the employee should receive 1½ times the hourly rate for the additional hours above 40. The taxes deducted from the wages should be according to the following table:

Number of Dependents	Percent Deducted
0	28
1	26
2	24
3	22
4	20
5	18
6	16
7 or more	14

The insurance deducted should be according to the following table:

Code	Meaning	Amount Deducted
0	No insurance	$ 0
1	Insurance for self only	5
2	Insurance for family	10

Have the following table prepared:

Employee Number	Gross Wages	Tax Deducted	Insurance Deducted	Net Pay
Totals	_____	_____	_____	____

Prepare the DATA statement for 10 employees and execute the program.

```
920 DATA 6044,0,37,3.50,1,4411,2,42,3.75,2
930 DATA 7158,1,40,4.10,2,1142,0,47,4.50,1
940 DATA 6482,8,45,2.80,2,1231,4,50,2.50,1
950 DATA 7111,2,40,3.00,1,1421,5,42,2.60,2
960 DATA 8421,7,38,4.25,2,1333,0,41,2.80,0
```

6.14 Write a program that reads in a product number, quantity ordered, and unit price, and have the computer print a table with the following heading:

PRODUCT NO. PRICE QUANTITY DISCOUNT AMOUNT

A discount of 10 percent is given on all orders of at least 100 items. The amount is equal to price times quantity less discount. There is no discount on orders of fewer than 100 items. Use the following data:

Product Number	Price	Quantity
101	$2	250
210	6	95
330	3	110

6.15 Write a program that reads in four numbers and prints one of the following messages as appropriate:

"All of the numbers are equal to each other"

or

"Not all of the numbers are equal to each other"

6.16 What would Program 6.8 do if line 75 were changed to line 58?

6.17 What would Program 6.9 do if line 55 was changed to line 72?

6.18 Write a program that will compute federal and state tax deductions, based on the gross wages given below, and also the net wage after all taxes have been deducted.

Federal Deduction		State Deduction	
Gross Wage	%	Gross Wage	%
Less than or equal $200	15	Less than or equal $200	2
Greater than $200 but less than $301	20	Greater than $200	3
Greater than $300	22		

Have a heading that looks like this:

GROSS WAGE	FEDERAL TAX	STATE TAX	TOTAL DEDUCTIONS	NET WAGE

Use these data values: 200, 350, 300, 250, 100, 500.

6.19 Using the concept of the counter and the GO TO statement, write the program for exercise 4.5.

6.20 Using the GO TO statement, do exercise 4.11.

6.21 The following table shows the first quarter sales of the EXACT Company, by division. Sales are in thousands of dollars.

Division	January	February	March
1	$1,000	$ 750	$ 750
2	1,200	800	1,000
3	1,300	500	1,200
4	500	1,050	950

Write a program that outputs this table with total sales for each month at the bottom of each column.

6.22 Revise Program 6.11 so that the output will have a heading:

EL. EMP.   AGE   YRS. EMPL.   SALARY

with all the relevant data following.

6.23 Revise Program 6.11 so that the READ/DATA statements are replaced by an INPUT statement.

6.24 The bank your company uses for checking has the following method for checking account charges each month:

a. If the end of the month balance is $400 or more, there is no charge for the month regardless of the number of checks written.

b. If the end of the month balance is less than $400, there is a 25¢ per check charge for checks written during the month.

These charges are deducted from the balance in the account. There is already a $500 starting balance from the previous month to be carried over to month one.

Using the monthly data given below, write a program that generates output as follows:

Month	Checks Written	Ending Balance	Monthly Charges
1	xxxx	xxxxx	xxxx
2	xxxx	xxxxx	xxxx
.			
.			
.			
5	xxxx	xxxxx	xxxx

Data:

Month	Amount of Each Check Written	Deposits
1	$25, 500, 300, 75, 20, 10, 1500, 200, 700	$300, 200, 1000, 1500
2	$575, 500, 75, 725, 50, 65, 300, 55, 15	$750, 1200, 800
3	$30, 1200, 45, 55, 700, 1500, 400	$500, 1800, 1200
4	$1075, 125, 350, 60, 1440, 560, 200, 50	$1500, 1000, 1600
5	$75, 1025, 750, 35, 25, 165, 450, 565, 20	$1250, 1700, 1300

6.25 Many airlines have computerized reservation systems for their flights. As reservations are taken, the number of seats available begins to decline. It is important to be forewarned when the number of seats on a particular flight get low so as to prevent overbooking.

Suppose Goodflight Airlines has three daily flights as follows:

Flight No.	No. Seats Available at This Hour
381	25
402	15
283	30

In the last 4 hours the following number of reservations have been made for each of these flights:

Hour	No. Seats Reserved per Flight		
	381	402	283
1	5	7	0
2	7	1	2
3	5	3	3
4	5	2	5

Assume that at the end of every hour these figures are fed into the computer by a clerk to get an update on the seats available. If for any flight the number of seats is 10 or less, a warning for that flight is printed out on the computer terminal. Your job is to write and run a conversational program that a nonprogramming clerk will run so that at the end of each hour the current seating status for each flight is obtained. Your program should utilize the above information and be neatly structured with fully labeled output in your own format.

6.26 Write a program that will read 10 persons' application numbers, annual salary, rent, years employed at same job, and years living at same address. Have the computer print the application numbers of people who are eligible for a credit card. To be eligible, one must have a salary of over $25,000 per year, or have an annual salary of over $20,000 and pay a rent of less than one-quarter of a month's salary, or have an annual salary of over $15,000 and be living at the same address for more than 5 years, or have an annual salary of at least $10,000 and be living at the same address for at least 5 years and be employed at the same job for at least 3 years. All other applications are rejected. To write this program, it will be helpful to draw a flowchart.

Use the following data:

Application Number	Salary	Rent	Years Employed	Years Residing
605	$21,000	$560	4	5
610	18,000	500	10	14
614	35,000	750	2	10
656	11,000	280	20	19
678	15,500	400	6	2
692	8,000	200	10	11
694	32,000	850	3	3
697	12,500	375	4	6
698	40,000	950	15	8
700	20,000	395	5	5

6.27 What will the following program print when it is run?

```
10 LET I = 1
15 ON I GO TO 40, 20, 30
20 PRINT "IS",
25 GO TO 45
30 PRINT "EASY"
35 GO TO 45
40 PRINT "PROGRAMMING",
45 LET I = I + 1
50 IF I < = 3 THEN 15
55 END
```

6.28 Modify the program in exercise 6.27 to have it print "IS PROGRAM-MING EASY." Change only line 15.

6.29 If we replaced line 55 in the program in exercise 6.27 with

```
                    55 STOP
```

what would the computer print?

7

FOR/NEXT

THE FOR AND NEXT STATEMENTS

Any time we wish to perform an operation or several operations a fixed number of times, the FOR/NEXT statements can be used. For example, in Program 6.8 we wanted to read five numbers from the DATA statement and add them and their squares. That program logic could have been set up much more easily with the FOR/NEXT statements. This will be done in Program 7.3. To introduce the FOR/NEXT statements, let us write a program that prints the numbers from 1 through 10, first using the IF statement.

PROGRAM 7.1   Printing the Numbers 1 through 10 Using IF/THEN

```
10 LET N=1
15 PRINT N;
20 IF N>=10 THEN 35
25 LET N=N+1
30 GO TO 15
35 END


RUN
 1   2   3   4   5   6   7   8   9   10
```

We will now rewrite the program using the FOR/NEXT statements.

PROGRAM 7.2   Printing the Numbers 1 through 10 Using FOR/NEXT

```
10 FOR N=1 TO 10
15 PRINT N;
20 NEXT N
25 END


RUN
 1   2   3   4   5   6   7   8   9   10
```

The FOR statement in line 10 initializes the variable N to 1. Line 15 then prints the number 1. The NEXT statement in line 20 compares the current value of the variable N (the number 1) to the upper limit mentioned in the FOR statement, namely, the number 10. If the variable N is less than 10, it will be incremented by 1, and execution will continue with the line following the FOR statement. Thus, the number 2 will be printed by line 15. This will continue until the variable N is finally equal to 10, at which time execution will continue with the statement following the NEXT statement, which in this case is the END statement.

Suppose we wished to have the computer print all the odd numbers between 1 and 10. To alter Program 7.1, we would replace line 25 with

$$25 \text{ LET } N = N + 2$$

That is, we would like to have the variable N incremented by 2 rather than 1. This change can also be accomplished with the FOR/NEXT statements by replacing line 10 in Program 7.2 with

$$10 \text{ FOR } N = 1 \text{ TO } 10 \text{ STEP } 2$$

That is, if we wish the index variable N to be changed by any number other than the number 1, we can add the word STEP at the end of the FOR statement and specify by how much we would like the index variable to be changed. Note that Program 7.1 would stop printing with the number 11, while Program 7.2 would stop printing with the number 9. The difference in logic is that Program 7.1 increments N by 2, prints N, and then tests N to see if it is greater than 10; whereas Program 7.2 increments N by 2, then tests to see if N is greater than 10, and then prints N. Some examples of FOR statements follow:

1. FOR K = 2 TO 8
2. FOR R = 1 TO M STEP .5
3. FOR L = S TO Q STEP Z
4. FOR J = A+B TO C+D−E/3 STEP F*G+8.7
5. FOR P = 10 TO −7 STEP −2

There is less variety possible with the NEXT statement. Some examples are NEXT K, NEXT R, etc.

The generalized form of the FOR statement is

$$\text{line \# FOR \{variable\}} = \begin{Bmatrix} \text{constant} \\ \text{variable} \\ \text{expression} \end{Bmatrix} \text{TO} \begin{Bmatrix} \text{constant} \\ \text{variable} \\ \text{expression} \end{Bmatrix} \text{STEP} \begin{Bmatrix} \text{constant} \\ \text{variable} \\ \text{expression} \end{Bmatrix}$$

The word FOR must be followed by some variable. This variable need not have been previously given a value. If that variable had some value previously, its previous value would be lost.

Following the = sign and the word TO must be some constant, variable, or expression. The variable, as well as any variables in the expression, must have been previously given values.

The STEP is optional and may be omitted if you wish to increment the index variable by the number 1. Note that it is possible to have a STEP of a fraction as in example 2 above, and to have a negative STEP as in example 5 above. Whenever the STEP is negative, the starting value should be greater than the finishing value. The looping in that case will continue until the value of the index variable becomes less than or equal to the finishing value.

The form of the NEXT statement is

line # NEXT variable

For each FOR statement in a program there must exist one and only one NEXT statement using the same variable.

We will now rewrite Program 6.8 using the FOR/NEXT statements but omitting all of the REM statements. Note that the output in Program 7.3 is identical to that of Program 6.8.

PROGRAM 7.3   Rewriting Program 6.8 Using the FOR/NEXT Statement

```
10 LET S=0
15 LET S2=0
20 FOR N=1 TO 5
25 READ X
30 LET S=S+X
35 LET S2=S2+X↑2
40 PRINT X,X↑2
45 NEXT N
50 PRINT"---","---"
55 PRINT S,S2
100 DATA 7,2,3,4,1
999 END


RUN
 7              49
 2               4
 3               9
 4              16
 1               1
---             ---
 17             79
```

An illustration of the FOR/NEXT statements is found in Program 7.4, which is based on Case 7.1. This case describes a situation where the FOR/NEXT loop should never be completed.

CASE 7.1 Suppose we have 10 product numbers, each followed by the amount in inventory of that product in DATA statements. A salesperson will input a product number and we want the computer to print the amount of that product in inventory. If the salesperson inputs an incorrect product number (i.e., one that is not listed in the DATA statements), we will inform him of this and allow him to try again. When the salesperson has completed asking questions, he can type in a zero for the product number, signaling the computer that he is done.

A flowchart that helps to plan out the program for this case is shown in Figure 7.1.

PROGRAM 7.4   Case 7.1, Inventory Search

```
10 REM INVENTORY PROGRAM
15 PRINT "WHAT IS THE PRODUCT NUMBER";
20 INPUT N
25 IF N=0 THEN 999
30 FOR I=1 TO 10
35 READ P,A
40 IF P=N THEN 60
45 NEXT I
50 PRINT "NO SUCH PRODUCT NUMBER AS";N;"TRY AGAIN"
55 GO TO 65
60 PRINT " THE AMOUNT OF PRODUCT";P;"IN INVENTORY IS";A
65 RESTORE
70 GO TO 15
75 DATA 1234,100,2345,150,1345,50,1432,75,3214,25,4321,10
80 DATA 3241,250,2233,80,1144,200,3311,500
999 END


RUN
WHAT IS THE PRODUCT NUMBER ?2345
  THE AMOUNT OF PRODUCT 2345 IN INVENTORY IS 150
WHAT IS THE PRODUCT NUMBER ?3311
  THE AMOUNT OF PRODUCT 3311 IN INVENTORY IS 500
WHAT IS THE PRODUCT NUMBER ?2233
  THE AMOUNT OF PRODUCT 2233 IN INVENTORY IS 80
WHAT IS THE PRODUCT NUMBER ?1122
NO SUCH PRODUCT NUMBER AS 1122 TRY AGAIN
WHAT IS THE PRODUCT NUMBER ?1144
  THE AMOUNT OF PRODUCT 1144 IN INVENTORY IS 200
WHAT IS THE PRODUCT NUMBER ?0
```

Note that in Program 7.4 we do not wish to complete the FOR/NEXT loop 10 times. If the program does complete the loop without branching

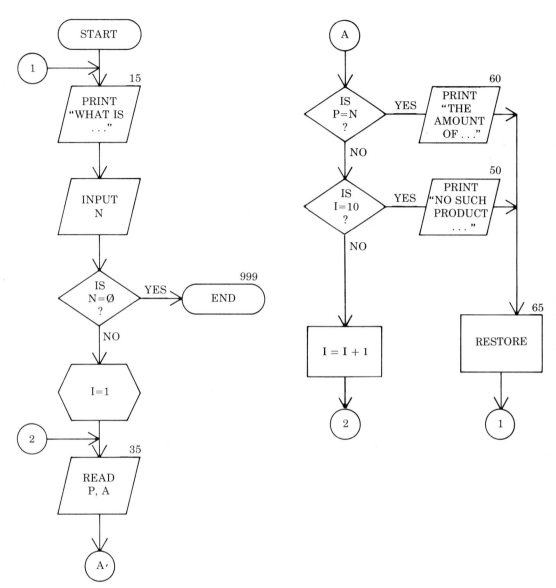

FIGURE 7.1 Flowchart for Program 7.4, Case 7.1, Inventory Search

out of it, it means that we have not found a product number in the DATA statements that matches the one that was INPUT.

Thus, we see that we can branch out of a FOR/NEXT loop. However, we should never branch into a FOR/NEXT loop from the outside. For example, if we would have a GO TO 35 on line 17 or on line 55, it would immediately cause an error message to be printed out.* We can branch to a statement in a FOR/NEXT loop from some other statement in the same loop without any difficulty. (See, for example, Program 7.7.)

NESTED LOOPS

Consider Program 7.5.

PROGRAM 7.5 Nested Loops

```
10 FOR I=1 TO 3
15 FOR J=1 TO 5
20 PRINT I;J,
25 NEXT J
30 NEXT I
35 END

RUN
 1  1          1  2          1  3          1  4          1  5
 2  1          2  2          2  3          2  4          2  5
 3  1          3  2          3  3          3  4          3  5
```

Whenever we have one FOR/NEXT loop (lines 15–25) contained entirely within another FOR/NEXT loop (lines 10–30), these loops are called *nested loops*. One loop may not overlap another loop. There is no limit to the number of levels of nesting. Some examples follow.

Valid Loops		Invalid Loops	
FOR I ⌐	FOR I ⌐	FOR I ⌐	FOR I ⌐
FOR J ⌐	FOR J ⌐	FOR J ⌐	FOR J ⌐
FOR K ⌐	NEXT J ⌐		FOR K ⌐
NEXT K ⌐	FOR K ⌐	NEXT I ⌐	
NEXT J ⌐	NEXT K ⌐		NEXT I ⌐
NEXT I ⌐	NEXT I ⌐	NEXT J ⌐	NEXT J ⌐
			NEXT K ⌐

Note that in Program 7.5 the variable *J* goes from 1 to 5 each time variable *I* assumes a value. Note also that the NEXT J statement comes *before* the NEXT I statement since the FOR J = 1 TO 5 statement is *after* the FOR I = 1 TO 3 statement.

---

*On some systems it may be possible to branch into a FOR/NEXT loop from the outside.

The output further aids in understanding how the nested loops are working. First the outer loop FOR statement in line 10 is executed. The value of $I = 1$ is fixed. This can be seen in the first row of output. The inner loop FOR statement in line 15 is executed and varies from $J = 1$ TO 5, while I is fixed at 1. Again look at the first line of output. Line 20, the PRINT statement, generates the fixed value of the outer loop and the varying values of the inner loop. Each row of output follows a similar pattern. The row value from the outer loop is fixed, while the column value derived from the inner loop changes.

Nested loop operations can also be seen in Programs 7.6 and 7.7. Program 7.6 prints a 5×5 multiplication table.

PROGRAM 7.6 A 5 × 5 Multiplication Table

```
10 FOR I=1 TO 5
15 FOR J=1 TO 5
20 PRINT I*J,
25 NEXT J
30 NEXT I
35 END
```

```
RUN
 1        2        3        4        5
 2        4        6        8       10
 3        6        9       12       15
 4        8       12       16       20
 5       10       15       20       25
```

Program 7.7 prints a 10×10 table of zeros with ones along the major diagonal.

PROGRAM 7.7 Branching in a FOR/NEXT Loop

```
10 FOR I=1 TO 10
15 FOR J=1 TO 10
20 LET X=0
25 IF I<>J THEN 35
30 LET X=1
35 PRINT X;
40 NEXT J
45 PRINT
50 NEXT I
55 END
```

```
RUN
 1  0  0  0  0  0  0  0  0  0
 0  1  0  0  0  0  0  0  0  0
 0  0  1  0  0  0  0  0  0  0
 0  0  0  1  0  0  0  0  0  0
 0  0  0  0  1  0  0  0  0  0
 0  0  0  0  0  1  0  0  0  0
 0  0  0  0  0  0  1  0  0  0
 0  0  0  0  0  0  0  1  0  0
 0  0  0  0  0  0  0  0  1  0
 0  0  0  0  0  0  0  0  0  1
```

The kind of table output by Program 7.7 is called the *identity matrix*. We will return to that and other matrices in Chapter 12. Program 7.7 illustrates the fact that we can branch from one part of a FOR/NEXT loop to another part of the same loop without difficulty because of line 25. Observe that the PRINT statement on line 45 is necessary to go to the next line after each line is complete.

Case 7.2 gives an application of nested FOR/NEXT loops.

CASE 7.2 The planning department for a large corporation prepares each year a 3 year projection, by division, of sales. Presently, they are assuming a 12 percent growth rate compounded annually. The sales figures for this year by division are:

Division	Sales (Million $)
1	$5.25
2	6.10
3	4.75
4	8.70
5	6.75
6	3.30

Program 7.8 generates a table with the required projections. This table is derived from the nested FOR/NEXT loop in the program. The outer loop (lines 25, 100) represents each of the six divisions. The inner loop (lines 40, 80) supplies the value for the variable Y which is found in the compounding formula in line 60. Note the placement of line 33 between the FOR statements. By placing this PRINT statement here, the division numbers can be outputted as part of the table.

PROGRAM 7.8 Case 7.2, Sales Projections, Nested FOR/NEXT Statements

```
2 REM GROWTH PROJECTION PROGRAM
5 PRINT " ","DIVISIONS SALES PROJECTIONS - MILLIONS $"
10 PRINT " ","CURRENT","     PROJECTION YEARS"
15 PRINT "DIVISION","YEAR",1,2,3
20 LET R=.12
22 REM OUTER LOOP FOR EACH DIVISION
25 FOR D=1 TO 6
30 READ S
33 PRINT D,S,
35 REM INNER LOOP FOR CURRENT & PROJ. SALES
40 FOR Y=1 TO 3
60 LET P=S*(1+R)↑Y
70 PRINT "$";P,
80 NEXT Y
90 PRINT
100 NEXT D
110 PRINT "   PROJECTION TABLE PREPARED BY PLANNING DEPARTMENT"
120 DATA 5.25,6.1,4.75,8.7,6.75,3.3
190 END
```

Program 7.8 continued

```
RUN
        DIVISIONS SALES PROJECTIONS - MILLIONS $
        CURRENT              PROJECTION YEARS
DIVISION  YEAR         1               2               3
1         5.25      $ 5.88        $ 6.5856       $ 7.37587

2         6.1       $ 6.832       $ 7.65184      $ 8.57006

3         4.75      $ 5.32        $ 5.9584       $ 6.67341

4         8.7       $ 9.744       $ 10.9133      $ 12.2229

5         6.75      $ 7.56        $ 8.4672       $ 9.48326

6         3.3       $ 3.696       $ 4.13952      $ 4.63626

   PROJECTION TABLE PREPARED BY PLANNING DEPARTMENT
```

A flowchart showing the logic of Program 7.8 is shown in Figure 7.2.

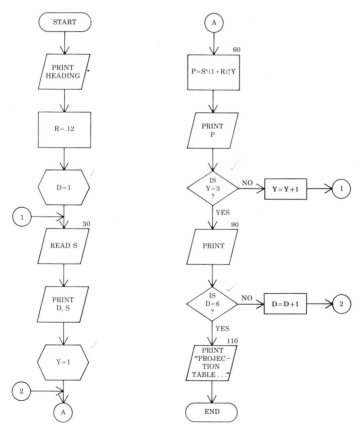

FIGURE 7.2 Flowchart for Program 7.8, Case 7.2, Sales Projections

SUMMARY

Whenever one wants to perform an operation a fixed number of times, the FOR/NEXT statements should be used. The FOR/NEXT statements are equivalent to a LET, an IF THEN, and a GO TO. The STEP option allows the programmer to increment the index variable by numbers other than one.

Nested FOR/NEXT loops are permissible as long as they don't overlap.

EXERCISES

7.1 What will the following program do?

```
10 READ A,B,C,
15 FOR I = A TO B/C STEP C*A
20 PRINT I;
25 NEXT I
30 DATA 1, 10, 1
35 END
```

7.2 What will the program in exercise 7.1 do if line 30 is changed to:
a. 30 DATA 2, 12, 1
b. 30 DATA .5, 5, 1
c. 30 DATA 10, 1, − .5
d. 30 DATA 1, 2, 3

7.3 Write a program that will print all of the even numbers between 1 and 20. Use FOR/NEXT statements.

7.4 Rewrite Program 6.11 so that data for exactly 10 employees are processed without having the program test if $N = 0$ to signal the end. Use FOR/NEXT statements.

7.5 Rewrite the programs in the following exercises using the FOR/NEXT statements:
a. exercise 6.11
b. exercise 6.12
c. exercise 6.13
d. exercise 6.18
e. exercise 6.21

7.6 What will the following program print when it is run?

```
10 FOR I = 1 TO 20 STEP 6
15 FOR J = 3 TO 10 STEP 2
20 PRINT I; J,
25 NEXT J
30 PRINT
35 NEXT I
40 END
```

7.7 What will the following program print when it is run?

```
10 FOR I = 1 TO 11 STEP 3
15 FOR J = 5 TO −1 STEP −2
20 FOR K = 2 TO 3 STEP .25
25 PRINT I; J; K,
30 NEXT K
35 PRINT
40 NEXT J
45 PRINT
50 NEXT I
55 END
```

7.8 Write a program that will print a 10×10 table with zeros everywhere except along the major and minor diagonals. That is, have the computer print an "X" of ones in a field of zeros.

7.9 What will Program 7.4 do if line 55 is changed to 55 GO TO 15?

Subscripted Variables and Dimensioning

SUBSCRIPTED VARIABLES

In Chapter 2 it was pointed out that in BASIC the set of variable names consists of the alphabetic letters A to Z (26 names) plus each of these letters combined with a single number $A0, \ldots, A9, B0, \ldots, B9, \ldots, Z0, \ldots, Z9$ (260 names), which gives a total of 286 possible variable names. For simple programs this may be a sufficient number of names. For more complex programs, a much larger list of names may be necessary. For example, it is not unusual for a company, a bank, or any large organization to have hundreds of employees, thousands of accounts, or thousands of customers. Each account, customer, and employee could require its own variable name. With only 286 variable names presently available, it would be very difficult to handle any problem dealing with hundreds or thousands of items.

The way out of this predicament is by using subscripted variables. A subscripted variable could be B_1 (B sub 1) or M_{25} (M sub 25). The letters B and M are the names of groups of similar items. Such a group of similar items having a single name is referred to as an *array*.

With subscripted variables a complete storage area is set aside for the values read in. This storage area has a single name and each value in the array has a subscript giving it a position in the storage area. If 20 values were to be treated as an array having a common name, N, read in and assigned by subscripting, Figure 8.1 would represent the storage area being discussed.

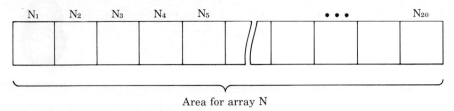

Area for array N

FIGURE 8.1 Storage Area for an Array with Subscripts

In Figure 8.1 the subscripts show that position in the array follows from left to right (low to high). The subscripts are always whole numbers, never fractional or decimal.

Each of the 286 "regular" variable names can be treated as an array having individual values identified with a subscript. For example, if each of 286 arrays had 100 items, the result would be 28,600 subscripted variables. With this many possible variables it becomes less difficult to "handle any problem dealing with hundreds or thousands of items." The way that subscripted variables are programmed in BASIC follows.

Suppose a company has insurance policies in various amounts for its 20 senior executives. We can assign a single variable name to these policies, say P. The mathematical notation and the BASIC notation for these 20 policies are as follows:

Mathematical	BASIC	Policy Face Value
P_1	P(1)	$20,000
P_2	P(2)	25,000
P_3	P(3)	15,000
$\vdots$	$\vdots$	$\vdots$
P_{20}	P(20)	28,000

The subscript in the mathematical notation is slightly below the variable name. Since the terminal keyboard does not permit such notation, the subscript identification number is placed in parentheses next to the variable name. When these policy amounts are read into the computer, each is assigned to a location referred to by the P, and given a position with a specific (unique) identification number. In this way P(1) will be set equal to $20,000, P(2) will be set equal to $25,000, and so on through to P(20).

For only 10 policies a simple program illustrating how values are read, printed, and stored as subscripted variables is shown in Program 8.1. The FOR/NEXT loop provides the identification numbers for each of the P

variables. When line 15, READ P(I), is executed, each data value gets the same variable name, *P,* but a different identification number. To print out the values of these variables we need a PRINT statement as shown in line 20.

PROGRAM 8.1 Reading, Printing, and Storing Subscripted Variables

```
10 FOR I=1 TO 10
15 READ P(I);
20 PRINT P(I);
25 NEXT I
30 DATA 20000,25000,15000,16500,18500,32000,19500,17500,22000,26000
99 END
```

```
RUN
 20000   25000   15000   16500   18500   32000   19500   17500   22000   26000
```

The 10 values in Program 8.1 formed an array named *P.* Each value is now stored in a specific location, P(1), . . . , P(10). If lines 15 and 20 in Program 8.1 had been

15 READ P

20 PRINT P;

the output obtained would have been the same. The difference in programs is reflected in the variables used. An "ordinary" variable such as *P* provides only a single storage location for a single value at any one time. The subscripted variable P(I) provides a storage area that can contain more than a single value at any one time. In addition, specific values of a subscripted array can be printed and used in subsequent processing if need be. With the ordinary variable approach mentioned above, it would not be possible to print out a specific *P* value, say the fourth or sixth value.

Program 8.2 shows in line 27 how the fourth, sixth, second, and seventh policy values are printed out because each has been assigned to a subscripted variable.

PROGRAM 8.2 Printing Specific Array Values

```
10 FOR I=1 TO 10
15 READ P(I)
20 PRINT P(I);
25 NEXT I
27 PRINT P(4),P(6),P(2),P(7)
30 DATA 20000,25000,15000,16500,18500,32000,19500,17500,22000,26000
99 END
```

```
RUN
 20000   25000   15000   16500   18500   32000   19500   17500   22000   26000
 16500           32000           25000           19500
```

At times, subscripted variables may be stated directly rather than using FOR/NEXT loops to give identification numbers. Values may be assigned to subscripted variables by using one of the following:

READ/DATA statements,

$$10 \text{ READ } M(1), M(2), M(3)$$
$$20 \text{ DATA } 2, 3, 70$$

INPUT statement,

$$10 \text{ INPUT } M(1), M(2), M(3)$$

or LET statements,

$$10 \text{ LET } M(1) = 2$$
$$20 \text{ LET } M(2) = 3$$
$$30 \text{ LET } M(3) = 70$$

From this discussion it can be seen that other subscripts are possible besides $P(I)$. In BASIC, examples of acceptable subscripts are $S(4)$, $X2(37)$, $M(I+6)$, $L(2*J)$, and $E(B-1)$. Thus, a subscript can be any expression that uses the operators $\uparrow$, $*$, $/$, $+$, and $-$. In addition, it is possible to subscript a subscripted variable so that if $B(I)$ is a value we can have the variable $N(B(I))$.

DIMENSIONING

When subscripted variables are read into the computer they are placed in storage with a specific memory location. You are permitted up to 10 "free" subscripted variables for each of the variable names in your program. But since total storage available is limited, if you have more than 10 subscripted variables you must reserve storage space for them in the computer. Such reservations are made by using a DIM (dimension) statement at the start of your program. This statement will be illustrated within the discussion of lists and tables that follows.

Lists

A single column or row of values comprises a list or array. Such a list was the 10 policies in Program 8.2. Since the list did not have more than 10 values, no dimension statement was required. If the list were larger, a DIM statement in the following form would be needed:

line # DIM variable name (# of storage spaces desired)

Examples of such statements are:

$$20 \ DIM \ B(35)$$

suitable for a single list; or dimensioning for more than one list,

$$20 \ DIM \ B(35), K(20), M(42)$$

Program 8.3 illustrates, for the amounts of the 20 insurance policies shown earlier, how these values can be stored and might be printed out.

PROGRAM 8.3   Dimensioning for a List of 20 Insurance Policies

```
 5 DIM P(20)
11 FOR I= 1 TO 20
15 READ P(I)
30 NEXT I
32 PRINT "POLICY","AMOUNT","POLICY","AMOUNT"
33 PRINT
34 FOR I= 20 TO 1 STEP -2
35 PRINT I,"$";P(I),I-1,"$";P(I-1)
38 NEXT I
40 DATA 20000,25000,15000,16500,18500,32000,19500,17500,22000,26000
45 DATA 18000,22000,16500,21500,22500,20000,18000,17000,19000,28000
99 END
```

```
RUN
POLICY          AMOUNT          POLICY          AMOUNT

20              $ 28000         19              $ 19000
18              $ 17000         17              $ 18000
16              $ 20000         15              $ 22500
14              $ 21500         13              $ 16500
12              $ 22000         11              $ 18000
10              $ 26000         9               $ 22000
8               $ 17500         7               $ 19500
6               $ 32000         5               $ 18500
4               $ 16500         3               $ 15000
2               $ 25000         1               $ 20000
```

Line 5 indicates that 20 storage areas are to be reserved for variable P. If the DIM statement was left out of the program, an error message would occur upon running the program. The DIM specification should always be equal to or greater than the size of the data list. Overdimensioning is permissible; underdimensioning is an error. Note the use of the variable designation $P(I-1)$ in line 35. With this designation the program prints out the amount of each odd-numbered policy starting with the 19th and continuing down until the first policy.

Program 8.4, using the information of Case 8.1, incorporates dimensioning and subscripted variables.

CASE 8.1 The B and N Department Store Company wants to estimate the average amount of a charge sale as well as the percent of charges that are above the average. A random sample of 15 charges was recorded one day last week as follows:

Charge	Amount	Charge	Amount
1	$ 3.47	9	$33.21
2	97.74	10	57.60
3	16.76	11	18.18
4	12.56	12	25.62
5	55.59	13	23.42
6	16.22	14	52.36
7	84.42	15	37.85
8	63.01		

Program 8.4 shows how the desired results for Case 8.1 can be obtained. With subscripting, all that is needed is a loop like lines 30–50, and a comparison test as in line 35. Remarks within the program explain what each of the statements following them (REM) does. A flowchart for the program is shown in Figure 8.2.

PROGRAM 8.4   **Case 8.1, B and N Department Store Company, Percent of Charges Above the Average**

```
1 DIM C(15)
2 PRINT "CHARGE","AMOUNT"
5 LET T1 = 0
6 LET T2 = 0
8 FOR I = 1 TO 15
10 READ C(I)
12 PRINT I,"$";C(I)
13 REM FIND THE TOTAL OF ALL CHARGES
15 LET T1=T1+C(I)
20 NEXT I
22 REM GET THE AVERAGE:DIVIDE TOTAL BY NUMBER OF CHARGES
25 LET A1=T1/15
30 FOR I=1 TO 15
32 REM TEST TO COMPARE WHICH CHARGES ARE GREATER THAN AVERAGE
35 IF C(I)>A1 THEN 45
40 GO TO 50
42 REM COUNT NUMBER OF CHARGES ABOVE AVERAGE
45 LET T2=T2+1
50 NEXT I
55 PRINT " ","--------"
60 PRINT "SAMPLE TOTAL $";T1
65 PRINT "EST.AVE.CHARGE $"A1
70 PRINT "% OF CHARGES ABOVE THE AVERAGE";(T2/I)*100
80 DATA 3.47,97.74,16.76,12.56,55.59,16.22,84.42,63.01,33.21,57.60
82 DATA 18.18,25.62,23.42,52.36,37.85
99 END
```

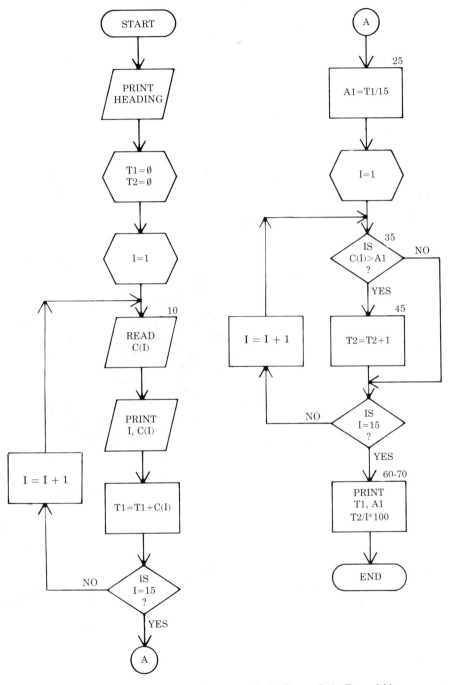

FIGURE 8.2 Flowchart for Program 8.4, Case 8.1, B and N Department Store Company

PROGRAM 8.4   continued

```
RUN
CHARGE          AMOUNT
  1            $  3.47
  2            $ 97.74
  3            $ 16.76
  4            $ 12.56
  5            $ 55.59
  6            $ 16.22
  7            $ 84.42
  8            $ 63.01
  9            $ 33.21
 10            $ 57.6
 11            $ 18.18
 12            $ 25.62
 13            $ 23.42
 14            $ 52.36
 15            $ 37.85
               --------
SAMPLE TOTAL $ 598.01
EST.AVE.CHARGE $ 39.8673
% OF CHARGES ABOVE THE AVERAGE 40
```

A problem may have multiple data lists. Case 8.2 is such a situation.

CASE 8.2   An investment advisor wants to compute the present total market value of one of the portfolios he manages. He has the number of shares of each of 12 stocks and its current market price. These figures are as follows:

Stock	Number of Shares	Market Price
1	300	$50
2	400	42
3	500	32
4	900	5
5	300	31
6	500	17
7	500	77
8	100	98
9	800	52
10	100	49
11	400	80
12	800	83

Program 8.5 illustrates how the present total market value for the stocks in Case 8.2 is obtained. Note the DIM statement in line 5 that is required

for the two lists, *N* and *P*. The program contains four FOR/NEXT loops in a series. The first loop (lines 12–14) reads in the number of shares; the second loop (lines 18–22) reads in the market price; the third loop (lines 24–32) causes the printing of stock numbers, number of shares, and market price, and then accumulates the market price. The last loop results in the underlining by dashes across the page.

PROGRAM 8.5 Portfolio

```
5 DIM N(15),P(15)
10 PRINT "STOCK","# SHARES","MARKET PRICE"
11 LET T=0
12 FOR I=1 TO 12
13 READ N(I)
14 NEXT I
18 FOR I= 1 TO 12
20 READ P(I)
22 NEXT I
24 FOR I=1 TO 12
25 PRINT I,N(I),"$";P(I)
30 LET T=T+N(I)*P(I)
32 NEXT I
40 FOR A=1 TO 45
45 PRINT "-";
50 NEXT A
55 PRINT
60 PRINT "THE PRESENT VALUE OF PORTFOLIO IS $";T
70 DATA 300,400,500,900,300,500,500,100,800,100,400,800
75 DATA 50,42,32,5,31,17,77,98,52,49,80,83
99 END
```

```
RUN
STOCK             # SHARES        MARKET PRICE
  1                 300            $ 50
  2                 400            $ 42
  3                 500            $ 32
  4                 900            $ 5
  5                 300            $ 31
  6                 500            $ 17
  7                 500            $ 77
  8                 100            $ 98
  9                 800            $ 52
 10                 100            $ 49
 11                 400            $ 80
 12                 800            $ 83
-------------------------------------------------
THE PRESENT VALUE OF PORTFOLIO IS $ 263300
```

Program 8.6 is a simple illustration of how it is possible to have values assigned to subscripted variables using the INPUT statement (line 20). Note how line 35 causes the inputted values to be printed out in reverse sequence.

PROGRAM 8.6   Subscripting Variables Using the INPUT Statement

```
10 FOR I= 1 TO 5
20 INPUT A(I)
25 NEXT I
30 PRINT
35 FOR I= 5 TO 1 STEP -1
40 PRINT A(I);
50 NEXT I
99 END


RUN
 ?22
 ?25
 ?38
 ?46
 ?59

 59   46   38   25   22
```

Case 8.3 is based on the idea of using INPUT to assign values to sub-scripted variables.

CASE 8.3   Town Food Stores, Inc., has a sophisticated management infor-mation system (MIS) that keeps track of daily operations for its 13 stores. At the end of each day, each store telephones in the total daily receipts to the main computer room clerk. The clerk then responds to a conversa-tional program that requests the sales figures for each store. This infor-mation is stored and a daily summary giving a total for the day for all the stores is printed out. Today's sales figures are:

Store	Sales	Store	Sales
1	$3,696	2	$4,281
3	5,650	4	6,969
5	3,854	6	4,955
7	5,724	8	1,695
9	7,864	10	1,947
11	4,417	12	5,092
13	2,611		

Program 8.7 shows a conversational program that carries out the objectives of Case 8.3. Line 30, INPUT D(I), is within a FOR/NEXT loop that causes values to be assigned to variables D(1) through D(13).

**PROGRAM 8.7   Case 8.3, Town Food Stores, Inc., Conversational
Program**

```
5 DIM D(15)
10 PRINT "PLEASE TYPE IN THE DAILY SALES FOR EACH STORE AFTER"
12 PRINT "THE ? MARK."
15 LET S1 =0
20 FOR I= 1 TO 13
25 PRINT "STORE";I;
30 INPUT D(I)
40 LET S1 = S1 + D(I)
45 NEXT I
50 PRINT "    TODAY'S SALES REPORT"
55 PRINT "    --------------------"
60 PRINT "STORE","SALES"
65 FOR I = 1 TO 13
70 PRINT I,"$";D(I)
75 NEXT I
80 PRINT
85 PRINT "TOTAL","$";S1
99 END
```

```
RUN
PLEASE TYPE IN THE DAILY SALES FOR EACH STORE AFTER
THE ? MARK.
STORE 1   ?3696
STORE 2   ?4281
STORE 3   ?5650
STORE 4   ?6969
STORE 5   ?3854
STORE 6   ?4955
STORE 7   ?5724
STORE 8   ?1695
STORE 9   ?7864
STORE 10  ?1947
STORE 11  ?4417
STORE 12  ?5092
STORE 13  ?2611
    TODAY'S SALES REPORT
    --------------------
STORE          SALES
  1            $ 3696
  2            $ 4281
  3            $ 5650
  4            $ 6969
  5            $ 3854
  6            $ 4955
  7            $ 5724
  8            $ 1695
  9            $ 7864
 10            $ 1947
 11            $ 4417
 12            $ 5092
 13            $ 2611

TOTAL          $ 58755
```

Tables

Many times, data takes the form of a table that is simply several lists grouped
together. Rather than reading each list as a separate variable, it is easier to

treat them all as a single variable with two subscripts instead of one. In this manner we have a table with one subscript representing the row locations, and the other representing the column locations.

As was the case with lists, tables containing data must be appropriately dimensioned to reserve storage space. The general form of the statement to be used is

line # DIM variable name (table size: # rows, # columns)

An example for a single table five rows by eight columns could be:

10 DIM C(5,8)

If there are several tables in a program, the following statement could apply:

10 DIM C(5,8), A(12,8), R(10,20)

With tables and lists in a program, this statement may be used:

10 DIM C(5,8), S(15), R(10,20), B(50), X(35)

Suppose the Better Gum Company has test marketed a new chewing gum in five types of outlets (candy store, gum machine, supermarket, etc.) in three regions for one month and has obtained the following sales figures in dozens of units sold:

Type of Outlet	Region		
	1	2	3
1	15	17	13
2	18	15	16
3	12	18	15
4	14	15	14
5	17	12	13

This table data has five rows with three columns. If the table is given the name "G," a program can then be written to read in and store the table. The "reading" of all the table will follow a row-by-row sequence, going from left to right across each column. The operation of nested loops does this reading process for us.* In Program 8.8 the outer loop bounded by lines 20 and 60, provides the row designation, and the inner loop (lines 30 through 50) provides the column designation.

---

*It may be useful for you at this point to review the material in Chapter 7 covering the operation of nested FOR/NEXT loops.

Line 10 in Program 8.8 shows the appropriate dimension, G(5,3), for a 5 x 3 table. The data in line 70 shows each row in sequence.

PROGRAM 8.8   Reading and Storing a 5 x 3 Table

```
10 DIM G(5,3)
20 FOR I= 1 TO 5
30 FOR J= 1 TO 3
40 READ G(I,J)
50 NEXT J
60 NEXT I
65 PRINT G(3,2), G(5,1)
70 DATA 15,17,13,18,15,16,12,18,15,14,15,14,17,12,13
99 END

RUN
18            17
```

When the program is executed, each data value is represented by the variable name followed by a unique identification number corresponding to its row, I, and column, J, location. Variable G(3,2) is assigned the value 18, variable G(5,1) is assigned the value 17, and similarly for the rest of the data. The PRINT statement in line 65 shows how the values of individual subscripted variables like G(3,2) and G(5,1) can be printed out. To print all of Table G a PRINT statement such as line 45, PRINT G(I,J), in Program 8.9 is required.

Figure 8.3 shows Table G subscripted variables and their values.

To obtain a total for all of the data in Table G an accumulator needs to be added to Program 8.8. To accomplish the task, lines 12 and 42 are added to the program. The revised program and resulting output are shown as Program 8.9.

		J:Columns 1	2	3
I:Rows	1	G(1,1) = 15	G(1,2) = 17	G(1,3) = 13
	2	G(2,1) = 18	G(2,2) = 15	G(2,3) = 16
G(I,J)	3	G(3,1) = 12	G(3,2) = 18	G(3,3) = 15
	4	G(4,1) = 14	G(4,2) = 15	G(4,3) = 14
	5	G(5,1) = 17	G(5,2) = 12	G(5,3) = 13

FIGURE 8.3   Table G Variables and Values

PROGRAM 8.9 Finding the Total Value of Table *G*

```
10 DIM G(5,3)
12 LET T1=0
15 PRINT " ","              REGION"
16 PRINT "OUTLET", 1,2,3
17 PRINT
20 FOR I= 1 TO 5
25 PRINT I,
30 FOR J= 1 TO 3
40 READ G(I,J)
42 LET T1= T1 + G(I,J)
45 PRINT G(I,J),
50 NEXT J
55 PRINT
60 NEXT I
65 PRINT "TOTAL SALES";T1;"GROSS"
69 DATA 15,17,13,18,15,16,12,18,15,14,15,14,17,12,13
99 END
```

```
RUN
                          REGION
OUTLET          1           2           3

1              15          17          13
2              18          15          16
3              12          18          15
4              14          15          14
5              17          12          13
TOTAL SALES 224 GROSS
```

A flowchart of Program 8.9 is shown in Figure 8.4.

After values have been read in and stored as a table, it is possible to manipulate them. For instance, it may be desired to retrieve a part of a table. This can be accomplished by changing the starting point of the nested loops. Program 8.10 shows how the sales data for outlets 3 to 5 in regions 2 and 3 of the Better Gum Company test marketing could be printed out. Lines 70 and 80 are responsible for the partial output of Table *G*. The outer loop restricts printing to rows 3 through 5, while the inner loop restricts printing to columns 2 through 3.

PROGRAM 8.10 Printing Out Part of Table *G*

```
10 DIM G(5,3)
20 FOR I= 1 TO 5
30 FOR J= 1 TO 3
40 READ G(I,J)
50 NEXT J
60 NEXT I
69 DATA 15,17,13,18,15,16,12,18,15,14,15,14,17,12,13
70 FOR I= 3 TO 5
80 FOR J= 2 TO 3
90 PRINT G(I,J),
100 NEXT J
110 PRINT
115 NEXT I
199 END
```

```
RUN
 18             15
 15             14
 12             13
```

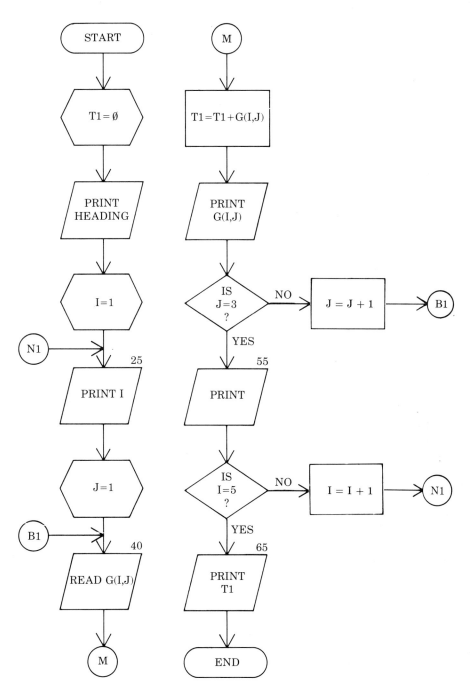

FIGURE 8.4   Flowchart of Program 8.9, Finding the Total Value of Table G

To obtain a specific row or column of a table that has been read in and stored (such as Table *G*), several approaches can be used. With only a few columns a statement such as

73 PRINT G(2,1), G(2,2), G(2,3)

would output the values of row 2 of Table *G*(18, 15, and 16, respectively). This could have also been done with the following statements:

77 FOR J = 1 TO 3
78 PRINT G(2,J),
80 NEXT J

Notice that G(2,J) holds the printing to row 2, while the columns, *J*, vary from 1 to 3. The same approach could be used to obtain a single column of a table. To print out the third column of Table *G* would require the following statements:

84 FOR I = 1 TO 5
85 PRINT G(I,3)
86 NEXT I

In the PRINT statement with G(I,3), the rows will vary from 1 to 5, while the printing is fixed on the third column. Program 8.11 summarizes these ideas based on the program (8.8) shown earlier.

PROGRAM 8.11   Printing Out a Row and Column of Table G

```
10 DIM G(5,3)
20 FOR I= 1 TO 5
30 FOR J= 1 TO 3
40 READ G(I,J)
50 NEXT J
60 NEXT I
69 DATA 15,17,13,18,15,16,12,18,15,14,15,14,17,12,13
70 PRINT
71 PRINT "OUTLET 2:"
73 PRINT G(2,1),G(2,2),G(2,3)
75 PRINT
76 PRINT "OUTLET 2:"
77 FOR J= 1 TO 3
78 PRINT G(2,J),
80 NEXT J
81 PRINT
82 PRINT "REGION 3:"
84 FOR I= 1 TO 5
85 PRINT G(I,3)
86 NEXT I
199 END

RUN

OUTLET 2:
 18              15              16

OUTLET 2:
 18              15              16
REGION 3:
 13
 16
 15
 14
 13
```

The following case (8.4) requires a single program that uses data in the form of two tables and one list.

CASE 8.4 The Computer Components Company pays its workers according to the number of units of each type of component (*A*, *B*, or *C*) they have assembled. The piecework rate is as follows:

Component	A	B	C
Rate per unit	$.25	$.35	$.50

Each worker's gross wages are based on a 2-week period. Output for the last 2 weeks is as follows:

	Week 1			Week 2		
	Components			Components		
Worker	A	B	C	A	B	C
1	200	100	20	185	110	22
2	150	125	30	160	115	35
3	320	75	15	275	100	30
4	275	100	15	275	90	20
5	100	200	10	150	150	10

Program 8.12 shows how two tables (one for each week) and one list (the rates) are treated so as to obtain the gross wage per worker.

Program 8.12 Case 8.4, Computer Components Company, Gross Wage Calculations

```
5 DIM W1(5,3), W2(5,3), A(5,3)
10 FOR I= 1 TO 5
15 FOR J= 1TO 3
20 READ W1(I,J)
30 NEXT J
32 NEXT I
33 FOR I = 1 TO 5
34 FOR J = 1 TO 3
35 READ W2(I,J)
36 NEXT J
37 NEXT I
40 FOR J= 1 TO 3
45 READ R(J)
50 NEXT J
55 FOR I= 1 TO 5
60 LET G=0
65 FOR J= 1 TO 3
69 LET A(I,J)=W1(I,J)+W2(I,J)
70 LET G= G + A(I,J)*R(J)
75 NEXT J
80 PRINT "WORKER";I, "GROSS WAGE $";G
85 NEXT I
90 DATA 200,100,20,150,125,30,320,75,15,275,100,15
95 DATA 100,200,10,185,110,22,160,115,25,275,100,30
100 DATA 275,90,20,150,150,10,.25,.35,.50
199 END
```

PROGRAM 8.12 continued

```
RUN
WORKER 1         GROSS WAGE $ 190.75
WORKER 2         GROSS WAGE $ 189
WORKER 3         GROSS WAGE $ 232.5
WORKER 4         GROSS WAGE $ 221.5
WORKER 5         GROSS WAGE $ 195
```

In the program, line 5 provides the necessary dimensioning for each of the two tables. The "output" for week 1 is designated Table $W1$, and the "output" for week 2 is Table $W2$. Note the dimensioning for a Table A. The values in this table are developed further on in the program, and since they are to be stored, dimensioning prior to their creation is necessary. Table $W1$ is read in with a nested FOR/NEXT loop (lines 10–32). Table $W2$ is read in with a nested FOR/NEXT loop (lines 33–37). The piecework rates are list designated R, and are read in with a single FOR/NEXT loop (lines 40–50).

Within the nested FOR/NEXT loops (lines 55–85), the following calculations occur: In the inner loop (lines 65–75), line 69 accumulates the number of units each worker produced, by component for 2 weeks; in line 70 the "gross wage" for each worker is calculated by multiplying the total number of units of each component produced by the piecework rate for each component.

Below are the step-by-step calculations carried out for "Worker 1." Assume that line 65 has been executed, then $I = 1$, $J = 1$.

line 69: $A(1,1) = W1(1,1) + W2(1,1) = 200 + 185 = 385$
line 70: $G = G + A(I,J)*R(J) = 0 + A(1,1)*R(1)$
          $G = 0 + 385*.25 = 96.25$

The NEXT J brings us to $I = 1$, $J = 2$,

line 69: $A(1,2) = W1(1,2) + W2(1,2) = 100 + 110 = 210$
line 70: $G = 96.25 + A(1,2)*R(2) = 96.25 + 210*.35$
          $G = 96.25 + 73.5 = 169.75$

The NEXT J brings us to $I = 1$, $J = 3$,

line 69: $A(1,3) = W1(1,3) + W2(1,3) = 20 + 22 = 42$
line 70: $G = 169.75 + A(1,3)*R(3) = 169.75 + 42*.50$
          $G = 169.75 + 21 = 190.75$

After $J = 3$, line 80 is executed, causing the results for Worker 1 to be printed out. The execution of line 85, the NEXT I, starts the process over again, but this time for $I = 2$, the second worker. Note how line 60 reinitializes G at zero before starting the next worker. This process ensures that the accumulation for G starts at zero for each worker.

SUMMARY

This chapter introduced the concept of subscripted variables. Such variables identify individual storage locations. The subscripting process can be accomplished within a single FOR/NEXT loop if the data consists of a list; or within nested FOR/NEXT loops if the data forms a table.

Subscripted variables may be stated directly with READ/DATA, INPUT, or LET statements. To reserve storage space for subscripted variables, dimensioning is necessary. The DIM statement is used to dimension both lists and tables of data.

EXERCISES

8.1 Revise Program 8.5 for Case 8.2 to add a column showing the present market value for each stock along with a total for this column.

8.2 Suppose for the 12 stocks listed in Case 8.2 there are also available the following purchase prices: $46, $42, $32, $5, $31, $17, $77, $98, $52, $49, $79, and $83. Revise Program 8.5 so that two additional columns will be produced, one showing the cost of purchase of each stock, and the other showing the gain or loss for each stock. The output should end with the total gain or loss for the entire portfolio.

8.3 Revise Program 8.5 (Case 8.2) such that the data lines are in this form:
    70 DATA 300, 50, 400, 42, 500, 32, 900, 5, 300, 31, 500, 17
    75 DATA 500, 77, 100, 98, 800, 52, 100, 49, 400, 80, 800, 83

Use READ N(I), P(I).

8.4 Revise Program 8.7 (Case 8.3) to add an additional column that shows for each store the "% of total sales."

8.5 Using the weekly data shown in Case 8.4, write a program that reads in both tables, stores them, prints out each one, and shows for each week how many units each worker has produced (row totals).

8.6 Using the weekly data shown in Case 8.4, write a program that reads in and stores this data, prints out each table, and generates how many units of each type were produced (column totals).

8.7 Write a single program that carries out the requirements of exercises 8.5 and 8.6, and in addition, gets a grand total for each weekly table.

8.8 Using the weekly data shown in Case 8.4, write a program that reads in and stores both tables, and then generates a new table that gives the combined week 1 and week 2 output by worker and component. This new table should also have column and row totals as well as a grand total.

8.9 Below are the prices at which four models of minicomputers are sold. Also shown are the numbers of units sold by the five salespersons selling these products. Prepare a program that will store this information and generate the total dollar volume for each salesperson. This total is equal to price per unit times number of units sold.

Model	1	2	3	4
Price	$10,000	$12,500	$17,200	$20,000

Salesperson	No. of Units Sold This Month, by Model			
	1	2	3	4
1	6	8	2	1
2	5	4	3	1
3	7	6	1	2
4	3	9	5	0
5	4	2	4	3

8.10 Write a program for exercise 8.9 and in addition have it obtain the total dollar sales volume for all the salespersons.

8.11 For the information given in exercise 8.9 prepare a program that will generate the following:
a. the total number of units of each model sold
b. the total dollar value of each model sold
c. the total dollar value of all the units sold
d. the percent of the total number of units sold, by model
e. the percent distribution of the total dollar value for each model sold

8.12 Assume in exercise 8.9 that each salesperson telephones in monthly sales figures to company headquarters. Write a conversational program that a clerk could run so as to generate a monthly sales report for the items requested in exercises 8.10 and 8.11.

8.13 The following table shows the sales (millions of dollars) for the first 6 months of the XYZ Company, by division.

Month	Division			
	1	2	3	4
1	2.1	3.2	1.8	.9
2	2.0	2.7	1.4	.8
3	1.7	3.1	1.5	.6
4	2.3	3.3	1.7	.7
5	1.8	3.0	1.9	.9
6	1.4	3.1	2.0	.9

Write a program that will do the following:
a. Read in and store this information.
b. Output the data for the 1st quarter (months 1–3).
c. Output the data for the 2nd quarter (months 4–6).
d. Output the data for divisions 2, 3, and 4.
e. Output the data for divisions 1 and 3.
f. Output the data for months 1 and 6.
g. Provide total sales by each quarter for all divisions.

Functions and Subroutines

STORED FUNCTIONS

There are a number of mathematical operations that the computer can perform directly without being given detailed instructions. For example, we can get the square root of a number directly without giving the computer detailed instructions. Such stored functions (library functions) are summarized below:

Function	Description
SIN(X)	The trigonometric sine function
COS(X)	" " cosine "
TAN(X)	" " tangent "
COT(X)	" " cotangent "
ATN(X)	" " arctangent "
LOG(X)	The natural logarithm function
EXP(X)	e raised to the X power
INT(X)	The greatest integer less than or equal to X
SGN(X)	The sign of X
ABS(X)	Absolute value of X
SQR(X)	The square root of X
RND(X)	Random number between 0 and 1.
	X is a dummy argument.

We confine our attention to the last five functions. The (X) is referred to as the argument.

The INT function (integer function) will assign the greatest integer that is less than or equal to its argument. For example,

X	INT(X)
5	5
7.2	7
6.9	6
0.5	0
-2.3	-3
-1.7	-2
$-.4$	-1

Note that INT$(6.9) = 6$. The number is not rounded off. Note also that INT $(-2.3) = -3$ since -3 is the greatest integer less than -2.3.

The SGN function (sign function) gives three possible values: $-1, 0$, and $+1$. If $X > 0$, SGN(X) $= 1$; if $X = 0$, SGN(X) $= 0$; and if $X < 0$, SGN (X) $= -1$.

X	SGN(X)
5	$+1$
-5.7	-1
1.0	$+1$
0.5	$+1$
0	0
-4	-1
-1	-1

The ABS function (absolute value function) returns the number in the parentheses without any sign. If $X > = 0$, ABS (X) $= X$; if $X < 0$, ABS(X) $= -1*X$.

X	ABS(X)
-4.8	4.8
0	0
5.1	5.1
$-.5$	.5
1.1	1.1

Note that SGN(X) * ABS(X) $= X$ for any X.

The SQR function gives the positive square root of any number or variable in the parentheses. The value in the parentheses should be positive, although some systems will allow negative numbers but ignore their sign. Programs 9.1 and 9.2 summarize the INT, ABS, SGN, and SQR functions. In Program 9.1 the square roots of negative numbers were not printed.

PROGRAM 9.1 Library Functions

```
10 PRINT "NUMBER","INTEGER","SIGN","ABS. VALUE","SQ. ROOT"
20 READ A,B,C,D,E,F
30 PRINT A,INT(A),SGN(A),ABS(A),SQR(A)
40 PRINT B,INT(B),SGN(B),ABS(B),SQR(B)
50 PRINT C,INT(C),SGN(C),ABS(C),SQR(C)
60 PRINT D,INT(D),SGN(D),ABS(D),SQR(D)
70 PRINT E,INT(E),SGN(E),ABS(E)," -"
80 PRINT F,INT(F),SGN(F),ABS(F)," -"
100 DATA 2,1.44,.09,0,-10.6,-5.1
110 STOP
199 END
```

```
RUN
NUMBER          INTEGER         SIGN            ABS. VALUE      SQ. ROOT
 2               2               1               2               1.41421
 1.44            1               1               1.44            1.2
 .09             0               1               .09             .3
 0               0               0               0               0
-10.6           -11             -1               10.6            -
-5.1            -6              -1               5.1             -
```

The parentheses may enclose a single variable, a constant, or an expression. The variable must have been given a value previously, as in the LET statement. The parentheses may also enclose another function as illustrated in Program 9.2.

PROGRAM 9.2 Function of Functions

```
10 READ X,Y,Z
15 DATA 5,-1.7,3.8
20 PRINT ABS(Y),SGN(Z),INT(Y)
25 LET W=SGN(X)+ABS(X)
30 PRINT INT(W*2),SGN(INT(ABS(Y)))
35 END
```

```
RUN
 1.7             1               -2
 12              1
```

Note that in line 30 of Program 9.2 we wish to print the sign of the greatest integer less than or equal to the absolute value of variable *Y*.

A practical application of the INT function is when we want to *round off* a number *to the nearest* integer or tenth. We can use the INT function to accomplish this as shown in Program 9.3.

PROGRAM 9.3 Rounding Numbers

```
10 READ A,B,C,D,E
15 DATA 5.11,3.63,9.37,4.46,2.58
20 PRINT "ROUNDING TO THE NEAREST WHOLE NUMBER"
25 LET A0 = INT(A+.5)
30 LET B0 = INT(B+.5)
35 LET C0 = INT(C+.5)
40 LET D0 = INT(D+.5)
45 LET E0 = INT(E+.5)
50 PRINT A,B,C,D,E
51 PRINT A0,B0,C0,D0,E0
55 PRINT
60 PRINT "ROUNDING TO THE NEAREST DECIMAL"
65 LET A1 = INT((A+.05)*10)/10
70 LET B1 = INT((B+.05)*10)/10
75 LET C1 = INT((C+.05)*10)/10
80 LET D1 = INT((D+.05)*10)/10
85 LET E1 = INT((E+.05)*10)/10
95 PRINT A,B,C,D,E
96 PRINT A1,B1,C1,D1,E1
100 END


RUN
ROUNDING TO THE NEAREST WHOLE NUMBER
 5.11         3.63         9.37         4.46         2.58
 5            4            9            4            3

ROUNDING TO THE NEAREST DECIMAL
 5.11         3.63         9.37         4.46         2.58
 5.1          3.6          9.4          4.5          2.6
```

Note that when we round off a number to the nearest whole number, we add ½ or .5 to it and take the INT function of the sum. For example, to round off 4.7 to the nearest whole number, we add .5 to 4.7 giving 5.2, and when we take INT of 5.2 we get 5. To round off 6.3 to the nearest whole number, we add .5 to 6.3 getting 6.8, and when we take INT of 6.8 we get 6. To round a number to the nearest tenth, we just add .05 to the number, multiply the sum by 10, take the INT function of that product, and then divide by 10. For example, to round 3.46 to the nearest tenth, we get $3.46 + .05 = 3.51$, $3.51 * 10 = 35.1$, $INT(35.1) = 35$, and $^{35}/_{10} = 3.5$.

Another program that rounds numbers to the nearest whole number and uses the SGN, ABS, and INT functions is given in Program 9.4. Note that the intermediate values are given as well. Programs 9.3 and 9.4 work for both positive and negative numbers.

PROGRAM 9.4 Rounding Numbers Using SGN, INT, and ABS

```
 5 PRINT "X","SGN(X)","INT(ABS(X+.5))","NEAREST WHOLE NUMBER"
10 READ X
15 LET S=SGN(X)
20 LET R=INT(ABS(X)+.5)
25 LET N=S*R
30 PRINT X,S,R,N
35 DATA -1.6,-5.4,7.5
36 GO TO 10
40 END
```

```
RUN
X                 SGN(X)        INT(ABS(X+.5)) NEAREST WHOLE NUMBER
-1.6               -1            2                 -2
-5.4               -1            5                 -5
 7.5                1            8                  8

OUT OF DATA- LN #  10
```

Program 9.5, based on the case (9.1) that follows, makes use of the SQR function.

CASE 9.1 The management of many firms involves the development of inventory policies that keep the total costs of ordering and carrying inventory at a minimum. Two useful formulas for inventory analysis and control are:

$$(1)\ Q_o = \sqrt{\frac{2\,R\,S}{I\,C}} \quad \text{and} \quad (2)\ T_{min} = \sqrt{2\,R\,I\,S\,C}$$

where

Q_o = the optimum order quantity or the number of units to order that will minimize the firm's total inventory costs; also referred to as the *economic order quantity* (EOQ)

C = the total cost of a single unit

R = the number of units required per year

S = the cost of placing a single order

I = the inventory carrying costs which are a percentage figure based on the value of the average inventory

T_{min} = the minimum total cost for carrying and ordering Q_o

A conversational program is needed to compute Q_o and T_{min} whenever such information is required.

Program 9.5 carries out the computation of Q_o and T_{min}. The values for C, R, S, and I that were inputted were $2.00, 4000 units, $15.00, and 10%, respectively.

Note lines 80 and 85 in the program. Since formulas (1) and (2) require a square root operation, these two lines and the LET statements in them carry out the evaluation required by using the SQR function.

PROGRAM 9.5 Case 9.1, Economic Order Quantity

```
10 PRINT "*****INVENTORY ANALYSIS PROGRAM*****"
25 PRINT "INSTRUCTIONS:  AFTER EACH ? MARK TYPE THE INFORMATION"
26 PRINT "REQUESTED FOLLOWED BY A RETURN."
35 PRINT "WHAT IS THE COST OF A SINGLE UNIT";
40 INPUT C
45 PRINT "HOW MANY UNITS ARE REQUIRED FOR THE YEAR";
50 INPUT R
55 PRINT "WHAT IS THE COST OF PLACING AN ORDER";
60 INPUT S
65 PRINT "WHAT IS THE PERCENTAGE OF THE AVERAGE INVENTORY VALUE"
66 PRINT "THAT IS FOR CARRYING COSTS";
70 INPUT I
75 REM COMPUTE EOQ AND T-MIN
80 LET Q=SQR(2*R*S/(I*C))
85 LET T=SQR(2*R*I*S*C)
90 PRINT
95 PRINT "*****INVENTORY ANALYSIS REPORT*****"
105 PRINT "THE OPTIMUM ORDER QUANTITY,EOQ IS";Q;"UNITS PER ORDER"
115 PRINT "THE MINIMUM TOTAL COST FOR ORDERING AND CARRYING THE"
116 PRINT "EOQ IS $";T
120 PRINT
125 PRINT "THE ABOVE RESULTS ARE BASED ON THE FOLLOWING:"
130 PRINT "A COST PER UNIT OF $";C;
135 PRINT " NUMBER OF UNITS REQUIRED";R;" UNITS"
140 PRINT "A COST OF PLACING AN ORDER OF $";S
150 PRINT "A CARRYING COST PERCENT OF AVG. INVENTORY VALUE";
151 PRINT "OF";I*100;"%"
190 END


RUN
*****INVENTORY ANALYSIS PROGRAM*****
INSTRUCTIONS:  AFTER EACH ? MARK TYPE THE INFORMATION
REQUESTED FOLLOWED BY A RETURN.
WHAT IS THE COST OF A SINGLE UNIT ?2
HOW MANY UNITS ARE REQUIRED FOR THE YEAR ?4000
WHAT IS THE COST OF PLACING AN ORDER ?15
WHAT IS THE PERCENTAGE OF THE AVERAGE INVENTORY VALUE
THAT IS FOR CARRYING COSTS ?.10

*****INVENTORY ANALYSIS REPORT*****
THE OPTIMUM ORDER QUANTITY,EOQ IS 774.597 UNITS PER ORDER
THE MINIMUM TOTAL COST FOR ORDERING AND CARRYING THE
EOQ IS $ 154.919

THE ABOVE RESULTS ARE BASED ON THE FOLLOWING:
A COST PER UNIT OF $ 2  NUMBER OF UNITS REQUIRED 4000  UNITS
A COST OF PLACING AN ORDER OF $ 15
A CARRYING COST PERCENT OF AVG. INVENTORY VALUEOF 10 %
```

The RND function generates a random number between 0 and 1. A random number is a number selected "at random." Imagine the computer having a round card with a spinner at the center and a scale going from 0 to 1 around the edge of the card. When the RND function is used, the spinner spins and the number to which the spinner points is recorded and RND takes that value. Thus, every number between 0 and 1 has an equal chance of being selected each time the RND function is used. (In point of fact, there is no spinner inside the computer. The actual method used to generate random numbers is beyond the scope of this book.) This function is useful when it is necessary to create artificial data.

The meaning of the argument depends on the system being used. For whatever system you are using, consult the "BASIC Manual" to see what role the argument plays in the RND function. On the RAPIDATA System, any numeric value can be placed in the brackets in place of the X. The results generated are not related to the argument. Random numbers will be generated from the same starting point each time this function is used. If different sets of random numbers are desired, the RAPIDATA System requires the following statement preceding the RND function:

line # RANDOMIZE

Programs 9.6 and 9.7 show the use of the RND function; Program 9.6 is without the RANDOMIZE statement and Program 9.7 is with it.

PROGRAM 9.6   RND without RANDOMIZE

```
10 LET N1=RND(12)
20 LET N2=10*RND(15)
30 LET N3=INT(10*RND(4))
34 PRINT N1,N2,N3
36 PRINT
40 PRINT RND(17),10*RND(17),INT(10*RND(17))
99 END


RUN
 .499592        5.27804         6

 .272735        6.0196          1
```

PROGRAM 9.7   RND with RANDOMIZE

```
5 RANDOMIZE
10 LET N1=RND(12)
20 LET N2=10*RND(15)
30 LET N3=INT(10*RND(4))
34 PRINT N1,N2,N3
36 PRINT
40 PRINT RND(17),10*RND(17),INT(10*RND(17))
99 END


RUN
 1.02444E-2     .611917         2

 9.89777E-2     1.19311         8
```

Variable $N1$ in line 10 of both programs will be a number between 0 and 1. Variable $N2$ in line 20 will be a number between 0 and 10, exclusive. Variable $N3$ in line 30 will be an integer number between 0 and 9, inclusive. Line

40 of these programs shows the three RANDOM number functions described above placed in a PRINT statement.

Because the RND function gives numbers *between* 0 and 1, it is necessary to use the following procedure if *exact* limits are required.

If the range of values desired is from low (L) to high (H), inclusive, then the RND function should look like this:

$$INT((D+1)*RND(X) + L)$$

where D is equal to the difference or range between H and L. For example, if random numbers from 10 to 20, inclusive, had to be generated, an appropriate statement would be:

$$40\ LET\ R = INT(11*RND(3) + 10)$$

Since RND(X) gives numbers between 0 and 1, or from .000001 to .999999, then 11*RND(3) will produce values from .000011 to 10.999989. By adding 10 to this range, we have values from 10.000011 to 20.999989. The integer part of this range is from 10 to 20, which is the desired range of values.

Case 9.2 requires a program using numbers that are generated by the RND function.

CASE 9.2 In order to check the quality of the product coming off its assembly line, the National Electronics Company quality control department examines samples of output twice a day. One inspection is in the morning between 9 a.m. and 12:59 p.m. The other is in the afternoon between 1 p.m. and 5:59 p.m. The times that the samples are taken each day are selected at random.

Program 9.8 shows how times can be randomly obtained for the quality control department. The program will generate the hours and minutes for each time interval by using the RND functions in lines 15, 25, 30, and 45.

PROGRAM 9.8 Case 9.2, Random Inspection Times

```
10 RANDOMIZE
15 LET H1=INT(4*RND(1)+9)
25 LET M1=INT(60*RND(2))
30 LET H2=INT(5*RND(3)+1)
45 LET M2=INT(60*RND(4))
60 PRINT "  **********INSPECTION TIMES*************"
70 PRINT "MORNING TIME";H1; ":" ;M1
75 PRINT
80 PRINT "AFTERNOON TIME";H2; ":" ;M2
99 END


RUN

   **********INSPECTION TIMES*************
MORNING TIME 10 : 31

AFTERNOON TIME 4 : 16
```

THE DEF STATEMENT

The DEF statement allows the programmer to define functions. For example, suppose you are interested in the amount of money that would be on deposit if $100 were invested at 6 percent compounded annually after n years for $n = 1, 5, 10,$ and 20. We would use the compound interest formula described in Chapter 2 under *Constants and Variables*.

$$A = P(1 + r)^n$$

Without the DEF statement we could write Program 9.9.

PROGRAM 9.9   Compound Interest without DEF

```
10 READ P,R
15 PRINT P*(1+R)†1,P*(1+R)†5,P*(1+R)†10,P*(1+R)†20
20 DATA 100,.06
25 END
```

```
RUN
 106            133.823          179.085         320.714
```

With the DEF statement, we have Program 9.10.

PROGRAM 9.10   Compound Interest with DEF

```
10 READ P,R,N
15 DEF FNA(N)=P*(1+R)†N
20 PRINT FNA(1),FNA(5),FNA(10),FNA(20)
25 DATA 100,.06,5
30 END
```

```
RUN
 106            133.823          179.085         320.714
```

The statement on line 15 defines the function of the dummy variable N. The variable N need not have been given a value previously. Line 20 then prints the values of the function for the values of the numbers in parentheses. That is, FNA(1) assigns the value of 1 to N and evaluates the function on line 15.

The form of the DEF statement is

$$\text{line \# DEF FN} - (V) = \text{expression}$$

The dash can be any letter. Thus, we can have at most 26 different functions in any one program – one designated by each letter of the alphabet. V can be any variable. Normally the variable would appear in the expression to the right of the equal sign.

If we would replace line 15 in Program 9.10 with

$$15 \ DEF \ FNA(P) = P * (1+R) \uparrow N$$

line 20 would print the amount on deposit after 5 years if $1, $5, $10, and $20 were deposited at 6 percent interest compounded annually. Note that all we changed was the variable in parentheses, and now we are defining a function of P, the principal, rather than a function of N, the number of years.

THE GO SUB AND RETURN STATEMENTS

Suppose you wanted to find the largest of three numbers for two different sets of three numbers. You could write the program as Program 9.11. Note that lines 20–60 are almost identical to lines 70–110. It is wasteful to have those lines appear twice in the same program. To avoid this redundancy, we can use the GO SUB and RETURN statements, as in Program 9.12.

PROGRAM 9.11   The Largest of Three Numbers without GO SUB

```
10 READ A,B,C
15 DATA 1,2,3,4,1,2
20 LET D=A
25 IF D<B THEN 45
30 IF D<C THEN 55
35 PRINT A,B,C,D
40 GO TO 65
45 LET D=B
50 GO TO 30
55 LET D=C
60 GO TO 35
65 READ A,B,C
70 LET D=A
75 IF D<B THEN 95
80 IF D<C THEN 105
85 PRINT A,B,C,D
90 GO TO 999
95 LET D=B
100 GO TO 80
105 LET D=C
110 GO TO 85
999 END


RUN
 1               2               3               3
 4               1               2               4
```

PROGRAM 9.12   The Largest of Three Numbers with GO SUB

```
10 READ A,B,C
15 DATA 1,2,3,4,1,2
20 GO SUB 500
25 PRINT A,B,C,D
30 READ A,B,C
35 GO SUB 500
40 PRINT A,B,C,D
45 STOP
500 LET D=A
510 IF D<B THEN 525
515 IF D<C THEN 535
520 RETURN
525 LET D=B
530 GO TO 515
535 LET D=C
540 RETURN
999 END
```

```
RUN
1            2         3         3
4            1         2         4
```

The GO SUB 500 in line 20 transfers control to line 500, just like a GO TO 500 would. However, the 20 GO SUB 500 stores the number of the line following line 20 (in this case line 25) in a special location internally. When the computer encounters the RETURN statement (in line 540), control is transferred to line 25.

Similarly, when 35 GO SUB 500 is executed, the number 40 is put in that special location. When the RETURN is encountered (now in line 520), control is transferred to line 40. The RETURN returns control to the line following the most recently executed GO SUB.

The statements 500 to 540 are a subroutine. This particular subroutine finds the largest of three numbers *A, B,* and *C* and assigns the largest number to variable *D* as was done in Program 9.11. Note that there are two RETURN statements in one subroutine. In general, the number of GO SUB statements can be more, the same as, or less than the number of RETURN statements. There need *not* be a one-to-one correspondence as there must be with the FOR and NEXT statements. The statements in Program 9.12 are executed in the following sequence:

$$10, 15, 20, 500, 510, 525, 530, 515, 535, 540, 25, 30$$
$$35, 500, 510, 515, 520, 40, 45$$

There are two essential applications of subroutines. One, as illustrated in Program 9.12, is to allow a series of statements to be executed several times during a program without having to actually rewrite those statements. Thus, in Program 9.12, statements 500 through 540 are executed twice in the program although they appear only once.

The other application of subroutines is to aid in the writing of large computer programs. Thus, if we are writing a payroll program, for example, we could write one subroutine to determine FICA taxes, others to determine federal, state, and city income taxes, another to determine insurance deductions, etc. Each of the subroutines can be written independently of the main program and checked individually. Then, the main program would consist primarily of a series of GO SUB statements.

NESTED SUBROUTINES

It is possible for one subroutine to cause the program to branch to another subroutine. Observe Program 9.13.

PROGRAM 9.13 Nested Subroutines

```
10 READ A,B,D
15 DATA 3,4,0
20 GO SUB 100
25 PRINT A,B,C,D
30 GO SUB 200
35 PRINT A,B,C,D
40 STOP
100 LET C=A+B
105 GO SUB 200
110 RETURN
200 LET D=D+1
205 RETURN
300 END


RUN
3          4          7          1
3          4          7          2
```

The statements in Program 9.13 are executed in the following sequence:

$$10, 15, 20, 100, 105, 200, 205, 110, 25, 30, 200, 205, 35, 40$$

Note that the RETURN in 205 returns you first to 110 and then to 25. As before, the RETURN always returns you to the statement following the most recently executed GO SUB statement. That is, each GO SUB statement that is executed puts into that special location of memory (actually, an array) the line number of the following statement. If a second GO SUB is encountered before a RETURN statement, the line number of the statement following the second GO SUB statement is also put into that array. Then, when a RETURN is encountered, the last line number to be put into the array is the one to which control is transferred. In other words, last in, first out.

Note that the STOP statements in lines 45 and 40 in Programs 9.12 and 9.13, respectively, are necessary. For example, if line 45 were eliminated in

Program 9.12, the program would print:

```
1    2    3    3
4    1    2    4
```
RETURN ENCOUNTERED WITHOUT
PRIOR GO SUB IN LINE 520.

That is, after finishing the program as before, it would continue down to lines 500, 510, 515, 520. The RETURN in 520 does not know where to return to since the special location in memory mentioned above is empty.

SUMMARY

There are several stored functions in the BASIC language including SIN, COS, TAN, COT, ATN, LOG, EXP, SQR, INT, SGN, ABS, and RND. In addition, you can define your own specialized functions using the DEF statement. The GO SUB and RETURN statements are used to write subroutines. A subroutine is useful when you have a series of statements that are to be executed more than once in a program (not in a loop) or when a very large program is being written and it is desired to test the different parts of the program independently.

EXERCISES

9.1   What value is assigned to the variables shown below:
    a. LET P = INT(-61.49)
    b. LET C = INT($2*31.2 + .9$)
    c. LET W = SQR($.16$)
    d. LET Y = INT(SQR($.25$))
    e. LET X = SGN(-51.3)
    f. LET M = SQR(225) + INT($46/3$)
    g. LET R = ABS(-45.01)

9.2   What value is assigned to $V7$ in line 80?

```
50 LET M = .6
60 LET B = 2
70 LET A = 7
80 LET V7 = 10 * INT(M + B + A*.30)
```

9.3   What is the range of values in each case below:
    a. LET R = 10*RND(5)
    b. LET X = RND(3)*2.5
    c. LET L = $-.5$*RND(10)

    d. LET T = INT(10*RND(4))

    e. LET B9 = INT(RND(0)*5*1)

    f. LET C2 = INT(50 + 101*RND(5))

    g. LET K4 = INT(21*RND(3)+60)

9.4   Suppose the National Electronics Company (Case 9.2) is operating on an overtime schedule, that is, from 8 a.m. to 12:59 p.m. and from 1 p.m. to 8:59 p.m. Revise Program 9.6 to take these changes into account.

9.5   Your club has sold 500 raffles, numbered from 001 to 500. Write a program to randomly select a winning number using the RND function.

9.6   Write a program to read one number and print whether that number is even or odd. Use the INT function.

9.7   How would we change Program 9.10 so that it would print the amount on deposit after 5 years if $100 is deposited at 6%, 7%, 8%, and 8½%. Change only lines 15 and 20.

9.8   Write a program similar to Program 9.12, but with *D* set equal to the smallest of *A, B,* and *C* instead of the largest.

9.9   Write any program with three levels of nested subroutines and state in what order the line numbers will be executed.

9.10 What will the following program print:

```
10 READ X, Y, Z
15 PRINT ABS(X), SGN(Y+Z), INT(Y)
20 PRINT ABS(SGN(INT(X)))
25 PRINT INT(ABS(SGN(X)))
30 DATA −4.1, 7.8, −7.8
35 END
```

9.11 Write a program to read one number and print it rounded off to the nearest thousandth.

9.12 Write a program as in exercise 9.11 for three numbers. Use the DEF, GO SUB, and RETURN statements.

String Variables

Until now, the only data we were able to READ, PRINT, or compare was numeric data. Thus, for example, we could only refer to an employee via his employee number (as in Program 6.11), not the employee's name, which might be more useful. Or (as in Program 7.4), we referred to a product number, instead of a more meaningful product name. In this chapter we will correct this deficiency.

Suppose we have in DATA statements five employee names and social security numbers, each followed by the number of hours worked and the hourly rate. We wish to write a program (10.1) to PRINT employee names, social security numbers, and salaries, computed as number of hours worked multiplied by hourly rate. Let us assume that there is no overtime.

PROGRAM 10.1   String Variables

```
10 PRINT "NAME","S.S NUMBER","HOURS","RATE","SALARY"
15 FOR I = 1 TO 5
20 READ N$,S$,H,R
25 LET S=H*R
30 PRINT N$,S$,H,R,S
35 NEXT I
40 DATA J.SUTTON,"123-45-6789",40,15.55
41 DATA E.KAPLAN,"352-31-7896",35,7.70
42 DATA R.NENNER,"098-76-5321",41,3.80
43 DATA B.SIROTA,"212-17-6034",50,10.50
44 DATA P.KAMBER,"696-40-3117",30,8.50
45 END
```

```
RUN
NAME           S.S NUMBER      HOURS         RATE         SALARY
J.SUTTON       123-45-6789     40            15.55        622
E.KAPLAN       352-31-7896     35            7.7          269.5
R.NENNER       098-76-5321     41            3.8          155.8
B.SIROTA       212-17-6034     50            10.5         525
P.KAMBER       696-40-3117     30            8.5          255
```

Look at Program 10.1. Note that the variable to which we assign the name of the employee is $N\$$. Any variable to which we want to assign an alphabetic value (that is, a variable containing letters, as opposed to a numeric variable, which can contain only numbers) must consist of a single letter (or a single letter followed by a single digit) followed by a "$\$$" sign. If on line 20 in Program 10.1 we would have had

20 READ N, S, H, R

we would have gotten an error message since the variable N can only contain numeric data and the first item in the DATA statement is J. SUTTON, which is alphabetic data. $N\$$ and $S\$$ are called *string variables*. A string variable can contain alphabetic data exclusively as $N\$$, and it can also contain numeric data as $S\$$. A string variable can contain any string of characters, including the dashes in the social security number.

A string variable can appear in any statement in which a numeric variable can appear. Some examples follow:

Statement	Example
READ	READ N$, H, R
PRINT	PRINT N$, S
LET	LET G$="B+" or LET G$=Q$
IF	IF A$<B$ THEN 10 or
	IF R$ = "YES" THEN 10
INPUT	INPUT R$
DIM	DIM N$ (20)

Alphabetic data can also appear in DATA statements. Quotation marks around the alphabetic data are optional. They are only required when a comma is part of the data, or if trailing blanks are part of the data. Thus, if the DATA statement in Program 10.1 had the last names first, followed by a comma and the first initial, we would have been required to write

40 DATA "SUTTON, J.", "123–45–6789", 40, 15.55

Similarly, if we want a string variable to contain the letters *ABC* followed by two blanks, we would have in the DATA statement

60 DATA "ABC   "

Program 10.2 illustrates how dimensioned string variables are handled.

PROGRAM 10.2   Dimensioned String Variables

```
10 DIM M$(12),P(12)    / GIVE VARIABLES SUBSCRIPTS
20 FOR I = 1 TO 12 ✓
30 READ M$(I),P(I)
40 NEXT I
50 DATA JANUARY,1500,FEBRUARY,1200,MARCH,1750,APRIL,1600,MAY,1550
51 DATA JUNE,1350,JULY,1400,AUGUST,1750,SEPTEMBER,1200,OCTOBER,1250
52 DATA NOVEMBER,1300,DECEMBER,1500
60 FOR I = 1 TO 4
61 PRINT "QUARTER NUMBER";I
62 PRINT "MONTH","PRODUCTION"
70 FOR J = 1 TO 3
100 PRINT M$(3*(I-1)+J),P(3*(I-1)+J)
110 NEXT J
115 PRINT
120 NEXT I
999 END


RUN
QUARTER NUMBER 1
MONTH          PRODUCTION
JANUARY          1500
FEBRUARY         1200
MARCH            1750

QUARTER NUMBER 2
MONTH          PRODUCTION
APRIL            1600
MAY              1550
JUNE             1350

QUARTER NUMBER 3
MONTH          PRODUCTION
JULY             1400
AUGUST           1750
SEPTEMBER        1200

QUARTER NUMBER 4
MONTH          PRODUCTION
OCTOBER          1250
NOVEMBER         1300
DECEMBER         1500
```

Note that line 30 reads in data for the string variable array $M\$$ as well as the numeric variable array P. By dimensioning $M\$$, we can refer to the sixth month by $M\$(6)$, which will be printed out as JUNE. Note how the expressions in the parentheses in line 100 print the Jth month in the Ith quarter. Thus, for example, the second month in the third quarter corresponds to $J = 2$ and $I = 3$ and $3*(I-1)+J = 8$, which is the eighth month of the year (August).

We can also compare the values of string variables. Suppose we want to print two names stored in $A\$$ and $B\$$ in alphabetical order but we don't know which name shall come first. This situation is illustrated in Program 10.3.

PROGRAM 10.3   Comparing String Variables

```
10 READ A$,B$
15 IF A$>B$ THEN 30
20 PRINT A$,B$
25 GO TO 40
30 PRINT B$,A$
35 DATA JACKY,JACKSON
40 END


RUN
JACKSON          JACKY
```

Note that JACKSON is lower alphabetically than JACKY, so it should appear first in order, just as these names would appear in a telephone book. It makes no difference that JACKSON has more letters than JACKY.

An example illustrating string variables in the INPUT statement appears in Program 10.4. In that program, the square root of any number will be printed.

PROGRAM 10.4   Inputting String Variables

```
10 PRINT "TYPE IN ANY POSITIVE NUMBER AND SQUARE ROOT WILL BE GIVEN"
15 PRINT "NUMBER =";
20 INPUT N
25 PRINT "THE SQUARE ROOT OF";N;"IS";SQR(N)
30 PRINT "ANY MORE NUMBERS (TYPE YES OR NO)"
35 INPUT A$
40 IF A$="YES" THEN 15
45 END


RUN
TYPE IN ANY POSITIVE NUMBER AND SQUARE ROOT WILL BE GIVEN
NUMBER = ?4
THE SQUARE ROOT OF 4 IS 2
ANY MORE NUMBERS (TYPE YES OR NO)
 ?YES
NUMBER = ?25
THE SQUARE ROOT OF 25 IS 5
ANY MORE NUMBERS (TYPE YES OR NO)
 ?YES
NUMBER = ?256
THE SQUARE ROOT OF 256 IS 16
ANY MORE NUMBERS (TYPE YES OR NO)
 ?YES
NUMBER = ?3
THE SQUARE ROOT OF 3 IS 1.73205
ANY MORE NUMBERS (TYPE YES OR NO)
 ?NO
```

Note how line 40 carries out an IF test on the word "YES." The only way this program will continue is if YES is typed after the INPUT query.

Case 10.1 requires a program using subscripted string variables.

CASE 10.1 In a certain course, three class exams and a final exam are given. The final term average is based on the average of the three class exam grades averaged in with the final exam grade. A letter grade of A, $B+$, B, $C+$, C, $D+$, D, or F is also given. We wish to write a program to read the student's name, class, grades, and final grade, and print a table with the student's name, final term average, and letter grade. A letter grade of A is given to those whose term average is at least 90, a $B+$ is given to those whose term average is at least 85 and less than 90, etc. There are 10 students in the class. We also wish to print the number of people receiving each of the grades.

PROGRAM 10.5 Case 10.1, Grading Program

$N(0)$, $G\$(2)$

```
5 DIM N(8),G$(8)
10 FOR I=1 TO 8
15 READ G$(I)
16 DATA A,B+,B,C+,C,D+,D,F
20 LET N(I)=0
25 NEXT I
30 PRINT "NAME","TERM AVERAGE","GRADE"
35 FOR I= 1 TO 10
40 READ N$,G1,G2,G3,FINAL
45 LET A=((G1+G2+G3)/3+F)/2
50 IF A>=90 THEN 95
55 IF A>=85 THEN 105
60 IF A>=80 THEN 115
65 IF A>=75 THEN 125
70 IF A>=70 THEN 135
75 IF A>=65 THEN 145
80 IF A>=60 THEN 155
85 LET X=8
90 GO TO 160
95 LET X=1
100 GO TO 160
105 LET X=2
110 GO TO 160
115 LET X=3
120 GO TO 160
125 LET X=4
130 GO TO 160
135 LET X=5
140 GO TO 160
145 LET X=6
150 GO TO 160
155 LET X=7
160 LET N(X)=N(X)+1
165 PRINT N$,A,G$(X)
170 NEXT I
175 PRINT "GRADE","NUMBER"
180 FOR I=1 TO 8
185 PRINT G$(I),N(I)
190 NEXT I
200 DATA J.SAMBORN,65,76,80,90,P.FISHMAN,70,81,95,93,E.GOLD,76,84,68,78
210 DATA A.EINSTEIN,98,97,90,95,B.WEIN,86,88,89,89,S.LACHS,77,76,80,73
220 DATA M.FALIG,81,84,90,80,R.HERMAN,58,74,67,54,E.GILA,70,75,78,79
230 DATA J.LYNN,70,74,65,68
9999 END
```

AVG

PROGRAM 10.5 continued

```
RUN
NAME              TERM AVERAGE    GRADE
J.SAMBORN         81.8333         B
P.FISHMAN         87.5            B+
E.GOLD            77              C+
A.EINSTEIN        95              A
B.WEIN            88.3333         B+
S.DACHS           75.3333         C+
M.FALIG           82.5            B
R.HERMAN          60.1667         D
B.GILA            76.6667         C+
J.LYNN            68.8333         D+
GRADE             NUMBER
A                 1
B+                2
B                 2
C+                3
C                 0
D+                1
D                 1
F                 0
```

In Program 10.5 an array $G\$$ contains each of the possible grades A, $B+$, B, $C+$, C, $D+$, D, and F. Similarly, the array N will contain the number of students receiving each grade. Thus, $G\$(3) = B$ and $N(3) =$ the number of students receiving a B, and so on. Therefore, if the average is, say, at least 80 and under 85, the program branches to line 115 where X is set to 3. Then, we go to line 160 where $N(X)$ or $N(3)$ increases by 1, and then print the name of the student, his term average, and $G\$(X)$ or $G\$(3)$, which is B. The values of the array $G\$$ were read in at the beginning of the program (lines 10–25), and the initial zero values of the array N were also set to zero within these lines.

Instead of reading the values of the array $G\$$, we could have written

$$\text{LET } G\$(1) = \text{``A''}$$
$$\text{LET } G\$(2) = \text{``B+''}$$
$$\text{LET } G\$(3) = \text{``B''}$$

and so on. See also exercise 10.4 that replaces all of the 22 statements between lines 50 and 155, inclusive, with only 7 statements.

SUMMARY

String variables are variables that can be assigned strings of characters, such as names of people or products. String variables can appear in any statement in which numeric variables can appear, including READ, PRINT, LET, IF/THEN, INPUT, and DIM.

EXERCISES

10.1 Write a program to read five product names, their prices, and quantity ordered, and print a table containing the column headings, "Product Name," "Price," "Quantity," and "Amount." The amount is the price times the quantity. The total of the amount column should also be printed. The data lines for the program are:

```
60 DATA HAND SOAP,24,.69,TOOTH PASTE,35,.76
62 DATA BROWN SUGAR,16,1.25
65 DATA COLA,24,.55,RYE BREAD,50,.20
```

10.2 Rewrite Program 7.4 to use these data lines with product names instead of product numbers:

```
75 DATA SOAP,100,TISSUE,150,BREAD,50
77 DATA BRUSHES,25,ASPIRIN,12,SODA,250
80 DATA CHEESE,80,CEREAL,200,BEANS,500,SOUP,75
```

10.3 Write a program to read three names of people and print them out in alphabetical order.

10.4 Explain how the following 7 statements accomplish the same thing as the 22 statements between lines 50 and 155, inclusive, of Program 10.5:

```
50 IF A>94 THEN 70
55 IF A<60 THEN 80
60 LET X = INT((94−A)/5) + 1
65 GO TO 160
70 LET X = 1
75 GO TO 160
80 LET X = 8
```

10.5 What would Program 10.4 do if, in response to the question "ANY MORE NUMBERS (TYPE YES OR NO)," you typed
a. DEFINITELY NOT
b. SURE
c. OF COURSE
d. YES!
e. NO!

10.6 Write a program that will read a name from the terminal, one letter at a time, and print out the name backwards. End the name with a period. You must use a DIM statement to dimension the letters in the name.

10.7   The XYZ Company has five salespersons. They are listed below with the amount of goods each sold last month.

Salesperson	Amount Sold
Julie Shana	$12,000
Jay Joshua	17,500
Shirley Efram	14,500
Al Bennet	18,250
Ari Lee	16,250

Using the concept of string variables for the above names, write a program that will output all the above information with a column showing commissions on sales. Commissions are 10 percent of sales.

10.8   Do exercise 10.7 treating first names and last names as separate string variables. Have the output show last names and then first names. Also have the totals of the amounts sold and commissions printed.

10.9   In order to prepare a budget for next year, the NARCO Company estimates that each of its sales regions will show a growth in sales above this year of $8\frac{1}{2}$ percent. This year's sales by each region are as follows:

Region	Sales (million $)
Northern	4.65
Central	5.23
Western	2.81
Midwest	9.67
Eastern	3.56
Southern	8.89

Write a program which uses string variables for the regions and which outputs the expected sales for next year for each region.

10.10   Redo exercise 6.13, reading in the employee's name instead of number, using the idea of subscripting given in Case 10.1 to determine the tax rate, and using different subroutines to determine the gross wages, tax rate, and insurance premium.

PRINT USING and TAB

THE PRINT USING STATEMENT

The PRINT USING statement is a very useful feature of some BASIC systems. It allows greater control of the output. Note, for example, the output in Program 6.3. Some revised prices are whole numbers and some have several decimal positions. Suppose we wish all of the revised prices to be printed rounded to two decimal places. Also observe that the column containing the item numbers is 15 spaces wide where 8 would be more than enough. Finally, it would be nice if prices over $1000 were printed with commas. These difficulties can be corrected with the PRINT USING statement.

To improve the output in Program 6.3 we replace each PRINT statement with a PRINT USING statement and an associated image statement. Observe Program 11.1.

PROGRAM 11.1   Revising Prices with PRINT USING

```
 5 REM PROGRAM TO UPDATE PRICE LIST
10 PRINT USING 60
11 PRINT USING 61
15 READ I,P
20 LET R=P*1.066
30 PRINT USING 62,I,P,R
40 GO TO 15
50 DATA 218,200,233,1456,345,545,367,248,401,225,406,179
55 DATA 407,1000,557,267,679,470,887,359
60 FMT ITEM            CURRENT          REVISED
61 FMT NUMB@R          PRICE            PRICE
62 FMT ###          $##,###.##       $##,###.##
90 END
```

PROGRAM 11.1   continued

```
RUN
  ITEM            CURRENT           REVISED
  NUMBER          PRICE             PRICE
  218          $    200.00       $    213.20
  233          $  1,456.00       $  1,552.10
  345          $    545.00       $    580.97
  367          $    248.00       $    264.37
  401          $    225.00       $    239.85
  406          $    179.00       $    190.81
  407          $  1,000.00       $  1,066.00
  557          $    267.00       $    284.62
  679          $    470.00       $    501.02
  887          $    359.00       $    382.69

OUT OF DATA- LN #   15
```

The image statement associated with each PRINT USING statement begins with the letters FMT* and tells the computer how to print the variables (if any) of the PRINT USING statement. The image statement may also contain only headings. Thus, lines 10 and 11 which have no variables in them will print everything following the letters FMT in lines 60 and 61, exactly as it appears there. Line 30 will cause the values of the variables *I, P,* and *R* to be printed where the fields of the "#"** symbols are in the image statement. That is, the item number, *I,* will be printed in the first three columns, the current price will be printed where the second field of #'s is and with two zeros to the right of the decimal point since there is a decimal point before the last two #'s. Note that the prices are right justified and all of the decimal points are aligned. Finally, the revised prices will appear where the third field of #'s is. Note how the commas are printed only for numbers more than $1,000.00

Some other features of the PRINT USING statement are illustrated in Program 11.2. Note how readable the numeric output appears with the commas. Also note that if a field of #'s is surrounded with parentheses, the output will have the parentheses only if the number is negative, as in the profit (loss) column. Note also that all of the decimal points are aligned properly, the numbers are all right justified, and the zeros are filled in all printing positions to the right of the decimal.

---

*In some systems a full colon is used instead of the letters FMT.
**In some systems, a "9" is used instead of the "#."

PROGRAM 11.2 Profit (Loss) with PRINT USING

```
10 PRINT USING 400
15 FOR J=1 TO 5
20 READ N$,I,E
25 LET P=I-E
30 PRINT USING 401,N$,I,E,P
35 NEXT J
40 DATA HERGOLD REALTY CO.,500000,197000
45 DATA SUNBRITE DAIRY CO.,1209765,1340123
50 DATA ACE RENTAL CO.,546739,467654
55 DATA ARNOLD PAINT CO.,65000,36000
60 DATA CHEFA CATERING CO.,430000,739000
400 FMTCOMPANY          GROSS INCOME      EXPENSES   PROFIT(LOSS)
401 FMT################# ##,###,###.##   ###,###,###.##  (###,###.##)
999 END


RUN
COMPANY              GROSS INCOME        EXPENSES   PROFIT(LOSS)
HERGOLD REALTY CO.      500,000.00      197,000.00    303,000.00
SUNBRITE DAIRY CO.    1,209,765.00    1,340,123.00  (130,363.00)
ACE RENTAL CO.          546,739.00      467,654.00     79,135.00
ARNOLD PAINT CO.         65,000.00       36,000.00  ( 21,000.00)
CHEFA CATERING CO.      430,000.00      739,000.00  (359,000.00)

USED:    2.5 UNITS
```

Another very useful feature of the PRINT USING statement is the asterisk protection feature, illustrated in Program 11.3. Note the single asterisk (*) in Line 201.

PROGRAM 11.3 Asterisk Protection Feature

```
10 PRINT USING 200
20 FOR I=1 TO 5
25 READ N$,H,R
30 PRINT USING 201,N$,H,R,H*R
35 NEXT I
200 FMT NAME        HOURS        RATE        SALARY
201 FMT ##########    ###      $###.##    $*#,###.##
300 DATA F.BACK,50,21.00,H.BOOK,25,2.50
310 DATA C.RAICE,31,2.75,K.SHIRA,39,3.72
320 DATA P.SURI,37,3.86
999 END


RUN
NAME        HOURS        RATE        SALARY
F.BACK        50      $ 21.00    $*1,050.00
H.BOOK        25      $  2.50    $****62.50
C.RAICE       31      $  2.75    $****85.25
K.SHIRA       39      $  3.72    $***145.08
P.SURI        37      $  3.86    $***142.82
```

Observe that the asterisks fill in all blanks between the "$" and the first non-zero figure. This feature effectively prevents an unscrupulous employee from giving himself a raise in salary by adding a number in the blank space before his existing salary on a paycheck.

Be careful whenever using the PRINT USING statement to have enough # symbols in the image statement to accommodate the largest number or string that is to be printed in that field. If the number of characters or digits to be printed is less than the number of # symbols in the image statement, no harm is done. Numbers will be printed in the rightmost positions and strings will be printed in the leftmost positions. If the number of characters or digits to be printed is more than the number of # symbols in the image statement, an error message will be printed or, in some systems, the leading characters or digits will not be printed.

THE TAB FUNCTION

The TAB feature enables us to print output in any column that we like. For example, if we wanted to print "MARCH SALES REPORT" beginning in column 36, we would write the statement:

10 PRINT TAB(35); "MARCH SALES REPORT"

The TAB(35); will skip until the 36th space. Note the semicolon following the TAB(35). A comma there would have caused "MARCH SALES RE-PORT" to be printed in column 46 (i.e., the fourth column) since the fourth column is the next available column after the 36th position. Thus, the TAB statement should *always be used with a semicolon.*

The parentheses following the word TAB can contain any numerical expression. If the expression has a noninteger value, the number of spaces skipped will be the integer part of the value.

The number in parentheses always refers to the number of spaces skipped from the left-hand margin. Thus the statement:

10 PRINT TAB(10); "*"; TAB(35); "*"

will print an "*" in columns 11 and 36, not in columns 11 and 46. Program 11.4 illustrates the TAB feature.

PROGRAM 11.4 The TAB Feature

```
10 FOR I = 1 TO 9
15 PRINT "*";TAB(I);"*";TAB(10);"*"
20 NEXT I
25 END


RUN
```

Note that line 15 prints three asterisks. The first asterisk is in the first column, the second in the Ith column, and the third in column 11.

In Program 10.5, we had in array $G$$ the letters $A, B+, B, C+, C, D+, D,$ and F; and in array N, the number of students receiving a particular grade. That is, G(1) = "A"$ and $N(1) = $ the number of students receiving the grade of A, G(2) = "B+"$ and $N(2) = $ the number of students receiving the grade of $B+$, and so on.

Suppose we wanted to plot the frequency distribution of grades. The program segment lines 400–415 of Program 11.5 when inserted into Program 10.5 will accomplish this. We have also (1) used the GO SUB and RETURN statements in Program 11.5 to segment the report into sections by underlining, (2) used the STOP statement (line 499), (3) used the suggestion given in exercise 10.4, and (4) used the PRINT USING statements in place of the PRINT statements in lines 30 and 165 to further improve the appearance of the output.

PROGRAM 11.5 The Grade Program with a Plot

```
  5 DIM N(8),G$(8)
  7 GO SUB 500
 10 FOR I=1 TO 8
 15 READ G$(I)
 16 DATA A,B+,B,C+,C,D+,D,F
 20 LET N(I)=0
 25 NEXT I
 30 PRINT USING 300
 35 FOR I= 1 TO 10
 40 READ N$,G1,G2,G3,F
 45 LET A=((G1+G2+G3)/3+F)/2
 50 IF A>94 THEN 70
 55 IF A<60 THEN 80
 60 LET X=INT((94-A)/5)+1
 65 GO TO 160
 70 LET X=1
 75 GO TO 160
 80 LET X=8
160 LET N(X)=N(X)+1
165 PRINT USING 301,N$,A,G$(X)
170 NEXT I
171 PRINT
172 GO SUB 500
175 PRINT "GRADE","NUMBER"
180 FOR I=1 TO 8
185 PRINT G$(I),N(I)
190 NEXT I
195 PRINT
200 DATA J.SAMBORN,65,76,80,90,P.FISHMAN,70,81,95,93,E.GOLD,76,84,68,78
210 DATA A.EINSTEIN,98,97,90,95,E.WEIN,86,88,89,89,S.LACHS,77,76,80,73
220 DATA M.FALIG,81,84,90,80,R.HERMAN,58,74,67,54,E.GILA,70,75,78,79
230 DATA J.LYNN,70,74,65,68
300 FMT NAME              AVERAGE       GRADE
301 FMT ############     ###.##        ###
305 GO SUB 500
400 FOR I=1 TO 8
405 PRINT G$(I);TAB(N(I)*3+5);"*"
410 PRINT
415 NEXT I
420 FOR I=0 TO 10
425 PRINT TAB(4+3*I);I;
430 NEXT I
```

PROGRAM 11.5 continued

```
435 PRINT
440 PRINT TAB(7),"NO. OF STUDENTS"
450 GO SUB 500
499 STOP
500 PRINT
501 PRINT
505 FOR I=1 TO 70
510 PRINT "-";
515 NEXT I
520 PRINT
521 PRINT
525 RETURN
9999 END
RUN
```

```
------------------------------------------------------------------------

NAME             AVERAGE        GRADE
  J.SAMBORN        81.83          B
  P.FISHMAN        87.50          B+
  E.GOLD           77.00          C+
  A.EINSTEIN       95.00          A
  B.WEIN           88.33          B+
  S.DACHS          75.33          C+
  M.FALIG          82.50          B
  R.HERMAN         60.17          D
  B.GILA           76.67          C+
  J.LYNN           68.83          D+


------------------------------------------------------------------------

GRADE            NUMBER
A                  1
B+                 2
B                  2
C+                 3
C                  0
D+                 1
D                  1
F                  0


------------------------------------------------------------------------

A         *

B+            *

B            *

C+              *

C      *

D+     *

D      *

F      *
        0  1  2  3  4  5  6  7  8  9  10
              NO. OF STUDENTS

------------------------------------------------------------------------
```

SUMMARY

The PRINT USING statement along with its associated image statement is more flexible than the standard PRINT statement.

With the PRINT USING statement, you can

1. round off numbers to any number of decimal places,
2. align the decimal points and have numbers right justified instead of left justified,
3. have columns of any width instead of only 15 character width columns,
4. have commas printed indicating thousands, millions, etc., in very large numbers,
5. print and adjust column headings more easily,
6. have negative numbers printed surrounded by parentheses (as in profit/loss statements), and
7. have all leading blanks filled in with asterisks.

The TAB feature allows one to conveniently skip spaces, much the same as the tab key does on a typewriter. It also enables one to draw graphs and frequency distributions.

EXERCISES

11.1 Write a program using PRINT USING to print the square root of 2 correct to 1, 2, 3, 4, 5, and 10 decimal places.

11.2 Write a program using PRINT USING to print the powers of 2 between 1 and 26, inclusive. Allow eight digits for your answer. Be sure to have the output printed with commas separating the groups of three numbers.

11.3 Rewrite Program 10.4 with PRINT USING statements. Have all square roots printed correct to four digits.

11.4 Rewrite Program 7.8 using PRINT USING statements. The sales projections should all be printed correct to two decimal places. Have the heading also printed with PRINT USING statements.

11.5 Write a program that would print the following letters of the alphabet using asterisks and the TAB feature, as in Program 11.4.

a. *Z*   c. *T*   e. *P*   g. *W*
b. *H*   d. *U*   f. *V*

11.6   What will the following program print when it is run:

```
10 GO SUB 100
20 GO SUB 200
30 GO SUB 100
40 GO SUB 200
50 GO SUB 100
60 STOP
100 FOR I = 1 TO 10
105 PRINT "*";
110 NEXT I
115 PRINT
120 RETURN
200 FOR I = 1 TO 7
205 PRINT "*"
210 NEXT I
215 RETURN
300 END
```

11.7   Write a program using the subroutines in exercise 11.6 to print the letter *F*.

11.8   Write one PRINT statement using TAB to print "NAME" in columns 1–4, "SALARY" in columns 21–26, "DEDUCTIONS" in columns 35–44, and "NET PAY" in columns 50–56.

11.9   Modify Program 4.11 so that the column for sales for each day is 10 characters in width instead of 15 characters. Use the TAB feature.

12

Matrices and Matrix Operations

There are many programming situations where large data arrays—lists and/or tables—are involved, or where matrix algebra computations are required. The BASIC language has a set of statements to handle such situations. These *matrix statements** provide the programmer with a convenient and easy way to carry out operations that might require added statements if done in an alternate way.

A matrix can be either a list or a table of data, as covered in Chapter 8. This chapter explains reading, printing, and manipulation of data as matrices.

THE MAT READ STATEMENT

The general form of the MAT READ statement is:

line # MAT READ matrix name(s)

Examples of such statements are:

20 MAT READ A
30 MAT READ X1
45 MAT READ K, L, M

Assume there is a matrix *B:*

$$\begin{vmatrix} 27 & 36 & 78 \\ 47 & 14 & 49 \end{vmatrix}$$

---

*Not every system will have matrix statements.

Examples of MAT READ and DATA statements to read this data are:

> 10 MAT READ B
> 20 DATA 27, 36, 78
> 30 DATA 47, 14, 49

or

> 10 MAT READ B
> 20 DATA 27, 36, 78, 47, 14, 49

A MAT READ statement is equivalent to reading with nested FOR/NEXT loops as shown in Program 12.1.

PROGRAM 12.1   Reading a Matrix Using Nested FOR/NEXT Loops

```
5 DIM B(2,3)
10 FOR I=1 TO 2
15 FOR J=1 TO 3
20 READ B(I,J)
25 NEXT J
30 NEXT I
35 DATA 27,36,78,47,14,49
99 END
```

A single statement (line 10, MAT READ B, in Program 12.2) functions like lines 10–30 in Program 12.1. All the values read by MAT READ B in Program 12.2 can be treated as subscripted variables.

In order to specify the size of the matrix being read in, we use a DIM statement. Such a statement serves in the same way as the outer limits of the FOR statements in Program 12.1. A complete program for reading matrix B is shown in Program 12.2.

PROGRAM 12.2   Reading a 2 × 3 Matrix with MAT READ

```
5 DIM B(2,3)
10 MAT READ B
20 DATA 27,36,78,47,14,49
99 END
```

The DIM in line 5 indicates the size of the matrix—in this case, two rows and three columns. As a result, Program 12.2 yields the following assignment of data to a subscripted variable:

$B(1,1) = 27$	$B(1,2) = 36$	$B(1,3) = 78$
$B(2,1) = 47$	$B(2,2) = 14$	$B(2,3) = 49$

In Chapter 8 it was pointed out that overdimensioning was permitted, but underdimensioning would generate an error message. The same holds true for matrix reading. If the DIM statement is larger than the matrix actually being read, the correct matrix size must be shown in the MAT READ statement. Program 12.3 is a revision of Program 12.2 illustrating this point.

PROGRAM 12.3 Specifying the Size of the Matrix in MAT READ

```
 5 DIM B(10,12)
10 MAT READ B(2,3)
20 DATA 27,36,78,47,14,49
99 END
```

Line 10 in the revised program provides the correct row and column specifications. Two general situations for line 10 can be stated:

1. line # MAT READ matrix name (rows *or* columns)
2. line # MAT READ matrix name (rows, columns)

Examples for these statements are:

10 MAT READ X(5):	a single list of 5 items to be subscripted X(1), X(2), . . . , X(5)
30 MAT READ A(20,5):	a table of 100 items (20 rows and 5 columns) subscripted as A(1,1), . . . , A(1,5)

$$\vdots \qquad\qquad \vdots$$

A(20,1), . . . , A(20,5)

THE MAT PRINT STATEMENT

A statement of the following form can be used to print out a matrix:

line # MAT PRINT matrix name(s)

Examples of such statements are:

25 MAT PRINT A
35 MAT PRINT X1;
45 MAT PRINT K, L, M

Line 25 generates output in fields of 15 spaces, 5 fields on each line. Line 35 prints output packed across each line, row by row, because of the "dangling" semicolon. Line 45 prints out each matrix one at a time, first matrix K, then L, and then M, one beneath the other.

Several programs that read in and print out matrices using different MAT PRINT statements follow.

Program 12.4 illustrates handling a single list as a matrix with output generated by line 20.

PROGRAM 12.4 MAT READ and MAT PRINT for a List

```
5 DIM L(12)
10 MAT READ L
20 MAT PRINT L
30 DATA 2,4,6,8,10,1,3,5,7,9,11,13
99 END
```

RUN

2	4	6	8	10
1	3	5	7	9
11	13			

Program 12.5 illustrates the single list shown in Program 12.4, with line 20 ending with ";". Note how the output is packed onto a single line.

PROGRAM 12.5 MAT PRINT Ending with a Semicolon

```
5 DIM L(12)
10 MAT READ L
20 MAT PRINT L;
30 DATA 2,4,6,8,10,1,3,5,7,9,11,13
99 END
```

RUN

```
2   4   6   8   10   1   3.  5   7   9   11   13
```

Program 12.6 illustrates the reading in and printing out of a simple table, four rows by three columns.

PROGRAM 12.6 MAT READ and MAT PRINT for a Table

```
10 DIM X(4,3)
15 MAT READ X
20 MAT PRINT X
25 DATA 2,2,2,6,6,6,8,8,8,9,9,9
99 END
```

RUN

2	2	2
6	6	6
8	8	8
9	9	9

Program 12.7 illustrates what happens with a different DIM statement than that used in Program 12.6. Instead of a 4 × 3 table, a 6 × 2 table has been outputted. Note the ";" at the end of line 20 and the resulting output.

PROGRAM 12.7   Changing the DIM Statement and Packing Output

```
10 DIM X(6,2)
15 MAT READ X
20 MAT PRINT X;
25 DATA 2,2,2,6,6,6,8,8,8,9,9,9
99 END
```

```
RUN

2    2
2    6
6    6
8    8
8    9
9    9
```

Program 12.8 illustrates a single program with several lists and tables being read in and printed out. The program uses the following:

$$\begin{array}{ll} \text{List } A: & 5, 12, 13, 76, 12, 17 \\ \text{List } J: & -32, 68, -41, 68 \end{array}$$

$$\begin{array}{lccc} \text{Table } N: & .3 & .5 & .2 \\ & .6 & .7 & .8 \\ & .2 & .1 & .9 \end{array}$$

$$\begin{array}{lcccc} \text{Table } P: & 8 & 1 & 5 & 6 \\ & 3 & 2 & 9 & 7 \end{array}$$

Note that the data must be in the precise order that it is to be read. That is, lists A and J, then tables N and P, must agree with line 10.

PROGRAM 12.8   Reading and Printing Lists and Tables

```
5 DIM A(6),J(4),N(3,3),P(2,4)
10 MAT READ A,J,N,P
20 MAT PRINT A;J,N,P;
30 DATA 5,12,13,76,12,17,-32,68,-41,68
40 DATA .3,.5,.2,.6,.7,.8,.2,.1,.9
50 DATA 8,1,5,6,3,2,9,7
99 END
```

```
RUN

5    12   13   76   12   17


-32             68             -41             68


.3              .5             .2
.6              .7             .8
.2              .1             .9


8    1    5    6
3    2    9    7
```

Program 12.9 illustrates overdimensioning with the MAT READ (line 20) giving the row and column specifications for a 3×5 table.

PROGRAM 12.9 Overdimensioning and Table Specifications in MAT READ

```
10 DIM C(10,20)
20 MAT READ C(3,5)
30 MAT PRINT C;
50 DATA 2,3,6,-7,8,9,1,-3,5,9,2,0,1,-5,8
99 END


RUN

2   3   6  -7   8
9   1  -3   5   9
2   0   1  -5   8
```

Program 12.10 illustrates how the parts of a matrix that have been read in can be printed out. The program will read in the following matrix *M:*

$$\begin{vmatrix} 7 & 3 & 6 \\ -5 & 12 & 8 \\ 9 & 17 & 11 \\ 10 & -8 & 5 \end{vmatrix}$$

PROGRAM 12.10 Printing Parts of a Matrix

```
5 DIM M(4,3)
10 MAT READ M
15 DATA 7,3,6,-5,12,8,9,17,11,10,-8,5
20 PRINT "2ND ROW"
25 PRINT M(2,1);M(2,2);M(2,3)
26 PRINT
30 PRINT "COLUMNS 1 AND 2"
35 FOR I= 1 TO 4
40 FOR J= 1 TO 2
50 PRINT M(I,J),
55 NEXT J
60 PRINT
65 NEXT I
70 PRINT "ROWS 2,3,&4-COLS 2&3"
75 FOR I= 2 TO 4
80 FOR J =2 TO 3
85 PRINT M(I,J),
90 NEXT J
95 PRINT
100 NEXT I
199 END


RUN
2ND ROW
-5   12   8

COLUMNS 1 AND 2
 7              3
-5             12
 9             17
 10            -8
ROWS 2,3,&4-COLS 2&3
 12             8
 17            11
-8              5
```

The first output will be the second row of the matrix, based on line 25. The next output will be columns 1 and 2 based on lines 35–65. The last output (the values in rows 2, 3, and 4 but only columns 2 and 3) is based on lines 75–100.

THE MAT INPUT STATEMENT

In Chapter 4 we saw how data could be supplied to a program in response to an INPUT statement. Such a statement results in the symbol "?" being printed at a user's terminal. Then the computer system pauses so that the user can type data in.

It is also possible to enter a matrix of data using the input approach. The general statement to do this is:

line # MAT INPUT variable list

Specific examples are:

25 MAT INPUT C
40 MAT INPUT S,T,V

When a MAT INPUT statement is executed, the symbol "?" appears for each data line in the matrix. After the first "?", one line of data is to be typed. Then another "?" appears, to be followed by the next line of data, and so on. In the case of line 40 above, where there are several matrices to be inputted, each matrix is entered sequentially; first MAT S, then MAT T, and finally MAT V. All data can then be referred to by means of subscripted variables since we are dealing with matrices.

Matrix C below is a 3×2 table with the following data in it:

$$\begin{vmatrix} 17 & -6 \\ 25 & 7 \\ 20 & -8 \end{vmatrix}$$

Program 12.11 shows this matrix as an input. Line 10 provides for the inputting of the data.

PROGRAM 12.11   MAT INPUT Statement

```
5 DIM C(3,2)
10 MAT INPUT C
15 MAT PRINT C
20 PRINT "COL.1 TOTAL", "COL.2 TOTAL"
25 PRINT C(1,1)+C(2,1)+C(3,1),C(1,2)+C(2,2)+C(3,2)
99 END

RUN
 ?17,-6
 ?25,7
 ?20,-8

 17          -6
 25           7
 20          -8

COL.1 TOTAL  COL.2 TOTAL
 62          -7
```

Note that line 25 in Program 12.11 generates totals based on the subscripted variables of the matrix.

Inputting more than one matrix is illustrated in Program 12.12. The following data is used.

$$S = \begin{vmatrix} 78 & 30 \\ 25 & 62 \end{vmatrix} \qquad T = \begin{vmatrix} 17 \\ 21 \\ 9 \end{vmatrix} \qquad V = \begin{vmatrix} 2 & 6 & 9 \\ 7 & 8 & 1 \end{vmatrix}$$

Note that all of the data for each matrix can be inputted at one time, rather than line by line.

PROGRAM 12.12   MAT INPUT for Several Matrices

```
5 DIM S(2,2),T(3,1),V(2,3)
10 MAT INPUT S,T,V
15 MAT PRINT S;T;V;
20 PRINT "NORTHWEST VALUE IN EACH MATRIX";S(1,1);T(1,1);V(1,1)
25 PRINT "SOUTHEAST VALUE IN EACH MATRIX";S(2,2);T(3,1);V(2,3)
99 END


RUN
?78,30,25,62
?17,21,9
?2,6,9,7,8,1

78  30
25  62


17
21
9


2  6  9
7  8  1


NORTHWEST VALUE IN EACH MATRIX 78   17   2
SOUTHEAST VALUE IN EACH MATRIX 62   9   1
```

Lines 20 and 25 in Program 12.12 show how data items inputted into a matrix can be manipulated using subscripted variables.

MATRIX ADDITION, SUBTRACTION, AND MULTIPLICATION

In general all matrix operations have the form:

line # MAT name = operation

Only one operation is permitted in a statement. This means that no more than two matrices can be manipulated at any time in a statement.

Addition and Subtraction

Matrix addition and subtraction can be illustrated by the following statements using matrices A and B:

$$A = \begin{vmatrix} -2 & 3 \\ 7 & -6 \\ 9 & 1 \end{vmatrix} \quad \text{and} \quad B = \begin{vmatrix} 7 & 6 \\ 5 & -2 \\ 8 & 1 \end{vmatrix}$$

25 MAT C = A + B
35 MAT D = A − B

To perform these operations all the matrices must have the same dimensions. We see that both A and B are 3×2. Appropriate dimensioning must be supplied for the matrices to hold the results of the operations, namely, matrices C and D.

Program 12.13 shows the above matrices being added, then subtracted, and the resulting output. Note that line 5 contains dimensioning for matrices C and D.

**PROGRAM 12.13   Adding and Subtracting Matrices Using MAT
                  Operations**

```
 5 DIM A(3,2),B(3,2),C(3,2),D(3,2)
10 MAT READ A,B
15 DATA -2,3,7,-6,9,1,7,6,5,-2,8,1
20 MAT PRINT A;B;
22 PRINT "C=A+B"
25 MAT C=A+B
30 MAT PRINT C;
32 PRINT "D=A-B"
35 MAT D=A-B
40 MAT PRINT D;
99 END


RUN

-2   3
 7  -6
 9   1


 7   6
 5  -2
 8   1

C=A+B

 5   9
12  -8
17   2

D=A-B

-9  -3
 2  -4
 1   0
```

If more than two matrices are to be manipulated, an intermediate step such as line 25 in Program 12.14 is required. This program is adding together matrices X, Y, and Z, which have these values:

$$X = \begin{vmatrix} 2 & 7 \\ 1 & 9 \end{vmatrix} \qquad Y = \begin{vmatrix} 5 & -4 \\ 9 & 0 \end{vmatrix} \qquad Z = \begin{vmatrix} -2 & 8 \\ 7 & 2 \end{vmatrix}$$

First X and Y are added in line 25 to give matrix I. This result is then added to matrix Z in line 40 to produce matrix F, the final answer. Dimensioning for matrices I and F must be provided, as is shown in line 5.

PROGRAM 12.14   Adding Three Matrices

```
5 DIM X(2,2),Y(2,2),Z(2,2),I(2,2),F(2,2)
10 MAT READ X,Y,Z
15 MAT PRINT X;Y;Z;
20 REM LINE 25 INTERMEDIATE STEP
25 MAT I=X+Y
30 PRINT "INTERMEDIATE MATRIX I"
35 MAT PRINT I;
40 MAT F=Z+I
45 PRINT "FINAL RESULT: X+Y+Z"
50 MAT PRINT F;
60 DATA 2,7,1,9,5,-4,9,0,-2,8,7,2
99 END

RUN

 2   7
 1   9



 5  -4
 9   0



-2   8
 7   2


INTERMEDIATE MATRIX I

 7   3
10   9


FINAL RESULT: X+Y+Z

 5  11
17  11
```

Program 12.15 illustrates the use of MAT statements and nested FOR/NEXT loops. It generates the desired results for Case 12.1. Figure 12.1 represents the flowchart for Program 12.15.

CASE 12.1 The ABC Company has profit data for the last 2 years, month by month, for its four sales regions. This data is shown below. It is desired to aggregate (add together) the yearly data into one table. Also 2 year regional sales totals are wanted.

ABC Company: Profits by Region
Year 1 and 2—Jan. to Dec.
(All figures in 000 dollars)

Region	J	F	M	A	M	J	J	A	S	O	N	D
Year 1												
1	7	5	5	8	7	5	6	7	7	6	5	6
2	6	5	7	8	6	5	5	7	6	5	6	4
3	5	8	5	7	7	6	5	6	5	6	7	8
4	9	7	8	6	6	7	8	9	8	7	6	7
Year 2												
1	4	6	5	4	5	6	7	8	8	8	7	6
2	5	6	8	7	8	6	6	7	8	7	5	6
3	6	8	6	8	8	7	6	5	6	8	7	9
4	9	8	8	7	8	9	6	9	9	8	7	10

PROGRAM 12.15   Case 12.1, ABC Company Profits—MAT Statements and Nested FOR/NEXT Loops

```
 5 DIM Y1(4,12),Y2(4,12),A(4,12)
10 MAT READ Y1,Y2
15 MAT A=Y1+Y2
20 PRINT "ABC COMPANY-PROFITS BY REGIONS,FOR TWO YEARS"
30 PRINT
40 PRINT "REG J    F    M    A    M    J    J    A    S    O    N    D    TOT"
50 FOR I = 1 TO 4
60 LET T(I)=0
65 PRINT "";I;
70 FOR J = 1 TO 12
80 PRINT A(I,J);
85 LET T(I) = T(I) + A(I,J)
90 NEXT J
95 PRINT T(I)
100 NEXT I
150 DATA 7,5,5,8,7,5,6,7,7,6,5,6,6,5,7,8,6,5,5,7,6,5,6,4
155 DATA 5,8,5,7,7,6,5,6,5,6,7,8,9,7,8,6,6,7,8,9,8,7,6,7
160 DATA 4,6,5,4,5,6,7,8,8,8,7,6,5,6,8,7,8,6,6,7,8,7,5,6
165 DATA 6,8,6,8,8,7,6,5,6,8,7,9,9,8,8,7,8,9,6,9,9,8,7,10
199 END
```

```
RUN
ABC COMPANY-PROFITS BY REGIONS,FOR TWO YEARS

REG J    F    M    A    M    J    J    A    S    O    N    D    TOT
 1   11   11   10   12   12   11   13   15   15   14   12   12   148
 2   11   11   15   15   14   11   11   14   14   12   11   10   149
 3   11   16   11   15   15   13   11   11   11   14   14   17   159
 4   18   15   16   13   14   16   14   18   17   15   13   17   186
```

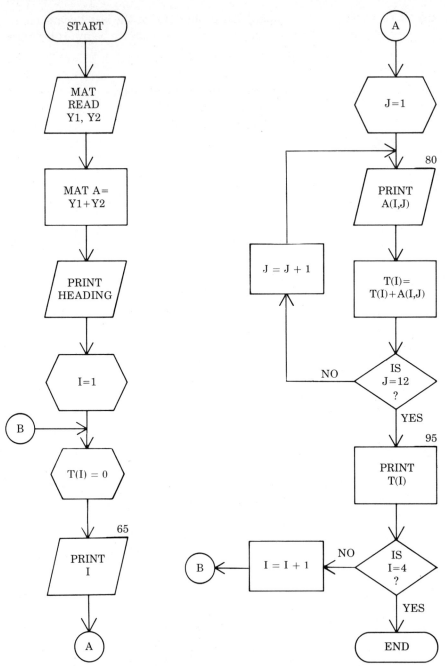

**FIGURE 12.1   Flowchart for Program 12.15, Case 12.1, ABC
Company Profits**

Multiplication

To multiply one matrix by another, the number of columns of the first matrix must be equal to the number of rows in the second matrix. The size of the resulting matrix is a matrix having the number of rows of the first matrix, and the number of columns of the second matrix. In general, if we multiply two matrices, $A \times B$, to get C, we then have

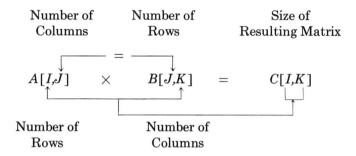

What follows are several examples of matrix multiplication using the following data:

$$A = |3\ 2\ 4| \qquad \text{a } 1 \times 3 \text{ list or row vector}$$

$$B = \begin{vmatrix} 5 \\ 4 \\ 3 \end{vmatrix} \qquad \text{a } 3 \times 1 \text{ list or column vector}$$

$$C = \begin{vmatrix} 2 & 5 & 1 \\ 1 & 8 & 2 \\ 7 & 3 & 5 \end{vmatrix} \qquad \text{a } 3 \times 3 \text{ table or matrix}$$

$$D = \begin{vmatrix} 2 & 4 & 3 \\ 5 & 4 & 1 \end{vmatrix} \qquad \text{a } 2 \times 3 \text{ table or matrix}$$

Example 1

Matrix A times matrix B (a 1×3 times a 3×1 results in a 1×1). The computation goes like this:

$$|3\ 2\ 4| \begin{vmatrix} 5 \\ 4 \\ 3 \end{vmatrix} = (3 \times 5) + (2 \times 4) + (4 \times 3) = |35|$$

In Program 12.16 this computation is done by line 20.

PROGRAM 12.16   Multiplying Matrices: A 1 × 3 Times a 3 × 1 Gives a 1 × 1

```
5 DIM A(1,3),B(3,1),X(1,1)
10 MAT READ A,B
15 MAT PRINT A;B;
20 MAT X=A*B
25 MAT PRINT X
50 DATA 3,2,4,5,4,3
99 END


RUN

 3   2   4



 5
 4
 3


35
```

Example 2

Matrix B times matrix A (a 3×1 times a 1×3 results in a 3×3). The computation goes like this:

$$\begin{vmatrix} 5 \\ 4 \\ 3 \end{vmatrix} |3\ 2\ 4| = \begin{vmatrix} (5 \times 3) & (5 \times 2) & (5 \times 4) \\ (4 \times 3) & (4 \times 2) & (4 \times 4) \\ (3 \times 3) & (3 \times 2) & (3 \times 4) \end{vmatrix} = \begin{vmatrix} 15 & 10 & 20 \\ 12 & 8 & 16 \\ 9 & 6 & 12 \end{vmatrix}$$

This computation is carried out by line 20 in Program 12.17.

PROGRAM 12.17   Multiplying Matrices: A 3 × 1 Times a 1 × 3 Gives a 3 × 3

```
5 DIM A(1,3),B(3,1),X(3,3)
10 MAT READ A,B
15 MAT PRINT B;A;
20 MAT X=B*A
25 MAT PRINT X
50 DATA 3,2,4,5,4,3
99 END


RUN

 5
 4
 3


 3   2   4


15          10          20
12          8           16
9           6           12
```

Example 3

Matrix A times matrix C (a 1×3 times a 3×3 results in a 1×3). Line 20 in Program 12.18 does the computation of $A \times C$:

$$|3\ 2\ 4| \begin{vmatrix} 2 & 5 & 1 \\ 1 & 8 & 2 \\ 7 & 3 & 5 \end{vmatrix} = \left| \begin{pmatrix} (3 \times 2) \\ +(2 \times 1) \\ +(4 \times 7) \end{pmatrix} \begin{pmatrix} (3 \times 5) \\ +(2 \times 8) \\ +(4 \times 3) \end{pmatrix} \begin{pmatrix} (3 \times 1) \\ +(2 \times 4) \\ +(4 \times 5) \end{pmatrix} \right| = |36\ 43\ 27|$$

PROGRAM 12.18 Multiplying Matrices: A 1 × 3 Times a 3 × 3 Gives a 1 × 3

```
 5 DIM A(1,3),C(3,3),X(1,3)
10 MAT READ A,C
15 MAT PRINT A;C;
20 MAT X=A*C
25 MAT PRINT X;
50 DATA 3,2,4,2,5,1,1,8,2,7,3,5
99 END


RUN

   3   2   4


   2   5   1
   1   8   2
   7   3   5


  36  43  27
```

Example 4

Matrix B times matrix C (a 3×3 times a 3×1 results in a 3×1). In Program 12.19 line 20 computes $C \times B$:

$$\begin{vmatrix} 2 & 5 & 1 \\ 1 & 8 & 2 \\ 7 & 3 & 5 \end{vmatrix} \begin{vmatrix} 5 \\ 4 \\ 3 \end{vmatrix} = \left| \begin{pmatrix} (2 \times 5) \\ +(5 \times 4) \\ +(1 \times 3) \end{pmatrix} \begin{pmatrix} (1 \times 5) \\ +(8 \times 4) \\ +(2 \times 3) \end{pmatrix} \begin{pmatrix} (7 \times 5) \\ +(3 \times 4) \\ +(5 \times 3) \end{pmatrix} \right| = \begin{vmatrix} 33 \\ 43 \\ 62 \end{vmatrix}$$

PROGRAM 12.19 Multiplying Matrices: A 3 × 3 Times a 3 × 1 Gives a 3 × 1

```
 5 DIM A(1,3),B(3,1),X(3,3)
10 MAT READ A,B
15 MAT PRINT B;A;
20 MAT X=B*A
25 MAT PRINT X
50 DATA 3,2,4,5,4,3
99 END
```

PROGRAM 12.19 continued

```
RUN

2   5   1
1   8   2
7   3   5



5
4
3



33
43
62
```

Example 5

Matrix D times matrix C (a 2×3 times a 3×3 results in a 2×3). Line 20 in Program 12.20 does the multiplication of $D \times C$:

$$\begin{vmatrix} 2 & 4 & 3 \\ 5 & 4 & 1 \end{vmatrix}\begin{vmatrix} 2 & 5 & 1 \\ 1 & 8 & 2 \\ 7 & 3 & 5 \end{vmatrix} = \begin{vmatrix} \begin{pmatrix} (2 \times 2) \\ +(4 \times 1) \\ +(3 \times 7) \end{pmatrix} & \begin{pmatrix} (2 \times 5) \\ +(4 \times 8) \\ +(3 \times 3) \end{pmatrix} & \begin{pmatrix} (2 \times 1) \\ +(4 \times 2) \\ +(3 \times 5) \end{pmatrix} \\ \begin{pmatrix} (5 \times 2) \\ +(4 \times 1) \\ +(1 \times 7) \end{pmatrix} & \begin{pmatrix} (5 \times 5) \\ +(4 \times 8) \\ +(1 \times 3) \end{pmatrix} & \begin{pmatrix} (5 \times 1) \\ +(4 \times 2) \\ +(1 \times 5) \end{pmatrix} \end{vmatrix} = \begin{vmatrix} 29 & 51 & 25 \\ 21 & 60 & 18 \end{vmatrix}$$

PROGRAM 12.20 Multiplying Matrices: A 2 × 3 Times a 3 × 3 Gives a 2 × 3

```
5 DIM D(2,3),C(3,3),X(2,3)
10 MAT READ D,C
15 MAT PRINT D;C;
20 MAT X=D*C
25 MAT PRINT X;
50 DATA 2,4,3,5,4,1,2,5,1,1,8,2,7,3,5
99 END


RUN

2   4   3
5   4   1


2   5   1
1   8   2
7   3   5


29   51   25
21   60   18
```

Several cases that follow illustrate the application of matrix multiplication.

CASE 12.2 The inventory of the Town Car Dealership consists of four models of a small car. Below are the quantities of each model in stock and the cost per car. It is desired to obtain the total dollar value for this inventory.

Car Model	1	2	3	4
Quantity	12	9	8	15
Cost	3150	3400	4100	3800

This case can be completed by letting the cost per model be a row vector, C, of size 1×4; and the quantity of each model a column vector, Q, of size 4×1. Line 35 in Program 12.21 obtains the total dollar value of the inventory by multiplying the cost vector C times the quantity vector Q. A 1×4 times a 4×1 produces a 1×1:

$$|3150 \ 3400 \ 4100 \ 3800| \begin{vmatrix} 12 \\ 9 \\ 8 \\ 15 \end{vmatrix} = |158200|$$

PROGRAM 12.21 Case 12.2, Inventory Valuation Using Matrix Multiplication

```
5 DIM C(1,4),Q(4,1),V(1,1)
10 MAT READ C,Q
12 PRINT " ","CAR MODEL"
14 PRINT " 1"," 2"," 3"," 4"
15 PRINT
16 PRINT " ","QUANTITY"
20 MAT PRINT C
22 PRINT " ","COST"
25 PRINT Q(1,1),Q(2,1),Q(3,1),Q(4,1)
26 PRINT
30 MAT V=C*Q
35 PRINT "TOTAL $ VALUE OF INVTY",
40 MAT PRINT V
50 DATA 12,9,8,15,3150,3400,4100,3800
99 END
```

```
RUN
               CAR MODEL
   1            2             3            4

               QUANTITY

  12            9             8            15

               COST
  3150          3400          4100         3800

TOTAL $ VALUE OF INVTY
 158200
```

CASE 12.3 Many investors in stocks evaluate their stocks from the price paid when purchased to the present date. Below is a stock portfolio with purchase price for each stock, present market price, and the number of shares of each stock. It is desired to see how the total value of the portfolio has changed over time.

Stock	No. Shares	Purchase Price	Present Price
ABC Co.	4800	$39\frac{1}{2}$	$37\frac{1}{2}$
AXZ	3800	$15\frac{7}{8}$	$14\frac{5}{8}$
BCE	1500	$10\frac{3}{8}$	$11\frac{1}{4}$
DITO	500	$4\frac{3}{4}$	$4\frac{3}{4}$
KLB	4300	$6\frac{1}{2}$	$7\frac{1}{8}$
LEZY	6700	$19\frac{7}{8}$	$23\frac{1}{2}$
TECH	1600	$1\frac{1}{2}$	$1\frac{3}{4}$
LOD	2300	$5\frac{1}{8}$	$6\frac{1}{8}$
DZ	900	$20\frac{1}{2}$	$23\frac{7}{8}$
FTC	1900	4	6

Case 12.3 can be completed if the number of shares is treated as a 1×10 matrix, N, and the price information a 10×2 matrix, P. By multiplying matrix N times matrix P, as shown in line 20 of Program 12.22, a 1×2 is obtained. This matrix is the result desired.

PROGRAM 12.22   Case 12.3, Portfolio Valuation Using Matrix Multiplication

```
5 DIM N(1,10),P(10,2),V(1,2)
10 MAT READ N,P
20 MAT V=N*P
30 PRINT "          PORTFOLIO VALUATION"
40 PRINT "PURCHASE VALUE","PRESENT VALUE","GAIN OR LOSS"
50 PRINT V(1,1),V(1,2),V(1,2)-V(1,1)
55 DATA 4800,3800,1500,500,4300,6700,1600,2300,900,1900
60 DATA 39.5,37.5,15.375,14.625,10.375,11.25,4.75,4.75,6.5,7.125
65 DATA 19.875,23.5,1.5,1.75,5.125,6.125,20.5,23.875,4,6
99 END
```

```
RUN
          PORTFOLIO VALUATION
PURCHASE VALUE PRESENT VALUE  GAIN OR LOSS
   469213.        492633.        23475
```

Note in line 50 how the results are printed out using subscripted variables, rather than a MAT PRINT statement.

CASE 12.4 The Apex Company manufactures four products. Below is their production cost budget. They want to determine the total costs for each product, as well as the total cost of direct materials, direct labor, and factory overhead.

Apex Company
Production Cost Budget
Current Year

Product	Direct Materials	Direct Labor	Factory Overhead
1	$260,000	$520,000	$400,000
2	292,000	438,000	325,000
3	200,000	400,000	350,000
4	300,000	630,000	385,000

Case 12.4 requires row totals and column totals for the production cost data given. If this data is treated as a matrix C, size 4×3, it is possible to obtain row and column totals by multiplying matrix C by two other matrices. A 1×4 matrix of ones times matrix C gives a 1×3 matrix that represents the column totals. Line 20 in Program 12.23 shows this multiplication as MAT H = K * C. Matrix K is a 1×4 containing ones. The multiplication looks like this:

$$K(1 \times 4) \qquad\qquad C(4 \times 3)$$

$$|1\ 1\ 1\ 1| \times \begin{vmatrix} 260000 & 520000 & 400000 \\ \cdots & \cdots & \cdots \\ \cdots & \cdots & \cdots \\ \cdots & \cdots & \cdots \end{vmatrix}$$

and results in $H(1 \times 3)|\cdots\ \cdots\ \cdots|$ column totals.

If matrix C is multiplied by a 3×1 matrix of ones (line 30), the result is a 4×1 matrix that represents the row totals. The multiplication looks like this:

$$C(4 \times 3) \qquad R(3 \times 1)\quad V(4 \times 1)$$

$$\begin{vmatrix} 260000 & 520000 & 400000 \\ \cdots & \cdots & \cdots \\ \cdots & \cdots & \cdots \\ \cdots & \cdots & \cdots \end{vmatrix} \times \begin{vmatrix} 1 \\ 1 \\ 1 \end{vmatrix} = \begin{vmatrix} \cdots \\ \cdots \\ \cdots \\ \cdots \end{vmatrix} \text{row totals}$$

The result is matrix V, a 4×1.

Note in the program that a nested FOR/NEXT loop (lines 40–90) is used to generate the original data and row totals. To generate the column totals, line 100 is used.

PROGRAM 12.23   Case 12.4, Production Cost Budget Using Matrix Multiplication and Nested FOR/NEXT Loops

```
5 DIM C(4,3),K(1,4),R(3,1),H(1,3),V(4,1)
10 MAT READ C,K,R
20 MAT H=K*C
30 MAT V=C*R
32 PRINT "       APEX CO.       "
34 PRINT "   PRODUCTION COST BUDGET"
36 PRINT "     CURRENT YEAR"
38 PRINT "PRODUCT","DIR MAT","DIR LABOR","FAC OH", "TOTAL"
40 FOR I = 1 TO 4
45 PRINT I,
50 FOR J = 1 TO 3
60 PRINT "$"C(I,J),
70 NEXT J
80 PRINT "$"V(I,1)
90 NEXT I
92 FOR U=1 TO 70
95 PRINT "-";
96 NEXT U
97 PRINT
100 PRINT "TOTALS",H(1,1),H(1,2),H(1,3)
140 DATA 260000,520000,400000,292000,438000,325000
145 DATA 200000,400000,350000,300000,630000,385000
150 DATA 1,1,1,1,1,1,1
199 END
```

```
RUN
     APEX CO.
   PRODUCTION COST BUDGET
     CURRENT YEAR
PRODUCT        DIR MAT         DIR LABOR       FAC OH          TOTAL
  1            $ 260000        $ 520000        $ 400000        $ 1.18E 6
  2            $ 292000        $ 438000        $ 325000        $ 1.055E 6
  3            $ 200000        $ 400000        $ 350000        $ 950000
  4            $ 300000        $ 630000        $ 385000        $ 1.315E 6
-----------------------------------------------------------------------
TOTALS         1.052E 6        1.988E 6        1.46E 6
```

OTHER MATRIX OPERATIONS

Several additional matrix operations are illustrated in this section. If a more detailed explanation is required for any of the illustrations or operations shown, you should refer to an introductory text that covers matrices.*

Multiplication by a Constant

Given a matrix A, to multiply every value in it by a constant K, we can use the following statement:

$$20 \text{ MAT } C = (K) * A$$

---

*See, for example, R. L. Childress, *Sets, Matrices, and Linear Programming* (Englewood Cliffs, N.J.: Prentice-Hall, 1974) or L. L. Schkade, *Vectors and Matrices* (Columbus, Ohio: Charles E. Merrill, 1967).

Suppose A is a 3×2 matrix:
$$\begin{vmatrix} 180 & 210 \\ 105 & 179 \\ 220 & 260 \end{vmatrix}$$

and K is equal to .80. Program 12.24 shows both program and output for a constant times a matrix.

PROGRAM 12.24 Multiplication of a Constant Times a Matrix

```
 5 DIM A(3,2),C(3,2)
1Ø MAT READ A
15 MAT PRINT A;
2Ø MAT C=(.8Ø)*A
25 PRINT ".8Ø TIMES MAT A"
3Ø MAT PRINT C;
4Ø DATA 18Ø,21Ø,1Ø5,179,22Ø,26Ø
99 END


RUN

 18 Ø   21Ø
 1Ø5   179
 22Ø   26Ø


 .8Ø TIMES MAT A

 144   168
 84   143.2
 176   2Ø8
```

Creating an Identity Matrix

An identity matrix has principal diagonal elements equal to one and all off-diagonal elements equal to zero. Such a matrix can be produced using a statement like this:

$$20 \, \text{MAT} \, D = \text{IDN}$$

Line 20 in Program 12.25 results in a 4×4 identity matrix (D).

PROGRAM 12.25 Identity Matrix

```
1Ø DIM D(4,4)
2Ø MAT D=IDN
3Ø PRINT "A 4 BY 4 IDENTITY MATRIX"
4Ø MAT PRINT D
99 END


RUN
A 4 BY 4 IDENTITY MATRIX

 1              Ø              Ø              Ø
 Ø              1              Ø              Ø
 Ø              Ø              1              Ø
 Ø              Ø              Ø              1
```

Transposing a Matrix

To interchange the rows and columns of a matrix use the following type of statement:

$$25 \text{ MAT E} = \text{TRN(P)}$$

If P is a 2 by 4,

$$\begin{vmatrix} 12 & 10 & -11 & 13 \\ 16 & 14 & 12 & -4 \end{vmatrix}$$

its transpose would be a 4×2. Program 12.26 illustrates such a transposition of P into E. Note that dimensioning must be provided for matrix E.

PROGRAM 12.26   Transpose of a Matrix

```
10 DIM P(2,4),E(4,2)
15 MAT READ P
18 PRINT "ORIGINAL MATRIX P, 2 BY 4"
20 MAT PRINT P;
25 MAT E=TRN(P)
30 PRINT "TRANSPOSE OF P, E IS A 4 BY 2"
35 MAT PRINT E;
50 DATA 12,10,-11,13,16,14,12,-4
99 END


RUN
ORIGINAL MATRIX P, 2 BY 4

 12  10 -11  13
 16  14  12 -4


TRANSPOSE OF P, E IS A 4 BY 2

 12  16
 10  14
-11  12
 13 -4
```

Inverse of a Matrix

An inverse of a matrix is analogous to obtaining the reciprocal of a quantity. To solve matrix problems that involve division it is necessary to find the inverse of at least one of the matrices in the problem. This is particularly true when solving sets of simultaneous linear equations by matrices (see exercise 12.20).

When it is necessary to use an inverted matrix, such a matrix can be developed using the following type of statement:

$$20 \text{ MAT F} = \text{INV(L)}$$

Assume L is a 2×2 matrix with values as follows:

$$\begin{vmatrix} 7 & 3 \\ 2 & 1 \end{vmatrix}$$

In Program 12.27 the inverse is obtained. The inverse matrix (F) must be dimensioned as shown in line 5.

PROGRAM 12.27 Inverse of a Matrix

```
5 DIM L(2,2),F(2,2)
10 MAT READ L
15 PRINT "ORIGINAL MATRIX L"
18 MAT PRINT L;
20 MAT F=INV(L)
25 PRINT "INVERSE OF L IS MATRIX F"
30 MAT PRINT F;
50 DATA 7,3,2,1
99 END


RUN
ORIGINAL MATRIX L

 7   3
 2   1


INVERSE OF L IS MATRIX F

  1.  -3.
 -2.   7.
```

Matrices of Zeros or Ones

To set every element of a matrix A to zero a statement such as this one can be used:

$$15 \text{ MAT } A = \text{ZER}$$

Matrix A will be set to zeros. To obtain a matrix B with every element a one, the following statement can be used:

$$25 \text{ MAT } B = \text{CON}$$

Matrix B will contain ones. Program 12.28 shows the result of a program creating a matrix of zeros and a matrix of ones.

PROGRAM 12.28   Matrices of Zeros or Ones

```
5 DIM A(5,8),B(7,7)
15 MAT A=ZER
25 MAT B=CON
30 MAT PRINT A;B;
99 END
```

```
RUN

0   0   0   0   0   0   0   0
0   0   0   0   0   0   0   0
0   0   0   0   0   0   0   0
0   0   0   0   0   0   0   0
0   0   0   0   0   0   0   0


1   1   1   1   1   1   1
1   1   1   1   1   1   1
1   1   1   1   1   1   1
1   1   1   1   1   1   1
1   1   1   1   1   1   1
1   1   1   1   1   1   1
1   1   1   1   1   1   1
```

SUMMARY

Large arrays of data can be easily handled with matrix operations. In this chapter reading and printing of matrices have been illustrated. In addition it has been shown how matrices can be added, subtracted, and multiplied.

Since a matrix is a table whose elements are referred to by means of subscripted variables, dimensioning is required.

A matrix can also be inputted. Other matrix operations that can be carried out are multiplication by a constant; creating an identity matrix; transposing a matrix; finding the inverse of a matrix; and creating a matrix of zeros or of ones.

EXERCISES

12.1   Treat the following data first as (a) a one-dimensional list of 20 items; then as (b) a 5 × 4 table:

1, 4, 5, 6, 7, 4, 1, 7, 9, 10, 6, 0, 8, 1, 7, 0, 4, 6, 8, 1

   a. Write a program that reads in the list as a matrix L.
   b. Write a program that reads in the table as a matrix T.

12.2   A 15 × 10 table is to be read in with the program below. The program is not complete. Why not? (The data lines are not shown, but can be assumed correct.)

    125 MAT READ M
    200 DATA . . . .
    299 END

12.3   A 12 × 30 table is to be read in with the program below. The program is not correct. Why not? (The data lines are not shown, but are correct.)

    10 DIM (30, 12)
    20 MAT READ A (50, 60)
    50 DATA . . . . .
    99

12.4   Write a program that reads in and prints out all of the following matrices:

$$\begin{vmatrix} 68 & 73 & 41 & 12 & 18 & 21 \\ 32 & 47 & 16 & -7 & 12 & 20 \\ 38 & 61 & 62 & 21 & 14 & -9 \end{vmatrix}, \begin{vmatrix} 2 & 7 \\ 3 & 9 \\ 6 & 11 \\ 12 & 8 \\ 14 & 7 \end{vmatrix}, \begin{vmatrix} 1.1 & .6 & .8 & .9 \end{vmatrix}$$

12.5   Write the program for the matrices in exercise 12.4 so that the output is "packed."

12.6   Treat the following table as a matrix when it is read in:

Student	Quiz Grades 1	2	3
1	9	8	9
2	7	9	8
3	6	7	8
4	7	7	8
5.	7	6	9
6	9	7	9
7	8	6	8
8	7	5	6
9	5	8	9
10	6	7	7
11	8	6	6

Write a single program that
a. Prints out the grades for each student with the student number showing in the output.

b. Prints out the grades for students 1–5.

c. Prints out for students 5–10, quiz grades 2 and 3.

d. Prints out for students 9, 10, 11, grades 1 and 3.

12.7 Compute gross pay for each worker in the table below:

Worker	Hours Worked	Rate Per Hour
1	32	$4.25
2	37	3.80
3	40	4.15
4	36	4.20
5	35	4.00
6	37½	3.75

The data should be treated as a matrix with each line an input.

12.8 At the beginning of the week the inventory in stock was as follows:

Item	Beginning Inventory (no. of units)	Units Sold During the Week
1	250	40
2	700	75
3	350	210
4	820	600
5	400	130
6	300	65
7	560	280

Determine what the ending inventory for each item is by treating beginning inventory and units sold as separate matrices. Your results should also be a matrix.

12.9 Below are the number of units shipped each week for each product the XYZ Company manufactures:

	Units Shipped — Product — (000)					
Week	M	N	O	P	Q	R
1	20	17	25	31	30	29
2	22	18	20	28	30	30
3	19	19	26	27	31	31
4	21	20	21	32	31	32

Treat each week as a separate matrix. Write a single program that generates the *total* number of units shipped for each product for (a) weeks 1 and 2, and (b) all 4 weeks.

12.10 Using the weekly data in exercise 12.9, compute the remaining inventory of units for the XYZ Company at the end of each week if the initial starting inventory for week 1 is:

Inventory on Hand — Product — (000)

M	N	O	P	Q	R
140	210	160	150	195	230

Assume no production has occurred during this 4 weeks.

12.11 Below are the number of units sold for the 10 leading foreign car imports in June of 1974 and 1975. Write a program that gives the total sales for all car types in June 1975 and June 1974. Treat the data as a matrix. Output all the data using the numbers 1 to 10 in place of the car names.

Import Sales Leaders

Car	June 1975	June 1974
Toyota	28,435	19,549
Datsun	23,867	13,656
Volkswagen	23,268	23,806
Honda	10,061	2,938
Fiat	9,466	7,182
Mazda	9,323	4,999
Colt	5,939	3,300
Volvo	5,629	4,232
Audi	4,789	3,980
Subaru	4,344	1,631

Source: *Automotive News.*

12.12 Use the sales data in exercise 12.11 and have your program generate total sales for each time period as well as the increase in sales between June 1974 and June 1975. A total for this difference should also be derived. Output all the data using the numbers 1 to 10 in place of the car names.

12.13 Perform the following matrix multiplications in a single program: A times B, B times A.

$$A = \begin{vmatrix} 4 & 6 & 3 & -1 \\ 0 & 1 & -2 & 1 \end{vmatrix}, \qquad B = \begin{vmatrix} 1 & 2 \\ -1 & 3 \\ 4 & -2 \\ 2 & 1 \end{vmatrix}$$

12.14 Perform the following matrix multiplications in a single program: C times D, D times C.

$$C = \begin{vmatrix} \tfrac{1}{4} \\ \tfrac{1}{2} \\ -\tfrac{1}{2} \\ \tfrac{3}{8} \end{vmatrix}, \qquad D = |16 \ 24 \ 20 \ 36|$$

12.15 Your stock portfolio contains seven stocks in the following amounts:

Stock	1	2	3	4	5	6	7
No. of Shares	110	200	100	150	200	250	100

Below are the prices for these stocks for three time periods:

		Price	
Stock	Jan. 2	May 1	July 25
1	3	$6\tfrac{1}{4}$	$6\tfrac{3}{8}$
2	$6\tfrac{7}{8}$	$13\tfrac{1}{4}$	17
3	$10\tfrac{7}{8}$	$16\tfrac{3}{4}$	$19\tfrac{1}{2}$
4	$2\tfrac{1}{2}$	$5\tfrac{7}{8}$	$7\tfrac{3}{8}$
5	$3\tfrac{3}{4}$	$8\tfrac{1}{4}$	$9\tfrac{1}{8}$
6	2	$4\tfrac{1}{8}$	$6\tfrac{3}{8}$
7	6	$10\tfrac{3}{4}$	12

Write a program using matrix operations to find the market value of the stock portfolio for each of the three dates.

12.16 The American Missile Corporation manufactures four antiaircraft missiles. Each missile contains a different number of components. These are as follows:

	No. of Components per Missile Type			
Component Type	1	2	3	4
X3	20	15	26	19
X4	7	8	11	10
X5	6	7	7	9

A new contract has been received to produce the following quantities of each missile:

Missile	Amount to Produce
1	1000
2	750
3	800
4	2000

Using matrix procedures, write a program that will generate how much of each type of component will be needed to complete the order.

12.17 Using matrix operations, write a program that will obtain row and column totals for the data below.

Sales by Quarters (Million Dollars)

Division	1st	2d	3d	4th
1	2.7	2.6	2.8	2.7
2	1.7	1.5	1.9	2.0
3	4.8	4.9	5.1	5.2
4	1.0	1.1	1.0	.9
5	8.6	8.6	8.7	8.8
6	5.2	5.4	5.6	5.8

12.18 Assume that a 5 percent increase in the sales shown in exercise 12.17 is required next year by each division. Write a program that generates estimated quarterly sales; i.e., this year's sales increased by 5 percent. Use matrix operations. (*Hint:* This is multiplication by a constant.)

12.19 Below are the production cost elements of the Ajax Company, and the quantity of each product to be produced.

Per Unit Costs

Cost Elements	Product 1 (200,000)	Product 2 (140,000)
Direct Materials	$2.00	$4.00
Direct Labor	4.00	6.00
Factory Overhead	3.00	4.50

Write a program that uses both matrix operations and FOR/NEXT loops to output:

a. A table with the three cost elements for each product based on the production figures given
b. Total costs for direct materials, direct labor, and factory overhead based on the production figures given
c. Total costs to produce 200,000 units of product 1, and 140,000 units of product 2
d. Total cost for *all* units of products 1 and 2 produced.

12.20 Matrix operations can be used to solve for variables in systems of linear equations.
Suppose we have the two equations

$$3x_1 + 2x_2 = 14 \quad \text{and} \quad 6x_1 - 2x_2 = 4$$

where x_1 and x_2 are unknowns. In matrix notation the solution for this type of system of equation is

$$X = A^{-1}B$$

where X is a matrix of solution values, A^{-1} is the inverse matrix of the matrix of coefficients of the variables in the equation, and B is a matrix of the values to the right of the equals.

Then for the equations above,

$$\begin{vmatrix} x_1 \\ x_2 \end{vmatrix} = \begin{vmatrix} \text{inverse matrix} \\ \text{of coefficients} \end{vmatrix} \times \begin{vmatrix} 14 \\ 4 \end{vmatrix}$$

where the inverse has not yet been obtained. The matrix of coefficients looks like this:

$$\begin{vmatrix} 3 & 2 \\ 6 & -2 \end{vmatrix}$$

Using matrix operations, write a program that solves for x_1 and x_2.

13

Data Files

Up to this point we have seen that each program has had its own set of data and data lines as an integral part of the program.

In this chapter we will see how it is possible to place data into a separate and distinct storage entity called a *data file*. Such files are typical of information systems where data is stored and retrieved as the situation requires. Once we have data in a file, any of numerous programs can then use it as though it were part of the program.*

CREATING A FILE

To create a data file the first step is to give it a name. A file name can be up to six characters in length starting with one of the alphabetic characters *A* to *Z*. Since a file being set up for the first time is like a new program, on the RAPIDATA System the creator of the file has to type in the command NEW, followed by the desired file name. The general form is:

NEW:file name

---

*The file instructions in this chapter are those of the RAPIDATA System. Refer to your system manual on this topic for exact specifications of statements to be used. It is also suggested that for a better understanding of files students refer to any one of a number of data-processing books that cover this topic. For example, J. G. Burch and F. R. Strater, Chapter 8, *Information Systems: Theory and Practice* (Santa Barbara, Calif.: Hamilton Publishing Co., 1974) or C. Mader and R. Hagin, Chapter 8, *Information Systems: Technology, Economics, Applications* (Chicago: Science Research Associates, 1974).

Specific examples are:

NEW:FILEA
NEW:XYZCO
NEW:YR1976
NEW:WAGES

After the naming of the file, the actual file creation is done. The structure of one line of a file is a line number, followed by a blank space, and then the data. Data may be either string or numeric. In general, a file line format looks like this:

line # (data list)

Specifically, a file may look like this:

NEW:GRADES
15 JACK, 80, 95, 76
20 BILL, 75, 70, 68
30 SALLY, 95, 75, 80
35 JOAN, 100, 80, 75

or like this:

NEW:PARTS
2 28, X1234
4 17, LM31K
6 101, BC7D
8 81, JA475

Notice that nowhere is the word DATA indicated. Since it is understood that a file will contain data, it is not necessary to type DATA on each line of a file. It is also important to remember to leave a blank between the line number and the data list. Otherwise the line number and the first item in the data list may be taken (incorrectly) as the line number. Observe the file named PARTS to see what would result in terms of line numbering if blanks were missing after any of the line numbers 2, 4, 6, 8.

The last step in the creation of a file is the "saving" aspect. After a file has been named and entered, the system command SAV (for save) must be typed.* This command ensures that the file is available for future use or for access by other programs.

---

*The system commands SAV and NEW, used to save and name files, are also used to save and name programs. (See Appendix B.)

If we have sales information for 5 years, as shown below, we could create a file to save such information.

XYZ Co. – Sales Data

Year	Millions of Dollars
1970	10.3
1971	11.4
1972	12.6
1973	13.7
1974	12.8

Figure 13.1 shows how the file SALESF is created and saved with the above sales data in it.

```
NEW:SALESF

10  1970,10.3
20  1971,11.4
30  1972,12.6
40  1973,13.7
50  1974,12.8

SAV
```

FIGURE 13.1   Creating a Data File

FILE READING

To make use of, or gain access to, a data file requires the appropriate BASIC statement in a program. The general format of the statement to read data from a file is:

line # INPUT:file name:data list

Typical file reading statements could be,

40 INPUT: GRADES: N$, G1, G2, G3

or

50 INPUT: PARTS: Q, P

which could be used in programs to deal with the files GRADES and PARTS that were shown earlier.

Program 13.1, named OTPTSF, reads and then prints out the entire contents of the previously created file, SALESF (Figure 13.1).

PROGRAM 13.1   Reading the Contents of a Data File

```
15 PRINT "YEAR","SALES(MILL.$)"
20 INPUT:SALESF:Y,S
25 PRINT Y,S
30 GO TO 20
99 END


RUN
YEAR           SALES(MILL.$)
 1970            10.3
 1971            11.4
 1972            12.6
 1973            13.7
 1974            12.8

FILE OUT OF DATA-- LN #  20
```

In the program (line 20) the data list variables *Y* and *S* correspond to the type of data in the file SALES, that is, numerical data for both year and sales. Note that line 25 (PRINT Y,S) is merely the way the programmer wants to have *Y* and *S* outputted. If only the sales data were desired as output, this could have been obtained by 25 PRINT S. Also note that without line 30 (GO TO 20), only the first line of the data file SALESF would be outputted. This is because of the sequential nature of the file process being used. The contents of the file are read from the first line, line by line, until out of data.

When working with files it is possible to have a program read from several files. All that is required is additional file INPUT statements in the program. This reading from several files is illustrated in Case 13.1.

CASE 13.1   The XYZ Company has sales data for the years 1970–74 in a file named SALESF (see earlier discussion). Below are the total sales for the industry group that the XYZ Company is a member of. This data is found in a file named INDSF. It is desired to obtain a report that shows XYZ Company sales as a percent of industry sales for the years 1970–74.

Industry Sales Data

Year	Millions of Dollars
1970	150.6
1971	175.2
1972	203.0
1973	230.8
1974	254.5

**PROGRAM 13.2   Case 13.1, XYZ Company, Reading Several Data
                Files in One Program**

```
25 PRINT "YEAR","XYZ CO.","INDUSTRY","% OF IND."
30 PRINT "      ","SALES(MILL.$)","SALES(MILL.$)"
35 PRINT "--------------------------------------------------------"
40 INPUT:SALESF:Y,S
50 INPUT:INDSF:N,D
60 PRINT N,S,D,(S/D)*100
65 GO TO 40
99 END
```

```
RUN
YEAR             XYZ CO.         INDUSTRY         % OF IND.
                 SALES(MILL.$)   SALES(MILL.$)
-------------------------------------------------------------
 1970            10.3             150.6            6.83931
 1971            11.4             175.2            6.50685
 1972            12.6             203              6.2069
 1973            13.7             230.8            5.93588
 1974            12.8             254.5            5.02947

FILE OUT OF DATA-- LN #  40
```

Program 13.2 reads from previously created data file SALESF and the
file INDSF (having the above information in it). The program using both
files generates the required output, as diagramed in Figure 13.2.

Lines 40 and 50 in the program obtain the data from the files SALESF
and INDSF, respectively. In line 60 the desired computation is carried out
based on the data from the two files. The GO TO in line 65 branches back to
the first file INPUT as though branching to a READ/DATA, as in programs
without files.

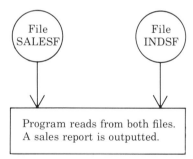

**FIGURE 13.2   Case 13.1, XYZ Company,
              Diagram of Files and Programs**

WRITING TO A FILE

In addition to reading from a file in a program, it is also possible to take the
results of a program and have them placed into a file. To transfer program

results to a file requires the following BASIC statement format:

line # PRINT: file name: list structure or expressions

Some typical statements are:

30 PRINT: XFILE: "TOTALS", A, B, C,
45 PRINT: YEARS: 1975, Y$, M$, L1, L2
170 PRINT: GNP: C + I + G, "YEAR"
185 PRINT: PAY: "HOURS WORKED × RATE"; H * R

Before writing to a file, it is important to remember that a file must be in existence to receive program results being sent to it. The file receiving program results could be either an empty one, or one with data already in it.

Figure 13.3 illustrates the creation of an empty file named EMPTY. Program 13.3 (SUMUP) generates output to the terminal as well as transferring results to the file EMPTY.

```
NEW:EMPTY


SAV
```

FIGURE 13.3   Creating an Empty File

PROGRAM 13.3   Writing to an Empty File

```
NEW:SUMUP



10 REM THIS PROGRAM ADDS UP VALUES, TRANSFERS THEM TO
11 REM A FILE,'EMPTY', WITH THE SUM OF THE VALUES
15 LET S=0
20 READ X
21 DATA 5,5,10,15,25,40,-999
22 IF X=-999 THEN 60
25 PRINT X
30 LET S=S+X
40 PRINT:EMPTY:"X VALUE";X
50 GO TO 20
60 PRINT "TOTAL=";S
70 PRINT:EMPTY:"TOTAL OF X IS";S
99 END


RUN
 5
 5
 10
 15
 25
 40
TOTAL= 100
```

In Program 13.3, lines 40 and 70 write to the file EMPTY the items shown, that is, the values X and S (the total, or sum, of the X values). Figure 13.4 is a listing that shows what the file EMPTY now contains.* Such a listing verifies the accuracy of the file.

```
OLD:EMPTY

:L
X  VALUE  5
X  VALUE  5
X  VALUE  10
X  VALUE  15
X  VALUE  25
X  VALUE  40
TOTAL OF X IS 100
```

FIGURE 13.4 Listing Contents of the File EMPTY

A file such as EMPTY is useless in terms of its being used by another program because the file does not have line numbers for the items in it. To provide line numbering for program output being written to a file, the following statement can be used:

line # PRINT: file name: LNM(X); list structure or expressions

where the X represents the line number in the file that the items following the semicolon will have. If the file contains more than one item the line numbering will increment by one. If X is less than a line number that already exists in the file, the line number assigned will be one more than the last line number in the file. Some examples of the file line numbering statement are:

45 PRINT: FILE 2: LNM(5); W, H, W*H
60 PRINT: IVEN: LNM(100); N\$, P\$, B—E
75 PRINT: XYZ: LNM(15); 1970 + I
100 PRINT: AB2: LNM(72); "TOTALS"; A + B

Program 13.3 has been revised by changing lines 40 and 70 to generate line numbers in the file EMPTY. Program 13.4 shows the revised program SUMUP. Figure 13.5 shows a list of the file EMPTY, now having the line numbers that are a result of program lines 40 and 70.

---

*To obtain a listing of a file or program that has been saved the system command OLD followed by the file or program name must be typed before the command LIST. (See Appendix B.)

PROGRAM 13.4   Writing to an Empty File and Providing Line Numbers

```
10 REM THIS PROGRAM ADDS UP VALUES, TRANSFERS THEM TO
11 REM A FILE, 'EMPTY', WITH THE SUM OF THE VALUES
15 LET S=0
20 READ X
21 DATA 5,5,10,15,25,40,-999
22 IF X=-999 THEN 60
25 PRINT X
30 LET S=S+X
40 PRINT:EMPTY:LNM(10);"X VALUE";X
50 GO TO 20
60 PRINT "TOTAL=";S
70 PRINT:EMPTY:LNM(20);"TOTAL OF X IS";S
99 END


RUN
  5
  5
 10
 15
 25
 40
TOTAL= 100
```

```
OLD:EMPTY


:L
10 X VALUE  5
11 X VALUE  5
12 X VALUE  10
13 X VALUE  15
14 X VALUE  25
15 X VALUE  40
20 TOTAL OF X IS 100
```

FIGURE 13.5   Listing Contents of the File EMPTY
Showing Line Numbers

Case 13.2 illustrates the use of several data files by different programs.

CASE 13.2 The Ajax Company has an employee payroll file named MASTER. The file structure contains employee name, social security number, number of dependents, and wage rate per hour for each person. A second file named HOURS contains employee social security number and the number of hours worked by the employee during the week.

Each week a payroll report for management is generated by a program named REPORT. This program makes use of the contents of the two files. The program REPORT also transfers to a file named GROSS the net wage after deductions of each employee. A summary wage report is required by management. This task is accomplished by using a program named SEGROS.

Below are the tax deductions used by the program REPORT based on an individual's number of dependents.

Number of Dependents	Deduction from Gross
1	10%
2	9
3	8
4	7
5 or more	6

Figure 13.6 shows a diagram of the files and programs in Case 13.2.

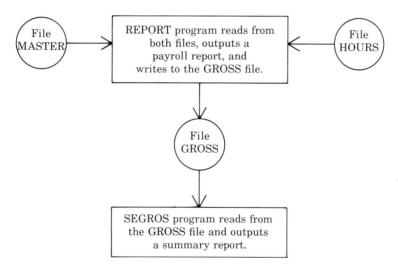

FIGURE 13.6   Case 13.2, Ajax Company, Schematic of Files and Programs

Figure 13.7 shows the two files, MASTER and HOURS, and the empty file GROSS. The contents for this file will be derived from the REPORT program.

The files, MASTER and HOURS, are used by Program 13.5 (REPORT) to generate the weekly payroll report. Line 75 of the REPORT program generates the contents of the GROSS file. This file is then used by Program 13.6 (SEGROS) to provide management with a summary payroll report.

```
NEW:MASTER

TAPE


10 J. STINE,1234567,2,3.50
20 B. O'HARA,8901234,3,5.25
30 M. BENNETT,5678901,1,4.75
40 J. LAKE,2345678,5,3.75
50 B. FARRONE,9012345,4,4.00
60 C. ERICSON,6789012,3,5.00
KEY

SAV

NEW:HOURS

TAPE


5 1234567,40
10 8901234,35
15 5678901,37
20 2345678,40
25 9012345,30
30 6789012,32
KEY

SAV

NEW:GROSS

SAV
```

**FIGURE 13.7   Case 13.2, Ajax Company, Data Files
MASTER, HOURS, and GROSS**

PROGRAM 13.5   Case 13.2, Ajax Company, REPORT Program

```
NEW:REPORT

5 REM PAYROLL REPORT PROGRAM
10 REM READ IN AND STORE TAX RATES
15 FOR I=1 TO 5
20 READ T(I)
25 NEXT I
30 DATA .10,.09,.08,.07,.06
32 REM GENERATE REPORT
35 PRINT TAB(10);"AJAX CO. WEEKLY PAYROLL REPORT"
37 PRINT
40 PRINT "NAME","SOC. SEC. NO.","GROSS WAGE","NET WAGE"
42 PRINT "----------------------------------------------------------"
45 FOR A=1 TO 6
50 INPUT:MASTER:N$,S$,D,P
55 INPUT:HOURS:S$,H
60 LET G=P*H
62 IF D>4 THEN 66
64 GO TO 70
66 LET D=T(5)
70 PRINT N$,S$,G,G-G*T(D)
75 PRINT:GROSS:LNM(5);N$;",",H;",",G
```

PROGRAM 13.5 continued

```
80 NEXT A
85 PRINT
90 PRINT TAB(20);"***PAYROLL REPORT COMPLETED***"
99 END


SAV


RUN
        AJAX CO. WEEKLY PAYROLL REPORT

NAME            SOC. SEC. NO.  GROSS WAGE    NET WAGE
-----------------------------------------------------
  J. STINE       1234567         140         127.4
  B. O'HARA      8901234         183.75      169.05
  M. BENNETT     5678901         175.75      158.175
  J. LAKE        2345678         150         141
  B. FARRONE     9012345         120         111.6
  C. ERICSON     6789012         160         147.2

            ***PAYROLL REPORT COMPLETED***
```

PROGRAM 13.6 Case 13.2, Ajax Company, SEGROS Program

```
NEW:SEGROSS

5 REM PROGRAM TO GENERATE OUTPUT BASED ON THE GROSS FILE
6 PRINT
7 PRINT "EMPLOYEE,HOURS WORKED THIS WEEK,GROSS PAYROLL"
8 PRINT
10 PRINT "NAME";TAB(12);"HOURS WORKED";TAB(28);"GROSS PAY"
12 PRINT "----------------------------------------------------"
15 LET W=0
20 LET P=0
25 FOR I=1 TO 6
30 INPUT:GROSS:N$,H,G
35 PRINT N$,H,G
40 LET W=W+H
45 LET P=P+G
50 NEXT I
70 PRINT "----------------------------------------------------"
75 PRINT "AVERAGE HOURS WORKED THIS WEEK";W/6
77 PRINT "TOTAL GROSS PAY THIS WEEK $";P
78 PRINT
80 PRINT TAB(10);"SUMMARY GROSS PAY REPORT COMPLETED"
99 END


RUN

EMPLOYEE,HOURS WORKED THIS WEEK,GROSS PAYROLL

NAME        HOURS WORKED    GROSS PAY
----------------------------------------------------
  J. STINE       40           140
  B. O'HARA      35           183.75
  M. BENNETT     37           175.75
  J. LAKE        40           150
  B. FARRONE     30           120
  C. ERICSON     32           160
----------------------------------------------------
AVERAGE HOURS WORKED THIS WEEK 35.6667
TOTAL GROSS PAY THIS WEEK $ 929.5

        SUMMARY GROSS PAY REPORT COMPLETED
```

SUMMARY

The concept of data files was introduced in this chapter. Such files can be used by many programs. A data file must first be created and saved. To obtain data from a file, an INPUT file statement is used. To have data written to a file, a PRINT file statement is used. It is important to study the appropriate system manual when working with files since the statements involved differ from system to system.

EXERCISES

13.1   For the following data create a data file. After it has been entered, list it out.

Plant	Units Produced
1	2400
2	3200
3	1800
4	2100
5	3000
6	4500

13.2   For the following data create a data file. After it has been entered, list it out.

Stock	Price: 7/7/75
ATT	$50\frac{3}{4}$
CBS	$53\frac{3}{4}$
GNMOT	$48\frac{1}{2}$
GTELEL	$25\frac{3}{8}$
IBM	204
PLAYBOY	5
XEROX	$67\frac{1}{4}$

13.3   For the following data create a data file. After it has been entered, list it out.

City	High Temperature (°F)	
	Yesterday	A Year Ago
Boston	65	61
New York	72	69
Washington, D.C.	71	68
Denver	49	55
Los Angeles	83	88
Honolulu	79	79
Phoenix	101	100

13.4   Write a program that reads the data file for exercise 13.1, outputs the data with headings, and computes the total units produced for all six plants.

13.5   Do exercise 13.4 but obtain the average production for the six plants.

13.6   For the data in exercise 13.1, assume that each unit produced costs $3.00, and that revenue per unit assuming all units are sold is $5.50. Write a program that reads the data in 13.1 from a file and outputs the total cost, total revenue, and net revenue obtained from the output of each plant.

13.7   Modify the program in exercise 13.6 to transfer all the results to a new file. List out this file to check its contents.

13.8   Write a program that can generate as output the contents of the file created in exercise 13.7.

13.9   a. For the data in exercise 13.2 create a file.
       b. Create another file for the number of shares held by the "National Bank."

Stock	No. of Shares
ATT	5000
CBS	4500
GNMOT	6000
GTELEL	2000
IBM	1200
PLAYBOY	2500
XEROX	1500

       c. Write a program that reads the files of (a) and (b) and outputs for each stock the market value (price times number of shares) as of 7/7/75.
       d. Revise the program in (c) to write the results of the program to a new file.
       e. Write a program that reads the file created in (d) and outputs its contents.

13.10 Suppose there already exist the following two separate data files:

       10 DIV A, 400, 15   10 DIV E, 380, 13
       20 DIV B, 500, 23   15 DIV F, 450, 25
       30 DIV C, 430, 20   20 DIV G, 300, 21
       40 DIV D, 330,30

       Write a program that will read and merge these separate files into a single file with appropriate line numbers. List out the file to check the line numbers. It is suggested that each file be read using subscripted variables to facilitate the merging.

13.11 Treat the following airline flight schedule as a data file:

747'S FROM NEW YORK TO GENEVA AND ZURICH

Day of Week	Leaves New York	Arrives Geneva (Nonstop)	Arrives Zurich
Mo/Th/Sa/Su	7:10 P.M.	7:30 A.M.	9:00 A.M.
	10:05 P.M.		10:40 A.M. (nonstop)
Tu/We/Fr	8:50 P.M.	9:10 A.M.	10:40 A.M.

Write a program that is conversational in nature, such that for any given day desired, Monday to Sunday, the flight schedule is printed out. Test your program by inputting these days: Wednesday, Monday, Friday, Tuesday, Thursday, Sunday, Saturday, Tuesday, Tuesday, Monday, Sunday. It is suggested that the file be read using subscripted variables. The subscript index can be used as a key to help generate the desired results.

13.12 The following airline schedule shows flight information from Seattle and Portland to various destinations. Treat the schedule as two separate files, one for Seattle and one for Portland.

To	Flt #	Leaves	Remarks
From Seattle			
Auckland	815	11:45 P.M.	707 Tu/Su
Tokyo	891/831	8:00 A.M.	707/747 Daily
Singapore	893/841	7:35 P.M.	747/707 Mo/We/Fr
Manila	893/841	7:35 P.M.	707/747 Tu/Th/Sa/Su
Sydney	893/811	7:35 P.M.	707 Mo
Melbourne	895	8:00 P.M.	707/747 We/Sa
From Portland			
Sydney	893/811	6:10 P.M.	707/Su/Mo/Tu 707/747/We/Th/Fr/Sa
Tokyo	891/831	9:15 A.M.	707/747 Daily
Singapore	893/841	6:10 P.M.	707/747 Mo/We/Fr
Manila	893/841	6:10 P.M.	707/747 Tu/Th/Sa/Su

Write a program that is conversational in nature and that, when given the city of departure (Seattle or Portland) and the destination, will print out the other flight information, that is, flight number, leaves, and remarks. (See the suggestion in exercise 13.11.) Test your program with the following input:

> Seattle, Tokyo
>   "   , Auckland
> Portland, Manila
>   "   , Tokyo
>   "   , Manila
> Seattle, Auckland
>   "   , Melbourne
>   "   , Manila
> Seattle, Sydney
>   "   ,   "
> Portland, Sydney
> Seattle, Manila

See what happens if you input Portland, Auckland.

13.13 Below are amounts, due dates, rates, and yields for a new bond issue. Treat this information as a data file. Write a conversational program that, when the due date is inputted, will print out the amount, rate, and yield for that date. (See the suggestion in exercise 13.11.) To test your program, input these dates: 1976, 1979, 1979, 1980, 1984, 1977, 1992, 1982, 1989, 1978, 1988. See what happens if you input 1969 or 1955.

Amount	Due	Rate	Yield
$290,000	1976	7.25%	4.25%
315,000	1977	7.25	4.50
335,000	1978	7.25	4.75
355,000	1979	7.25	5.00
385,000	1980	7.25	5.20
410,000	1981	7.25	5.35
440,000	1982	7.25	5.45
470,000	1983	7.25	5.60
505,000	1984	7.25	5.70
540,000	1985	7.25	8.85
580,000	1986	7.00	6.00
620,000	1987	7.00	6.10
665,000	1988	7.00	6.25
710,000	1989	7.00	6.40
755,000	1990	7.00	6.60
810,000	1991	7.00	6.75
1,005,000	1992	7.00	6.90

Case Application Problems and Programming Projects

In this chapter we show the programs for several longer and more involved case applications than we have seen so far. In addition, the chapter contains programming projects which will give students further opportunities to put their knowledge of the BASIC language to use.

CASE PROBLEM I PRODUCTION DECISIONMAKING

To determine how much of an item should be produced when production of the item is not continuous but in batches, a computer can be used to find which batch size is the most profitable to produce. In this case problem the number of batches to produce is based on total expected profit, which is the average profit that can be obtained given the probability of a demand and multiplying it by the profit for that demand. The total is obtained by summing up each expected profit for each demand. Symbolically, this can be written as

$$EP = \sum (P(D) \times \text{profit of } D)$$

where $\sum$ is sum of, EP is expected profit, and $P(D)$ is probability of demand (D).

Program 14.1 is based on the following relevant facts:

1. A company can make 1, 2, 3, 4, or 5 batches of a chemical a day.
2. The daily demand varies from 0 to 5 or more batches.
3. The company gains $3000 for each batch sold and loses $3500 for each batch made but not sold.
4. Actual sales for the last 10 days were 5, 7, 1, 0, 2, 3, 3, 1, 1, and 4 batches.

The program using the above information does the following:

1. Calculates the probability of demand based on the 10 days sales data.
2. Calculates and prints out the profits and expected profits for each day for each production level (that is, 1, 2, 3, 4, and 5 batches).
3. Determines the most profitable number of batches to be produced based on the total expected profit found for each batch size.

PROGRAM 14.1   Case Problem I Production Decisionmaking

```
60 REM INITIALIZE PROBABILITIES TO ZERO
70 FOR A=0 TO 5
72 LET X(A)=0
74 NEXT A
75 REM READ PAST DEMAND AND CALCULATE PROBABILITY
100 FOR I=1 TO 10
400 READ A
402 DATA 5,7,1,0,2,3,3,1,1,4
405 REM IF DEMAND IS MORE THAN 5, SET DEMAND = 5
500 IF A<=5 THEN 750
700 LET A=5
750 LET X(A)=X(A)+1
800 NEXT I
801 REM Q STANDS FOR THE BEST PROFIT SO FAR. INITIALIZED TO ZERO
805 LET Q=0
806 REM OUTER LOOP ON NUMBER OF BATCHES PRODUCED
810 FOR B=1 TO 5
820 PRINT "NO. OF BATCHES TO BE MADE";B
830 GO SUB 2000
835 PRINT
836 REM INITIALIZE TOTAL EXPECTED PROFIT TO ZERO
840 LET T=0
850 PRINT "DEMAND","PROB.","PROFIT","EXPECTED PROFIT"
851 REM INNER LOOP ON NUMBER OF BATCHES DEMANDED
900 FOR J = 0 TO 5
910 LET P=3000*B
920 IF J<B THEN 942
940 GO TO 960
942 LET P = 3000*J-3500*(B-J)
960 PRINT J,X(J)/10,P,P*(X(J)/10)
970 LET T = T + P*(X(J)/10)
980 NEXT J
990 GO SUB 2000
993 PRINT
995 PRINT TAB(23);"TOTAL EXPECTED PROFIT";T
996 REM COMPARE TOTAL EXPECTED PROFIT WITH BEST PROFIT SO FAR
997 REM SAVE IN VARIABLE K THE BEST NO. OF BATCHES TO BE MADE
999 IF Q>T THEN 1030
1000 LET Q=T
1010 LET K=B
```

```
1030 NEXT B
1040 PRINT "THE MOST PROFITABLE NO. OF BATCHES TO BE MADE IS";K
1050 STOP
2000 FOR I=1 TO 70
2010 PRINT "-";
2020 NEXT I
2030 RETURN
2040 END
```

```
RUN
NO. OF BATCHES TO BE MADE 1
```

DEMAND	PROB.	PROFIT	EXPECTED PROFIT
0	.1	-3500	-350
1	.3	3000	900
2	.1	3000	300
3	.2	3000	600
4	.1	3000	300
5	.2	3000	600

```
                    TOTAL EXPECTED PROFIT 2350.
NO. OF BATCHES TO BE MADE 2
```

DEMAND	PROB.	PROFIT	EXPECTED PROFIT
0	.1	-7000	-700
1	.3	-500	-150
2	.1	6000	600
3	.2	6000	1200
4	.1	6000	600
5	.2	6000	1200

```
                    TOTAL EXPECTED PROFIT 2750
NO. OF BATCHES TO BE MADE 3
```

DEMAND	PROB.	PROFIT	EXPECTED PROFIT
0	.1	-10500	-1050
1	.3	-4000	-1200
2	.1	2500	250
3	.2	9000	1800
4	.1	9000	900
5	.2	9000	1800

```
                    TOTAL EXPECTED PROFIT 2500
NO. OF BATCHES TO BE MADE 4
```

DEMAND	PROB.	PROFIT	EXPECTED PROFIT
0	.1	-14000	-1400
1	.3	-7500	-2250
2	.1	-1000	-100
3	.2	5500	1100
4	.1	12000	1200
5	.2	12000	2400

```
                    TOTAL EXPECTED PROFIT 950.
NO. OF BATCHES TO BE MADE 5
```

DEMAND	PROB.	PROFIT	EXPECTED PROFIT
0	.1	-17500	-1750
1	.3	-11000	-3300
2	.1	-4500	-450
3	.2	2000	400
4	.1	8500	850
5	.2	15000	3000

```
                    TOTAL EXPECTED PROFIT-1250.
THE MOST PROFITABLE NO. OF BATCHES TO BE MADE IS 2
```

CASE PROBLEM II PROCESS SIMULATION

Computer simulation is useful for management planning and analysis of certain kinds of operations. This case problem uses Monte Carlo simulation to examine the processing of mail bags in a mail order department.*

Monte Carlo simulation is a technique that generates artificial outcomes that represent the process being examined. The technique requires that the process being studied have probabilistic outcomes. From such information outcomes can be predicted by random sampling instructions included in the computer program. The results obtained can then be analyzed in terms of the management decisions that must be made.

Program 14.2 is designed to carry out a Monte Carlo simulation. The program is based on these relevant facts:

1. A mail order department has two employees who process bags of mail that are delivered during the night for processing that begins at 9 A.M. the next morning.
2. It takes an employee 1 hour to process the contents of one mail bag.
3. At the end of the day any unprocessed mail bags are left over for processing on the next day.
4. Each employee works 7 hours a day, 5 days a week.
5. Over the last 50 days the distribution of the number of bags arriving has been:

Number of Bags Arriving	Relative Frequency	Cumulative Frequency
12	.13	.13
13	.22	.35
14	.26	.61
15	.30	.91
16	.06	.97
17	.03	1.00
	1.00	

Note: The relative frequency represents the probability distribution. The cumulative frequency was obtained by adding each successive relative frequency value. These values are used in Program 14.2 to do the random sampling of outcomes (number of bags arriving).

The purpose of the simulation is to help answer these questions:

1. How many mail bags can arrive each day over a 50-day period?
2. How many mail bags remain unprocessed each day over a 50-day period?

---

*A reference for the Monte Carlo simulation technique is given in the opening REM statements of Program 14.2.

3. On the average, how many bags arrive each day?

4. On the average, how many bags are unprocessed each day?

5. Out of 50 days, on how many days were mail bags unprocessed?

The output of the computer simulation generates answers to these questions. Management can then decide whether to (a) hire additional employees; or (b) put the present employees on overtime; or (c) maintain the present operation.

PROGRAM 14.2 Case Problem II Process Simulation

```
 1 REM MONTE CARLO SIMULATION OF A MAIL ORDER
 2 REM DEPARTMENT PROCESSING OPERATION
 3 REM REFERENCE FOR TECHNIQUE: DECISION MAKING
 4 REM THROUGH OPERATIONS RESEARCH, R.J.THIERAUF
 5 REM & R.C.KLEKAMP, 2ND. ED., WILEY, 1975  CHAP. 14
 6 PRINT "SIMULATION OF MAIL ORDER DEPARTMENT PROCESSING"
 7 PRINT "OPERATION FOR FIFTY DAYS WITH TWO EMPLOYEES"
 8 PRINT "EACH WORKING SEVEN HOURS A DAY, PROCESSING ONE"
 9 PRINT "MAIL BAG PER HOUR EACH"
10 PRINT
12 PRINT "DAY","# MAIL BAGS","TOT # BAGS TO","NUMBER","MAIL BAGS"
14 PRINT "NUMBER","DELIVERED","BE PROCESSED","PROCESSED","UNPROCESSED"
16 GO SUB 275
20 READ E
22 DATA 2
25 LET C=E*7
30 REM INITIALIZE VARIABLES
35 LET A=0
40 LET U=0
45 LET L=0
48 LET Y=0
50 FOR D=1 TO 50
52 REM PICK A RANDOM NUMBER
54 RANDOMIZE
55 LET N=RND(X)
60 REM TEST OF THE RANDOM NUMBER
65 IF N<=.13 THEN 145
70 IF N<=.35 THEN 135
75 IF N<=.61 THEN 125
80 IF N<=.91 THEN 115
85 IF N<=.97 THEN 105
90 REM MATCH RANDOM # WITH # OF BAGS DELIVERED
95 LET B=17
100 GO TO 160
105 LET B=16
110 GO TO 160
115 LET B=15
120 GO TO 160
125 LET B=14
130 GO TO 160
135 LET B=13
140 GO TO 160
145 LET B=12
150 REM COMPUTATIONS FOLLOW
155 REM ACCUMULATE # BAGS DELIVERED
160 LET A=A+B
165 REM TOTAL TO BE PROCESSED=DELIVERED+UNPROCESSED
170 LET P=B+U
175 REM NUMBER PROCESSED CANNOT EXCEED CAPACITY,C.
180 IF P>C THEN 210
```

PROGRAM 14.2 continued

```
185 LET U=0
190 PRINT D,B,P,P,U
200 GO TO 230
205 REM WHEN CAPACITY,C, IS EXCEEDED
210 LET U=P-C
215 PRINT D,B,P,C,U
218 REM L= TOTAL NUMBER OF BAGS UNPROCESSED
220 LET L=L+U
222 REM COUNT NUMBER OF DAYS THERE ARE UNPROCESSED BAGS
225 LET Y=Y+1
230 NEXT D
255 REM COMPUTE AVERAGES, PRINT TOTALS
260 GO SUB 275
265 PRINT "TOTALS",A,TAB(60);L
270 PRINT "  AVERAGES",A/D,TAB(60);L/D
271 PRINT
272 PRINT "OUT OF";D;"DAYS,";Y;"DAYS HAD MAIL BAGS UNPROCESSED"
273 STOP
275 FOR I=1 TO 71
280 PRINT "-";
285 NEXT I
286 PRINT
287 RETURN
290 END


RUN
SIMULATION OF MAIL ORDER DEPARTMENT PROCESSING
OPERATION FOR FIFTY DAYS WITH TWO EMPLOYEES
EACH WORKING SEVEN HOURS A DAY, PROCESSING ONE
MAIL BAG PER HOUR EACH
```

DAY NUMBER	# MAIL BAGS DELIVERED	TOT # BAGS TO BE PROCESSED	NUMBER PROCESSED	MAIL BAGS UNPROCESSED
1	15	15	14	1
2	12	13	13	0
3	13	13	13	0
4	14	14	14	0
5	12	12	12	0
6	13	13	13	0
7	13	13	13	0
8	15	15	14	1
9	14	15	14	1
10	14	15	14	1
11	15	16	14	2
12	12	14	14	0
13	15	15	14	1
14	13	14	14	0
15	12	12	12	0
16	13	13	13	0
17	14	14	14	0
18	13	13	13	0
19	13	13	13	0
20	16	16	14	2
21	15	17	14	3
22	14	17	14	3
23	15	18	14	4
24	14	18	14	4
25	14	18	14	4
26	13	17	14	3
27	15	18	14	4
28	16	20	14	6
29	15	21	14	7
30	13	20	14	6
31	15	21	14	7
32	15	22	14	8
33	12	20	14	6

PROGRAM 14.2 continued

```
34          15          21          14          7
35          14          21          14          7
36          13          20          14          6
37          16          22          14          8
38          14          22          14          8
39          15          23          14          9
40          14          23          14          9
41          13          22          14          8
42          15          23          14          9
43          17          26          14          12
44          14          26          14          12
45          15          27          14          13
46          12          25          14          11
47          12          23          14          9
48          13          22          14          8
49          15          23          14          9
50          15          24          14          10
-----------------------------------------------------------------
TOTALS      699                                 229
   AVERAGES 13.98                               4.58
```

OUT OF 50 DAYS, 37 DAYS HAD MAIL BAGS UNPROCESSED

PROGRAMMING PROJECTS

Project I   Design of a Computerized Billing System

Background   The G&E Power Co., Inc. is a public utility that wants to set up a computerized billing system. You have been asked to design a program to meet their needs. Your program will be a prototype using only two customers. Customer 1 pays all bills on time. Customer 2 fails to pay his (her) bills on time. Even though only two customers are being billed, it is expected that this program will be able to handle several thousand customers.

Program Test Data   The following information is to be utilized to test out the program:

Customer Name/Address	ID No.	Gas (cu. ft.) Begin.	End	Elec. (KWH) Begin.	End	Mo.
Your Name	S. S.	1000	1500	300	400	Jan.
Your Address	No.	1500	2000	400	500	Feb.
		2000	2400	500	625	Mar.
		2400	2800	625	700	Apr.
Mr. Bill Due	999-00-6666	1200	1400	180	210	Jan.
Smogville,		1400	1650	210	290	Feb.
USA		1650	2000	290	350	Mar.
		2000	2400	350	400	Apr.

(Meter Readings)

Four months of test data are being used so that the logic of the program can be checked. This is necessary because of the "warning" notices that are printed out when bills are not paid (see below).

Computational Information   Rates and taxes are as follows:

Gas	$.10 (10¢) per cu. ft.
Electricity	$.03 (3¢) per KWH (kilowatthour)
Taxes	6% of total bill each month

Each month a bill is sent to each customer based on the following simple computation:

Total without taxes = gas total + electric total
                    = no. of cu. ft. × gas rate + no. of KWH
                     × electric rate
Amount due   = (total without taxes) + (total × tax rate)

Program Operation   Each month the meter readings as data are fed into the computer for each customer. The name, address, identification (I D) number, and rates have been previously stored by you as part of the program.

Output Requirements   The following printed output is desired: the present balance due showing the month and dollar amount for gas and electricity; the meter readings and usage for each item; the customer's name, address, and I D number; any previous balance due; the taxes; the total amount due. All of this output should appear as a billing statement. The form of it is up to you.

If the customer is in arrears, the following notices must be printed on the statement as appropriate:

1. First Notice (no payment received after 2 months of service)

> "Warning—No payment after 2 months.
> Your next notice will be for a cutoff of
> gas and electricity. Pay up now."

2. Second Notice (no payment received after 3 months of service)

> "Your gas and electricity has been cut off.
> Service will be restored when full payment
> is made of the amount due."

(Optional) A company record must also be printed for each customer. This record shows name, address, ID number, all meter readings, and usage for each month; all billing for each month by gas, electricity, and totals; and any warnings or cutoff notices. The company record design is up to you.

Summary Your billing system should consist of the following for 4 months:

1. A billing statement for each (two) customer for each month; with or without warnings or cutoff notices depending upon the circumstances. *Note:* Customer 1 pays all bills on time; customer 2 does not pay any bills. These facts should be built into your program so that the warning notices can be tested.
2. (Optional) A company record showing all of the above information for each month for each customer. You should have four company files for each customer as your output—one file for each month showing the previous months and then the present update.

Documentation A complete flowchart should be prepared for the program, including REM statements where appropriate.

Project II   Inventory Control System

Background Your firm, Top Knotch Management Consultants Inc., Jamaica, New York 11439, has been hired by the

> Good Toy Co., Inc.
> Fun And Games Street
> Any City, USA, 10000

to write an inventory system program for their 1000 different products. The ultimate system desired is one that will enable an inventory clerk at the end of each day to merely inform the computer via a terminal of the number of units of each product sold during the day. Such reporting of daily sales by product will provide a constant inventory updating for each product. When the inventory of any particular item reaches a specified low point, new goods will be ordered to replenish the stock. All new orders will arrive when the inventory level of the products reaches zero. Figure 14.1 shows how a typical system works for *each* product.

Programming Assignment You have been asked to write the prototype program for one of the products kept in the inventory. This program is to be conversational in design. Data is entered by means of INPUT statements.

The product is a small aboveground swimming pool 12 feet in diameter that has an item no. 738. It sells for $198 and has a purchase price of $100 from the wholesaler (Wet Pool Co., Inc., Lakeville, USA 20000). The pool can only be ordered 50 units at a time. Reordering is required when inventory reaches 20 percent of the order size. There are 25 units now in stock.

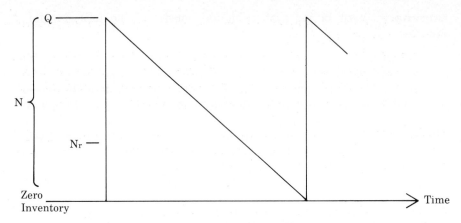

Q = order quantity of some product. New inventory.
N$_r$ = reorder point. Inventory is ordered when the stock level reaches this
point. (Q arrives when stock level reaches zero.)
N = inventory stock level as units are sold.

FIGURE 14.1 Inventory System

Generating Sales Data To test out the program, data for daily sales
for the product are obtained by using two predefined BASIC functions,
RND and INT. These functions together will generate random numbers
from 0 to 10. For example:

```
10 FOR I = 1 TO 10
20 PRINT INT(11*RND(0)),
30 NEXT I
99 END
```

The 10 numbers generated will represent sales data for each of the 10 days.

Program Requirements The Good Toy Co. would like this program
to accomplish the following:

1. The program should "ask" the clerk the item number, description of
   the item sold from inventory, and the number of units sold during
   the day.

2. The program should result in the following printouts:
   a. Current inventory *after* the clerk inputs the desired information.
   b. A summary table of the day-by-day inventory for the product at
      the end of each 5 day week. This table should show the total num-
      ber of units sold and the dollar value of these sales both day by day
      and for the whole week.

   c. When the reorder point, N_r, is reached, a warning that informs the clerk of this situation.
   d. An order form (when the reorder point is reached) that contains the supplier's address, the purchaser's address, the date of the order, the number of units being ordered, the item number, the item description, the retail unit cost, and the total retail cost of the order.

Documentation   Throughout your program use should be made of REM statements so that another programmer can easily follow what you have done. A final flowchart is also desired.

Project III   Design of a Computerized Payroll System

Background   The Alpha Co., Inc., wants to set up a computerized payroll accounting system that will be able to handle up to 30 employees. You have been hired to write a computer program to do the weekly payroll. Initially, you will only write a test program for two employees (see below).

Pertinent Information   Each employee will have a record containing the following items of information:

   1. Employee identification number (social security number)
   2. Employee name
   3. Number of dependents
   4. Hourly pay rate
   5. Pay period:
      a. Gross earnings
      b. Federal income tax; state income tax
      c. Social security tax
      d. Net earnings
   6. Year-to-date: all items in 5 above

   Each weekly pay period a paycheck is printed out for each employee. With the paycheck the employee gets a stub showing the items in 5 and 6 above.
   Weekly timecards are processed for each employee to obtain their gross wage (hours worked times hourly wage).

Computational Requirements

   1. To write the paychecks the federal income tax to be withheld is computed as follows:
      a. The tax base is determined by subtracting $30.00 times the number of dependents from gross earnings.

b. The amount to be withheld is computed from the following table:

If the amount of the tax base is:		The federal income tax to be withheld is:		
Over-	But not over-			
$ 0	$100	14%	of excess over	$ 0
100	200	$ 14 + 15%		100
200	300	29 + 16%		200
300	400	45 + 17%		300
400	800	62 + 19%		400
800		138 + 22%		800

2. To write the paychecks the state income tax to be withheld is computed based on the following table:

If the gross wage is:

Over-	But not over-	The state tax to be withheld is:		
$ 0	$100	2%	of excess over	$ 0
100	300	$2 plus 3%		100
300	500	8 plus 4%		300
500		16 plus 5%		500

3. Social security tax is 10.8 percent of gross earnings, not to exceed $1080.00 in any one year.
4. Overtime wages are at $1\frac{1}{2}$ times the hourly wage for more than 35 hours worked in one week.
5. Net earnings (the amount of the check) equals gross earnings less federal, state, and social security taxes.
6. Before writing the checks, pay-period figures should be added to year-to-date figures.

Computer Output   For each employee, for *each* week the program should generate printouts of the following:

1. A company record for each employee having all of the six items listed under "Pertinent Information."
2. A paycheck for each employee showing name, ID number, company name, week 1 or 2, and the net wage.
3. A check stub having all of the items 5 and 6 listed under "Pertinent Information."
   The design of the company record, pay check, and stub is up to you.

Program Test Data   The following information for two employees is to be used to test the program:

Name	ID No. (Soc. Sec. No.)	Number of Dependents	Wage/ Hour	Hours Worked Week 1	Week 2
Your name	Your number	1	$14	42	35
Any worker	111-88-9669	4	7	35	32

Documentation   A flowchart must be included with the final program, as well as a liberal amount of REM statements describing the various parts of it.

Project IV   Hotel Reservation System Simulation

Background   The Always Have A Room Motel Co., Inc., has motels in nine locations:

Atlanta, Ga.	New York, N.Y.
Baltimore, Md.	Raleigh, N.C.
Boston, Mass.	Richmond, Va.
Jacksonville, Fla.	Washington, D.C.
Miami, Fla.	

A person phones for a reservation in a certain city. Depending on the number of persons in the party, there may or may not be a vacancy. If there is no vacancy, he is told the two closest cities to the desired location—one north of it and the other south of it.

Programming Assignment   Write a program that will simulate the system using the Monte Carlo technique. The program should simulate 20 telephone calls. Assume that a call for each of the nine cities is equally likely (a one-ninth probability for each).

Data for the Program   All data for the program is generated internally using a random number function. This function is used to simulate the city desired by the caller, the number of people in the party (1 to 6), and whether or not there is a vacancy.

Use the following information (based on historical data) to simulate the number of persons in the party, and whether or not there is a vacancy:

If the no. of persons is:	The probability of no vacancy is:
1	.30
2	.40
3	.50
4 to 6	.60

Output Format   Your printed output might look like this: (as an illustration only)

Call	City Desired*	No. in Party	Vacancy Yes/No	Nearest Other Cities
1	NYC	8	No	XYZ and ABC
___	___	___	___	___
___	___	___	___	___
20	___	___	___	___

Documentation   A flowchart should be prepared for the program. REM statements should be used throughout the program to explain relevant segments of it.

---

*This list of cities is not in geographical sequence. Consult a map or atlas for the correct location of each one.

Paper Tape Preparation and Correcting Errors

This appendix summarizes the preparation of a paper tape and the correction of errors.

HOW TO PREPARE A PAPER TAPE

1. Turn the knob at the lower right-hand side of the terminal (Figure A.1) clockwise (to the right).
2. Push down the "ON" button of the paper tape punch. The punch is located on the left side of the terminal.
3. To get a 4- or 5-inch leader on your tape before typing the actual program, press the two keys REPT and RUB OUT at the same time. These two keys are located on the right side of the keyboard. (See Figure A.2.)
4. Now you are ready to type your program. . . .
   a. Begin each line with a line number.
   b. At the end of each line, hit the keys RETURN, LINE FEED and RUB OUT—in that order.

   Note: The "0" on the top row next to the 9 is a zero. The "O" on the second row between the "I" and "P" is the alphabetic letter. Don't mix them up.
5. When you are finished typing your program, repeat step 3 to get a tail on your tape, then gently rip the tape from the terminal upwards. Turn the tape punch OFF.

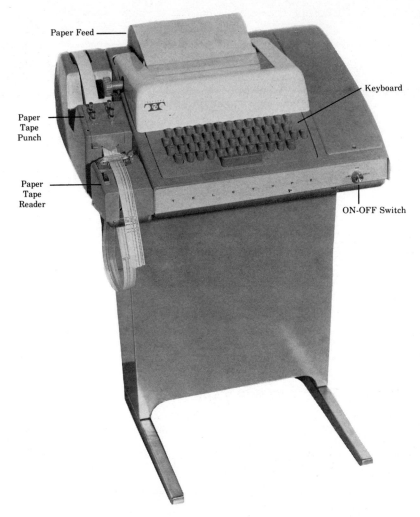

Paper Feed

Keyboard

Paper
Tape
Punch

Paper
Tape
Reader

ON-OFF Switch

**FIGURE A.1   Model 33 ASR Teletype (Courtesy of Teletype
Corporation)**

CORRECTING ERRORS

When preparing a program off-line (not connected to the computer), or
working on-line (connected to the computer), errors may be made. The
programmer may have (a) one or more characters to correct; (b) a line
presently being worked on to delete; or (c) a line previously completed that

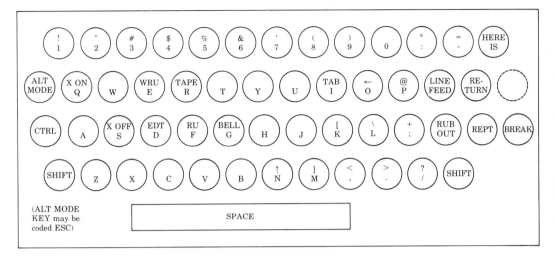

FIGURE A.2 Keyboard for Model 33 ASR Teletype

should be deleted. Each of these situations and the appropriate action to be taken will be explained.

Incorrect Characters While still working on a line, if something has been incorrectly typed it can be "erased" by holding down the SHIFT key and typing the letter "O" as many times as is necessary to reach and erase the incorrect character.

The combination of the SHIFT and "O" will produce a little arrow (←). If for instance the following error occurred:

10 PRIIT

the correction requires two arrows:

10 PRIIT ← ← NT

followed by the correct letters. The first arrow erases the *T*: the second arrow, the second *I*. When this line is executed by the computer, it is taken as

10 PRINT

Current Line Deletion If when working on a line there appears to be too many errors to correct, or it is impractical to use the arrow repeatedly, the entire line can be erased by typing the ALT MODE key. If this is done while on-line, a slash (\) will be printed.

Completed Line Correction   If it is necessary to delete or redo a line that has been completed, all that is required is to type the line number of the line to be deleted. This erases the entire line. If it is to be redone, continue typing the appropriate statement after the line number. This revised line replaces the previous line having the same line number. Such revisions can be made at any time you are working on a current problem.

System Commands

This appendix summarizes many of the most widely used system commands. For easy reference they are listed in alphabetical order. In many systems, only the first three letters of any word must be entered.

1. BYE or GOODBYE disconnects the terminal from the timesharing system. The amount of connect and/or CPU time used this session may also be printed at this time.

2. GOOD BYE (same as BYE, item 1).

3. KEY indicates that input to the computer will come from the keyboard. This command usually follows the TAPE command (see item 10).

4. LIST causes the most current version of the program or file to be printed on the teletype.
   LISTNH stands for LIST NO HEADING and means just what it says—it will do everything that LIST will do but will not print the heading, which includes the name of the program, if any, the time, and the date. Some timesharing systems include the name of the timesharing company as well. On the RAPIDATA System the command ":L" has the same effect as LISTNH.

5. NEW allows a new program to be entered into the timesharing system, while it erases the working copy of the current program. The system responds to the NEW command with a request for the NAME of the new program. If you wish to create a new program without naming it, you could just type SCR (see 9), and then begin typing the

new program. Such an unnamed program could not be SAVEd until it was NAMEd.

6. OLD introduces a new program that was previously saved (see 8) and destroys the working copy of the current program. The system responds to the OLD command with a request for the NAME of the OLD program that is to be loaded in.

7. RUN compiles and executes the current program. If there are any syntax errors in the program they will be indicated at this time. RUNNH is the same as RUN, but no heading will be printed.

8. SAVE saves the working copy of the current program by writing it onto a disc file. This program can then be recalled by typing OLD and then the name of the program.

9. SCRATCH erases the working copy of the current program. It is useful when you have run one program and then wish to create a new program. There will be no leftover line numbers from the previous program.

10. TAPE indicates that information will be entered via the tape reader. After the TAPE has been entered, the KEY command should be executed.

11. UNSAVE removes the current SAVEd program from the disc storage. After this command, the program can no longer be recalled by the OLD command.

Answers and Solutions to Selected Exercises

CHAPTER 2

2.2 Unacceptable BASIC variables are:
   a. Xll;   c. −M5;   d. C.2;   e. PI;   h. D+8

2.4 Numerical solutions:
   a. $\frac{1}{7}$ c. −19   e. $1\frac{1}{2}$ g. 240
   b. $15\frac{4}{7}$ d. 80   f. 20   h. 360

2.6 $(2*R*C/(U*P)) \uparrow .50$

CHAPTER 3

3.1 a. 20 PRINT "EARNINGS FOR 3RD QUARTER"
   b. 30 PRINT "   ", "DIVISION", "   ", "SALES"
   c. 40 PRINT "NAME", "S.S.#", "DATE OF BIRTH", "NO. OF
      DEP."

3.3 a. .00000528   c. 4,680,000.   e. 75,310,000,000.
   b. .000000153   d. .0341791   f. −.0123658

3.4
```
5 PRINT "ANY STUDENT'S NAME"
10 PRINT "124 UNIVERSITY PL."
15 PRINT "ANY TOWN, ANY STATE   ZIP CODE"
20 PRINT "COURSE IS - BUS 10"
99 END


RUN
ANY STUDENT'S NAME
124 UNIVERSITY PL.
ANY TOWN, ANY STATE   ZIP CODE
COURSE IS - BUS 10
```

3.7
```
10 PRINT "SALES","TAX","TOTAL"
12 PRINT "-------------------------------------------"
15 PRINT "$";5,"$";5*.05,"$";5+5*.05
20 PRINT "$";10,"$";10*.05,"$";10+10*.05
25 PRINT "$";15,"$";15*.05,"$";15+15*.05
99 END
```

```
RUN
SALES            TAX              TOTAL
-------------------------------------------
$ 5              $ .25            $ 5.25
$ 10             $ .5             $ 10.5
$ 15             $ .75            $ 15.75
```

3.12 Expressions have the following values:
     a. 5;   b. 3;   c. 27;   d. 11

3.15
```
1 REM   THIS PROGRAM FINDS THE AREA OF A TRIANGLE.
2 REM   NOTE THE USE OF COMPUTATIONAL PRINT.
5 PRINT "BASE","HEIGHT","AREA"
10 PRINT 5,7,5*7/2
15 PRINT 10.5,6.2,10.5*6.2/2
20 PRINT 100,78,100*78/2
99 END
```

```
RUN
BASE             HEIGHT           AREA
5                7                17.5
 10.5            6.2              32.55
 100             78               3900
```

CHAPTER 4

4.1 69
     304

4.3 a.
```
10 PRINT "SALES","TAX","TOTAL"
15 DATA 5,10,15
20 READ S1,S2,S3
25 PRINT S1,.05*S1,.05*S1+S1
30 PRINT S2,.05*S2,.05*S2+S2
35 PRINT S3,.05*S3,.05*S3+S3
99 END
```

```
RUN
SALES            TAX              TOTAL
5                .25              5.25
 10              .5               10.5
 15              .75              15.75
```

4.10
```
5 REM UNITED COMPUTER COMPANY
7 INPUT S1,P1,W1,S2,P2,W2,S3,P3,W3,S4,P4,W4
10 PRINT "SALESPERSON","AMOUNT SOLD","SALARY"
20 PRINT "1",S1,W1+P1*S1
25 PRINT "2",S2,W2+P2*S2
30 PRINT "3",S3,W3+P3*S3
35 PRINT "4",S4,W4+P4*S4
99 END
```

```
RUN
 ?13500,.015,1000,21000,.015,1000,9600,.015,1000,24400,.015,1000
SALESPERSON    AMOUNT SOLD    SALARY
1              13500          1202.5
2              21000          1315
3              9600           1144
4              24400          1366
```

4.14
```
10 REM THIS PROGRAM ILLUSTRATES THE PROPERTY OF THE SUM OF THE
15 REM DEVIATIONS ABOUT THE MEAN IS EQUAL TO ZERO
20 INPUT U
25 READ X1,X2,X3,X4,X5
30 PRINT "SUM OF THE DEVIATIONS ABOUT THE MEAN IS";
35 PRINT (X1-U)+(X2-U)+(X3-U)+(X4-U)+(X5-U)
40 DATA 5,-3,7,8,-2
45 END
```

```
RUN
 ?3
SUM OF THE DEVIATIONS ABOUT THE MEAN IS 0
```

CHAPTER 5

5.1   15.25   4   4   3

5.2   −2.75   .25   4   3

5.4
```
5 REM PROGRAM TO FIND TOTAL PROFITS. TOTAL PROFITS = TOTAL REVENUE-
10 REM TOTAL COST. WHERE T=TOTAL PROFIT, P=PRICE PER UNIT, C=COST
15 REM PER UNIT, U=# UNITS SOLD AND BOUGHT,T1=TOTAL REV.(P X U),
20 REM AND T2=TOTAL COST(C X U).
30 READ P,C,U
40 LET T1= P*U
50 LET T2= C*U
60 LET T = T1-T2
70 PRINT "TOTAL PROFIT REPORT"
75 PRINT
80 PRINT "NUMBER OF UNITS SOLD";U
85 PRINT "PRICE PER UNIT";P,"COST PER UNIT";C
86 PRINT "TOTAL REVENUE";T1
92 PRINT "LESS TOTAL COST";T2
95 PRINT "----------------------------------"
100 PRINT "TOTAL PROFIT";T
150 DATA 10,6.50,225
199 END
```

5.4   continued

```
RUN
TOTAL PROFIT REPORT

NUMBER OF UNITS SOLD 225
PRICE PER UNIT 10                        COST PER UNIT 6.5
TOTAL REVENUE 2250
LESS TOTAL COST 1462.5
-------------------------------------
TOTAL PROFIT 787.5
```

CHAPTER 6

6.1   a. The program would loop infinitely, printing out the same first line
         of results.
      b. Only the first line of output would result.

6.3   b. Variable S would always be set equal to zero, and the last column
         of output would have the values of X. The heading is repeated each
         time.
      e. Only the heading and the first line of output result. No "OUT OF
         DATA" occurs.
      i. Same as e.
      j. The variable S is not accumulated. Since S is equal to zero, the val-
         ues in the last column of output will be zero.

6.6   a. The output would not change.
      b. Omitting line 35 would not cause the output to change because A
         is greater than B. If A was less than B, both the B and A values
         would be printed out, each on a separate line.

6.17 The data value 999 would be processed in lines 60, 65, and 70. An addi-
      tional line of output results with these values: 99 and 998001. The
      column totals become: 1016 and 998080.

6.19
```
10 REM GO TO SOLUTION
12 PRINT "SALESPERSON","AM'T.SOLD","SALARY+COMM."
13 PRINT "------------","---------","-------------"
15 LET P=0
20 READ A
30 DATA 13500,21000,9600,24400
40 LET P=P+1
50 PRINT P,"$";A,"$";1000+.015*A
60 GO TO 20
90 END

RUN
SALESPERSON      AM'T.SOLD        SALARY+COMM.
------------     ---------        -------------
     1           $ 13500          $ 1202.5
     2           $ 21000          $ 1315
     3           $ 9600           $ 1144
     4           $ 24400          $ 1366

OUT OF DATA- LN # 20
```

6.25
```
10 LET S1=25
20 LET S2=15
30 LET S3=30
40 LET H=0
45 READ H
46 PRINT"FOR THE HOUR ";H
50 PRINT,"FLIGHT 381","FLIGHT 402","FLIGHT 283"
55 PRINT":::::::::::::::::::::::::::::::::::::::::::::::::::::::::::::::::::::"
60 PRINT"SEATS AVAILABLE";;S1,S2,S3
70 PRINT"WHEN ? APPEARS TYPE RES. FOR THIS HOUR"
80 INPUT F1,F2,F3
90 LET S1=S1-F1
100LET S2=S2-F2
110LET S3=S3-F3
120LET H =H+1
130IF H=5 THEN 299
140IF S1<=10 THEN 180
150IF S2<=10 THEN 200
160IF S3<=10 THEN 220
170GO TO 46
180PRINT"WARNING, FLIGHT 381 HAS 10 OR LESS SEATS AVAILABLE"
190GO TO 150
200PRINT"WARNING, FLIGHT 402 HAS 10 OR LESS SEATS AVAILABLE"
210GO TO 160
220PRINT"WARNING, FLIGHT 283 HAS 10 OR LESS SEATS AVAILABLE"
230GO TO 46
240 DATA 1
299 END
```

6.26
```
5 REM CREDIT CARD APPLICATION
7 LET I=0
8 LET I=I+1
10 IF I>10 THEN 999
15 READ N,S,R,Y,L
20 IF S>=25000 THEN100
30 IF S>=20000 THEN 55
40 IF S>=15000 THEN 70
45 IF S>=10000 THEN 80
50 GO TO 8
55 IF R<.25*S/12 THEN 100
60 GO TO 40
70 IF L>5 THEN 100
75 GO TO 8
80 IF L>5 THEN 90
85 GO TO 8
90 IF Y>=3 THEN100
95 GO TO 8
100 PRINT N
200 GO TO 8
900 DATA 605,21000,560,4,5,610,18000,500,10,14
910 DATA 614,35000,750,2,10,656,11000,280,20,19
920 DATA 678,15500,400,6,2,692,8000,200,10,11
930 DATA 694,32000,850,3,3,697,12500,375,4,6
940 DATA 698,40000,950,15,8,700,20000,395,5,5
999 END

RUN
 610
 614
 656
 694
 697
 698
 700
```

CHAPTER 7

7.1   1 2 3 4 5 6 7 8 9 10

7.5b.
```
10 READ N, A, Y, S
15 IF A>=62 THEN 40
20 IF Y>=25 THEN 40
25 IF A>=60 THEN 50
30 IF A>=58 THEN 60
35 GO TO 75
40 PRINT N
45 GO TO 75
50 IF Y>=20 THEN 40
55 GO TO 75
60 IF Y>=20 THEN 70
65 GO TO 75
70 IF S>=25000 THEN 40
75 NEXT J
80 DATA 1234, 40, 5, 12500, 1235, 61, 25, 15000
85 DATA 1236, 56, 21, 30000, 1237, 71, 15, 18000
90 DATA 1238, 62, 19, 41000, 1239, 59, 30, 11000
95 DATA 1240, 20, 10, 10000, 1241, 56, 22, 29000
100 DATA 1242, 57, 18, 31000, 1243, 62, 24, 35000
999 END
```

```
RUN
 1235
 1237
 1238
 1239
 1243
```

7.8
```
5 REM TABLE OF ZEROS
10 FOR I=1 TO 10
15 FOR J=1 TO 10
20 LET X=0
25 IF I=J THEN 40
30 IF I+J=11 THEN 40
35 GO TO 45
40 LET X=1
45 PRINT X;
50 NEXT J
55 PRINT
60 NEXT I
65 END
```

CHAPTER 8

8.8
```
5 REM TWO WEEK TOTALS FOR PRODUCTION
7 DIM W1(5,3), W2(5,3), A(5,3)
10 FOR I=1 TO 5
15 FOR J=1 TO 3
20 READ W1(I,J)
30 NEXT J
35 NEXT I
40 FOR I=1 TO 5
45 FOR J=1 TO 3
50 READ W2(I,J)
52 LET A(I,J)=W1(I,J)+W2(I,J)
55 NEXT J
60 NEXT I
65 FOR I=1 TO 5
```

8.8 continued

```
 70 LET B(I)=0
 75 FOR J=1 TO 3
 80 LET B(I)=E(I)+A(I,J)
 85 NEXT J
 90 NEXT I
100 PRINT "WORKER","  A","  E"," C","# UNITS"
110 FOR I=1 TO 5
120 PRINT I,
130 FOR J=1 TO 3
140 PRINT A(I,J),
150 NEXT J
160 PRINT B(I)
170 NEXT I
180 PRINT
190 FOR K=1 TO 65
200 PRINT "-";
210 NEXT K
212 PRINT
215 LET G=0
220 FOR J=1 TO 3
230 LET D(J)=0
240 FOR I=1 TO 5
250 LET D(J)=D(J)+A(I,J)
260 NEXT I
270 NEXT J
275 PRINT "TOTALS",
280 FOR J=1 TO 3
285 PRINT D(J),
290 LET G=G+D(J)
300 NEXT J
310 PRINT G
320 PRINT
400 DATA 200,100,20,150,125,30,320,75,15,275,100,15
410 DATA 100,200,10,185,110,22,160,115,25,275,100,30
420 DATA 275,90,20,150,150,10
999 END
```

RUN WORKER	A	B	C	# UNITS
1	385	210	42	637
2	310	240	55	605
3	595	175	45	815
4	550	190	35	775
5	250	350	20	620

TOTALS	2090	1165	197	3452

8.9

```
  5 REM DOLLAR VALUE FOR SALE OF MINI-COMPUTERS
 10 PRINT"SALESPERSON",,"TOTAL DOLLAR VALUE"
 20 DIM S(5,4)
 30 FOR J=1 TO 4
 40 READ P(J)
 50 NEXT J
 60 FOR I=1 TO 5
 70 LET T(I)=0
 80 FOR J=1 TO 4
 90 READ S(I,J)
100 LET T(I)=S(I,J)*P(J)+T(I)
120 NEXT J
140 PRINT I,,T(I)
160 NEXT I
900 DATA 10000,12500,17200,20000
950 DATA 6,8,2,1,5,4,3,1,7,6,1,2,3,9,5,0,4,2,4,3
999 END
```

8.9   continued

```
RUN
SALESPERSON                          TOTAL DOLLAR VALUE
    1                                    214400
    2                                    171600
    3                                    202200
    4                                    228500
    5                                    193800
```

CHAPTER 9

9.1   b. 63,   c. .4,   g. 45.01

9.2   40

9.3   b. between zero and 2.5
      d. from zero to 9, inclusive
      f. from 50 to 150, inclusive

9.5
```
5 REM PICKING A RANDOM NUMBER FROM 001 TO 500
10 LET W = INT(499*RND(B) + 1)
15 PRINT "THE WINNING NUMBER IS"; W
20 END


RUN
THE WINNING NUMBER IS 250
```

9.8
```
10 READ A,B,C
15 DATA 2,3,1,4,2,1
20 GO SUB 500
25 PRINT A,B,C,D
30 READ A,B,C
35 GO SUB 500
40 PRINT A,B,C,D
45 STOP
500 LET D=A
510 IF D>B THEN 525
515 IF D>C THEN 535
520 RETURN
525 LET D=B
530 GO TO 515
535 LET D=C
540 RETURN
999 END


RUN
    2              3              1              1
    4              2              1              1
```

CHAPTER 10

10.1
```
 5 DIM N$(5),P(5),Q(5)
10 PRINT "PRODUCT NAME","PRICE","QUANTITY","AMOUNT"
15 PRINT "------------","-----","--------","------"
20 LET A=0
25 FOR I=1 TO 5
30 READ N$(I),Q(I),P(I)
35 LET A=A+P(I)*Q(I)
40 PRINT N$(I),"$";P(I),Q(I),"$";P(I)*Q(I)
45 NEXT I
50 PRINT
55 PRINT "THE TOTAL AMOUNT IS ";"$";A
60 DATA HAND SOAP,24,.69,TOOTH PASTE,35,.76
62 DATA BROWN SUGAR,16,1.25
65 DATA COLA,24,.55,RYE BREAD,50,.20
99 END
```

```
RUN
PRODUCT NAME    PRICE           QUANTITY        AMOUNT
------------    -----           --------        ------
HAND SOAP       $ .69           24              $ 16.56
TOOTH PASTE     $ .76           35              $ 26.6
BROWN SUGAR     $ 1.25          16              $ 20
COLA            $ .55           24              $ 13.2
RYE BREAD       $ .2            50              $ 10

THE TOTAL AMOUNT IS $ 86.36
```

10.2
```
10 REM INVENTORY PROGRAM
15 PRINT "WHAT IS THE PRODUCT NAME ";
20 INPUT N$
25 IF N$="STOP" THEN 999
30 FOR I=1 TO 10
35 READ P$,A
40 IF P$=N$ THEN 60
45 NEXT I
50 PRINT "NO SUCH PRODUCT NAME AS ";N$;" TRY AGAIN"
55 GO TO 65
60 PRINT "THE AMOUNT OF ";P$;" IN INVENTORY IS ";A
65 RESTORE
70 GO TO 15
75 DATA SOAP,100,TISSUE,150,BREAD,50
77 DATA BRUSHES,25,ASPIRIN,12,SODA,250
80 DATA CHEESE,80,CEREAL,200,BEANS,500,SOUP,75
999 END
```

```
RUN
WHAT IS THE PRODUCT NAME ?CHEESE
THE AMOUNT OF CHEESE IN INVENTORY IS  80
WHAT IS THE PRODUCT NAME  ?TISSUE
THE AMOUNT OF TISSUE IN INVENTORY IS  150
WHAT IS THE PRODUCT NAME  ?ASPIRIN
THE AMOUNT OF ASPIRIN IN INVENTORY IS  12
WHAT IS THE PRODUCT NAME  ?CAVIAR
NO SUCH PRODUCT NAME AS CAVIAR TRY AGAIN
WHAT IS THE PRODUCT NAME  ?SOUP
THE AMOUNT OF SOUP IN INVENTORY IS  75
WHAT IS THE PRODUCT NAME  ?STOP
```

10.6
```
5 DIM N$(11)
10 FOR I=1 TO 11
15 INPUT N$(I)
20 NEXT I
25 FOR I=1 TO 11
30 PRINT N$(12-I);
35 NEXT I
36 PRINT
40 END


RUN
?P
?R
?O
?G
?R
?A
?M
?M
?E
?R
?.
.REMMARG ORP
```

CHAPTER 11

11.1
```
10 PRINT USING 55
15 PRINT USING 50
20 PRINT USING 60,2,SQR(2)
25 PRINT USING 65,2,SQR(2)
30 PRINT USING 70,2,SQR(2)
35 PRINT USING 75,2,SQR(2)
40 PRINT USING 80,2,SQR(2)
45 PRINT USING 85,2,SQR(2)
50 FMT --- -----------
55 FMT TWO  SQUARE ROOT
60 FMT #      #.#
65 FMT #      #.##
70 FMT #      #.###
75 FMT #      #.####
80 FMT #      #.#####
85 FMT #      #.##########
90 END


RUN
TWO  SQUARE ROOT
---  -----------
 2     1.4
 2     1.41
 2     1.414
 2     1.4142
 2     1.41421
 2     1.4142135624
```

11.2
```
1 PRINT USING 100
5 FOR I=1 TO 26
10 LET P=2↑I
15 PRINT USING 105,P
20 NEXT I
100 FMT POWERS OF 2 BETWEEN 1 AND 26 INCLUSIVE
105 FMT ##,###,###
199 END

RUN
  POWERS OF 2 BETWEEN 1 AND 26 INCLUSIVE
             2
             4
             8
            16
            32
            64
           128
           256
           512
         1,024
         2,048
         4,096
         8,192
        16,384
        32,768
        65,536
       131,072
       262,144
       524,288
     1,048,576
     2,097,152
     4,194,304
     8,388,608
    16,777,216
    33,554,432
    67,108,864
```

11.5a
```
5 FOR I=1 TO 10
10 PRINT "*";
15 NEXT I
20 PRINT "*"
25 FOR I=1 TO 9
30 PRINT TAB(10-I);"*"
35 NEXT I
40 FOR I=1 TO 10
45 PRINT "*";
50 NEXT I
55 PRINT "*"
99 END

RUN
***********
         *
        *
       *
      *
     *
    *
   *
  *
 *
***********
```

11.5b
```
5 FOR I=1 TO4
10 PRINT "*";TAB(10);"*"
15 NEXT I
20 FOR I=1 TO 9
25 PRINT "*";
30 NEXT I
35 FOR I=1 TO 5
40 PRINT "*";TAB(10);"*"
45 NEXT I
99 END


RUN
*         *
*         *
*         *
*         *
***********
*         *
*         *
*         *
*         *
```

11.5e
```
10 FOR I=1 TO 4
15 PRINT "*";
20 NEXT I
25 PRINT
30 PRINT "*";TAB(4);"*"
35 PRINT "*";TAB(5);"*"
40 PRINT "*";TAB(4);"*"
45 FOR I=1 TO 4
50 PRINT "*";
55 NEXT I
56 PRINT
60 FOR I=1 TO 4
65 PRINT "*"
70 NEXT I
75 PRINT
99 END


RUN
****
*   *
*    *
*   *
****
*
*
*
*
```

11.5f
```
5 PRINT "*";TAB(16);"*"
10 FOR I=1 TO 7
15 PRINT TAB(I);"*";TAB(16-I);"*"
20 NEXT I
25 PRINT TAB(8);"*"
99 END
```

```
RUN
*                    *
 *                  *
  *                *
   *              *
    *            *
     *          *
      *        *
       *      *
        *    *
         *  *
          *
```

11.5g
```
5 FOR I=1 TO 4
10 PRINT TAB(I);"*";TAB(26-I);"*"
15 NEXT I
20 PRINT TAB(5);"*";TAB(13);"*";TAB(21);"*"
25 FOR I=1 TO 3
30 PRINT TAB(5+I);"*";TAB(13-I);"*";TAB(13+I);"*";TAB(21-I);"*"
35 NEXT I
40 PRINT TAB(9);"*";TAB(17);"*"
99 END
```

```
RUN
 *                      *
  *                    *
   *                  *
    *                *
     *        *        *
      *      * *      *
       *    *   *    *
        *  *     *  *
         **       **
          *       *
```

11.7
```
10 GO SUB 100
20 GO SUB 200
30 GO SUB 100
40 GO SUB 200
60 STOP
100 FOR I=1 TO 10
105 PRINT "*";
110 NEXT I
115 PRINT
120 RETURN
200 FOR I=1 TO 7
205 PRINT "*"
210 NEXT I
215 RETURN
300 END
```

11.7 continued

```
RUN
**********
*
*
*
*
*
*
*
**********
*
*
*
*
*
*
*
```

11.8 `5 PRINT "NAME";TAB(20);"SALARY";TAB(34);"DEDUCTIONS";TAB(49);"NET PAY"`
`10 END`

```
RUN
NAME               SALARY      DEDUCTIONS     NET PAY
```

CHAPTER 12

12.2 A dimension statement is needed.

12.5 `05 REM MATRICES:PACKED OUTPUT`
`10 DIM A(3,6), B(5,2), C(4)`
`20 MAT READ A,B,C`
`30 MAT PRINT A; B; C;`
`40 DATA 68,73,41,12,18,21,32,47,16,-7,12,20,38,61,62,21,14,-9`
`50 DATA 2,7,3,9,6,11,12,8,14,7,1.1,.6,.8,.9`
`68   73`
`99 END`

```
RUN

68   73   41   12   18   21
32   47   16   -7   12   20
38   61   62   21   14   -9


2    7
3    9
6    11
12    8
14    7


1.1   .6   .8   .9
```

12.7
```
05 REM MAT INPUT:GROSS PAY
10 DIM H(6,1),R(1,6),P(6,6)
20 MAT INPUT H,R
30 MAT P=H*R
40 PRINT
50 PRINT "WORKER","HOURS WORKED","RATE PER HOUR","GROSS PAY"
60 PRINT "------","-------------","-------------","---------"
70 FOR I=1 TO 6
80 PRINT I,H(I,1),"$";R(1,I),"$";P(I,I)
90 NEXT I
99 END


RUN
 ?32,37,40,36,35,37.5
 ?4.25,3.80,4.15,4.20,4.00,3.75

 WORKER         HOURS WORKED    RATE PER HOUR  GROSS PAY
 ------         ------------    -------------  ---------
   1               32            $ 4.25         $ 136
   2               37            $ 3.8          $ 140.6
   3               40            $ 4.15         $ 166
   4               36            $ 4.2          $ 151.2
   5               35            $ 4            $ 140
   6               37.5          $ 3.75         $ 140.625
```

12.11
```
05 REM CAR SALES:MATRIX
10 DIM S(10,2),K(1,10),H(1,2)
20 MAT READ S,K
30 MAT H=K*S
40 PRINT " ","IMPORT SALES LEADERS"
50 PRINT " ","--------------------"
60 PRINT " "," JUNE"," JUNE"
70 PRINT "NUMBER","1975","1974"
80 PRINT "-----------------------------------"
90 FOR I=1 TO 10
100PRINT I,S(I,1),S(I,2)
110NEXT I
120PRINT "-----------------------------------"
130PRINT "TOTAL",H(1,1),H(1,2)
140DATA 28435,19549,23867,13656,23268,23806,10061,2938,9466,7182
150DATA 9323,4999,5939,3300,5629,4232,4789,3980,4344,1631
160DATA 1,1,1,1,1,1,1,1,1,1
999END


RUN
          IMPORT SALES LEADERS
          --------------------
             JUNE        JUNE
 NUMBER      1975        1974
 -----------------------------------
   1         28435        19549
   2         23867        13656
   3         23268        23806
   4         10061         2938
   5          9466         7182
   6          9323         4999
   7          5939         3300
   8          5629         4232
   9          4789         3980
  10          4344         1631
 -----------------------------------
 TOTAL       125121       85273
```

12.14
```
05 REM MATRIX MULT.
10 DIM C(4,1),D(1,4),M1(4,4),M2(1,1)
20 MAT READ C,D
30 MAT M1=C*D
40 MAT M2=D*C
50 MAT PRINT M1,M2
60 DATA .25,.5,-.5,.375,16,24,20,36
99 END


RUN
```

4	6	5	9
8	12	10	18
-8	-12	-10	-18
6	9	7.5	13.5

```
   19.5
```

12.15
```
05 REM STOCK VALUE:MATRIX
10 DIM N(1,7), P(7,3), V(1,3)
20 MAT READ N,P
30 MAT V=N*P
40 PRINT " ","PORTFOLIO EVALUATION"
50 PRINT " ","--------------------"
60 PRINT "JAN.2","MAY 1","JUL Y 25"
70 PRINT "-----","-----","--------"
80 MAT PRINT V
90 DATA 110,200,100,150,200,250,100
100 DATA 3,6.25,6.375,6.875,13.25,17,10.875,16.75,19.5
110 DATA 2.5,5.875,7.375,3.75,8.25,9.125,2,4.125,6.375,6,10.75,12
120 END


RUN
```

	PORTFOLIO EVALUATION	

JAN.2	MAY 1	JUL Y 25
-----	-----	--------
5017.5	9650	11776.3

CHAPTER 13

13.1
```
NEW:UNITF


5 1,2400
10 2,3200
15 3,1800
20 4,2100
25 5,3000
30 6,4500

SAV
```

```
13.4  5 PRINT "PLANT","UNITS PRODUCED"
      10 PRINT "-----","--------------"
      15 LET T=0
      20 LET N=0
      25 INPUT:UNITF:P,U
      30 LET N=N+1
      35 PRINT P,U
      40 LET T=T+U
      45 IF N=6 THEN 55
      50 GO TO 25
      55 PRINT "----------------------------"
      60 PRINT "TOTAL",T
      99 END
```

```
RUN
PLANT          UNITS PRODUCED
-----          --------------
  1               2400
  2               3200
  3               1800
  4               2100
  5               3000
  6               4500
----------------------------
TOTAL             17000
```

13.10 Data Files

```
NEW:DIV1


10 DIV A,400,15
20 DIV B,500,23
30 DIV C,430,20
40 DIV D,330,30
.SAV

NEW:DIV2


10 DIV E,380,13
15 DIV F,450,25
20 DIV G,300,21
SAV
```

Program and Listing

```
NEW:MERGEF


SAV


5 FOR I=1 TO 4
10 INPUT:DIV1:D$,A,B
15 PRINT:MERGEF:LNM(10);D$;",";A;",";B
20 NEXT I
25 FOR I=1 TO 3
30 INPUT:DIV2:D$,A,B
35 PRINT:MERGEF:LNM(10);D$;",";A;",";B
40 NEXT I
99 END
```

13.10 continued

```
RUN

USED:    3.0 UNITS


OLD:MERGEF


LIST
10 DIV A, 400 , 15
11 DIV B, 500 , 23
12 DIV C, 430 , 20
13 DIV D, 330 , 30
14 DIV E, 380 , 13
15 DIV F, 450 , 25
16 DIV G, 300 , 21
```

13.11 Data File

```
NEW:SCHED



10 MONDAY    , 7:10PM, 7:30AM, 9:00AM
11           ,10:05PM,        ,10:40AM NON STOP
12 TUESDAY   , 8:50PM, 9:10AM,10:40AM
13 , , , ,
14 WEDNESDAY , 8:50PM, 9:10AM,10:40AM
15 , , , ,
16 THURSDAY  , 7:10PM, 7:30AM, 9:00AM
17           ,10:05PM,        ,10:40AM NON STOP
18 FRIDAY    , 8:50PM, 9:10AM,10:40AM
19 , , , ,
20 SATURDAY  , 7:10PM, 7:30AM, 9:00AM
21           ,10:05PM,        ,10:40AM NON STOP
22 SUNDAY    , 7:10PM, 7:30AM, 9:00AM
23           ,10:05PM,        ,10:40AM NON STOP
SAV
```

Program

```
10 FOR I=1 TO 7
15 INPUT:SCHED:D$(I),N$(I),G$(I),Z$(I)
20 INPUT:SCHED:S$(I),T$(I),U$(I),V$(I)
25 NEXT I
30 PRINT "TYPE IN 1 FOR MONDAY, 2 FOR TUESDAY, 3 FOR WEDNESDAY,"
35 PRINT "..., 7 FOR SUNDAY, AND 0 TO TERMINATE, AFTER THE ? MARK"
40 PRINT "APPEARS";
45 INPUT N
50 IF N=0 GO TO 110
55 PRINT "747'S FROM NEW YORK TO GENEVA AND ZURICH"
60 PRINT "DAY","LEAVES N.Y.","ARRIVES GENEVA","ARRIVES ZURICH"
65 PRINT "---","------------","---------------","---------------"
70 GO TO 85
75 INPUT N
80 IF N=0 THEN 110
85 PRINT D$(N),N$(N),G$(N),Z$(N)
90 PRINT S$(N),T$(N),U$(N),V$(N)
95 PRINT
100 PRINT
105 GO TO 75
110 END
```

Index

Bruce Bosworth is Associate Professor of Quantitative Analysis at St. John's University, College of Business Administration (New York). He has devoted his research efforts to the use of the computer in business curricula. He is the author of *Programs in BASIC: a Lecture Notebook.* Dr. Bosworth is a member of the American Statistical Association and the American Institute for Decision Sciences. He received the B.S. degree from New York University, School of Commerce, and M.B.A. and Ph.D. degrees in business administration from New York University, Graduate School of Business Administration.

Harry L. Nagel, formerly a Management Sciences Analyst at Stauffer Chemical Company, is also currently at St. John's University, College of Business Administration (New York). He received a B.S. in mathematics Summa Cum Laude from Brooklyn College, and an M.S. and Ph.D. in operations research from New York University, School of Engineering and Science. He is a member of Phi Beta Kappa, Sigma Xi, Operations Research Society of America, American Statistical Association and The American Institute for Decision Sciences.

This book was set in 10-point Century School-
book with display lines in Zepplin and Michel
by Typothetae, Palo Alto, California. Artwork
was prepared by Carol Schwartzback and
Associates, San Francisco.

Sponsoring Editor	Robert L. Safran
Project Editor	Gretchen Hargis
Designer	Judith A. Olson

Summary of BASIC Statements (continued)

Statement (Chapter)	Purpose	Example
PRINT (3)	Prints literals and/or values	40 PRINT"ANS.";A+B+C
PRINT:FLNAM: (13)	Writes to a file	40 PRINT:TAX:D$,N
PRINT USING (11)	Prints using a format	20 PRINT USING 100, T
RANDOMIZE (9)	Causes different sets of random numbers to be generated	10 RANDOMIZE
READ (4)	Assigns values from DATA statements to variables	10 READ A,C,N$
REM (3)	Provides comments in a program	10 REM PAYROLL PROGRAM
RESTORE (4)	Causes data to be reread	40 RESTORE
RETURN (9)	Returns execution from sub-routine to line following GO SUB	450 RETURN
STOP (6)	Stops the execution of the program	80 STOP
TAB (11)	Specifies exact print position of output	20 PRINT TAB(35);"SALES"

Miscellaneous

Mathematical Operators (in hierarchy of execution) (2)

Symbol	Purpose	Example
↑	Exponentiation	X↑2
*,/	Multiplication, division	A*B/C
+, −	Addition, subtraction	K−L+M

Stored BASIC Functions (9)
SIN, COS TAN, COT, ATN, LOG, EXP, INT, SGN, ABS, SQR, RND

Relations (6)
<, <=, >, >=, =, <>

REORDER
NUMBER 13-4090